Suing Abusive Debt Collectors

Don't Get Mad, Get Even and Get Paid

Allen Harkleroad

Statesboro, Georgia, USA

ISBN : 0-9789997-7-0
ISBN-13: 978-0-9789997-7-3

Printed in the United States of America.

LEGAL INFORMATION IS NOT LEGAL ADVICE

Other Books by Allen Harkleroad

Stick it to Sue Happy Debt Collectors
The Care and Feeding of a Sucks.com
Confidential SEO Secrets

FOREWORD

The abuse of consumers by the debt collection industry has skyrocketed in the last several years. Federal and state regulators are slow to pursue actions against collection companies; it has now fallen on consumers to exact justice from abusive collectors.

The collection industry groups claim that collection abuse is rare, one only has to search online to find that consumer lawsuits against collectors has constantly risen year after year. If you have been a victim of collection abuse, you must fight back and hold these companies liable for their actions. Consumers can cause changes in the collection industry. We consumers have the power to force change upon them, and so we should hold them accountable.

The process of collecting evidence and filing suit is not complicated or overly burdensome. Anyone can do it. One thing is certain, the bigger the collection company, the faster they settle consumer generated lawsuits.

Contents

1

HOW TO USE THIS BOOK

This book is written with consumers in mind, primarily for those who have been harassed, or abused, by unscrupulous debt collectors. Much of the information included are from the authors own real-life experiences. The author will show you how to identify illegal collection tactics, how to prepare evidence and how to file a lawsuit against a debt collector.

The contents are not for exacting revenge on legitimate debt collection companies, it is for exacting justice for consumers that have been abused by debt collectors. If you are reading this book then you are probably at wits end and have been on the receiving end of bad debt collection tactics. It is time to turn the tables on illegal debt collections and hit them where it hurts, in the wallet.

The big secret in the debt collection industry is that in upwards of ninety-eight percent of legitimate consumer filed Fair Debt Collection Practices Act (FDCPA) lawsuits the collection company will settle before their case ever makes it to a courtroom. Many times an offer of settlement is made as soon as the collection company files an answer to your complaint. I will go into more detail as to why they often settle later in the book.

I know this personally. I have filed many FDCPA lawsuits against collectors and through my thousands of hours of legal research that I share, you may learn how to do the same. Nearly every day I am reading consumer FDCPA lawsuit filings and checking to see if they make it to trial. In only an extremely small number of cases, the consumer's complaint goes to the courtroom. This means you have a high chance of obtaining a settlement (and a check) shortly after you sue a debt collector.

While the Federal Trade Commission does regulate much of the collection industry, they are slow to hold abusive debt collectors accountable for abuse. It is up to consumers like you to fight collection abuse. The more of us that do, the less abuse will occur.

As you will soon discover by reading this book, catching debt collectors breaking the law and then filing suit against them is relatively simple. In fact, suing debt collectors is easy and many times monetarily rewarding.

MY MOTTO
"Don't Get Mad, Get Even and Get Paid!

I will teach you how to identify the different types of illegal debt collection, how to collect evidence, and then sue collectors for violating your rights and the law. Included are systematic instructions, detailed explanations and my own real-life examples to help illustrate different portions of the book.

Also included in this book are collectors' dirty little secrets that they prefer you never read, as it will cause them an inordinate amount trouble when confronted in court.

In chapter two, I will explain in detail many of the most frequent illegal collections tactics of the collection industry and how to use them against collectors in court. I will cover the Fair Debt Collection Practices Act (FDCPA), Fair Credit Reporting Act (FCRA), and some of the Telephone Consumer Protection Act (TCPA) violations. Several federal statutes (acts or laws) apply to third party debt collectors and original creditor collections.

In chapter three, I will cover various ways of "catching" collectors violating laws and gathering admissible evidence. Many of them are commonsense violations. However, the uninformed consumer may overlook several obvious items. I want to ensure that you have all the tools available to "stick it" to the abusive debt collectors.

In chapter four, I will explain the various aspects of filing a civil complaint, and preparing your documents in an easy to understand systematic process with explanations.

In chapter five, I will explain and illustrate the drafting of a complaint, how to file, as well as proper court procedure for serving a summons and complaint on the defendant.

In chapter six, I will cover whether or not to accept an offer of settlement from the collection company or to move forward in court with your complaint.

In chapter seven, I provide additional pro se litigation resources for legal research and legal citations to use in your filings. While I cannot cover every possible scenario, I do provide the additional resources so that you are able to locate additional factual allegations to your own complaint.

In chapter eight, you will find the full US code covering the Fair Debt Collection Practices Act (FDCPA) and the Fair Credit Reporting Act (FCRA). While this chapter is lengthy, it provides an easy reference to use in your cases against debt collectors.

Included throughout the book are my personal experiences dealing with debt collector harassment and abuse. Several of them in the past had me at wit's end and I do not want anyone else to endure the things that I have in the past. As you read this book, you will discover that being a pro se litigant is not difficult once each aspect is explained. I have sued several debt collectors and at the time of the writing of this book, I am contemplating accepting a collectors "amicable resolution" (as they put it), or to move forward with a civil action against them.

When I filed my first suit, I had no help and I had to learn how to do it myself. I made a few mistakes along the way, which of course helped me when filing subsequent lawsuits against other debt collectors. Since filing my first suit, I have researched on a nearly daily basis (for more than four and a half years) to gather legal "ammunition" in the event that I had to file future civil actions. I share much of what I have learned with you in this book.

Because of my experiences, you will benefit from my research and the cases that I have filed to date. I am arming you with information that will help you win against illegal debt collection tactics. Since the Federal Trade Commission and many states are slow to prosecute abusive collectors it rests on our shoulders to exact justice from them, rather than waiting on our government to do anything.

This is not my first book on the subject of dealing with debt collectors. In 2010, I published a book on how to defend a collection case in court and beat them. The book is titled; "Stick it to Sue Happy Debt Collectors" and it outlines from start to finish how to fight debt collectors and their attorneys in court and, win against them. If you are interested, you can read more about the book at www.beatdebtcollectors.com. The book is available in print, and PDF eBook, and in Kindle and Nook eReader formats.

While I cannot guarantee one hundred percent that you will win against a debt collector in court, I do know the information and tools in this book will give the upper hand in many cases. However, once you file a suit against collectors they will most likely not attempt any further collections against you. I have seen this repeatedly. Pro-se litigation is very powerful and will put the collection company on notice that you are educated and informed on how to deal with them.

HINT: Debt collection lawyers and law firms "hate" being sued more than you do. Consumer litigation generally stops them in their tracks (an attorney actually told

me this).

Nowadays when the phone rings and the number are not familiar, I lick my lips in anticipation of it being a bad collector. I am hoping that they leave a voice message on my phone, which is illegal, so that I can publicize it, and sue them for the violation(s).

During the writing of this book a debt collector that had left a voice mail several years ago claiming to have "fraud" papers on his desk concerning me, called back a couple of weeks ago and left a very similar voice mail (without proper disclosure I might add). He was the same person, three years apart, and continuing to leave fraudulent and misleading messages on my answering machine. I am in the process of drafting the civil complaint against the company and will be filing it shortly.

Filing lawsuits against abusive debt collectors are not that difficult and not expensive. It costs roughly one hundred to one hundred and fifty dollars to file and serve the lawsuit. Of course, all you need is your own time, diligence and patience to catch the debt collectors breaking the law.

TO BE NOTED: Consumers should never assume that a collector actually owns a debt or that that the collector is authorized to collect on a debt. Consumers have legal rights. You have the right to receive proper proof that a collection company owns the debt, or are authorized to collect on behalf of the debt owner. Chances are if it is a collection where the original creditor still owns a debt, it may be that they do not even own the debt as it was securitized, or sold without proper documentation, which means they may not have the right to collect. Now it is time to start hitting bad debt collectors where it hurts, in the wallet!

2

ILLEGAL COLLECTIONS

I imagine if debt collectors have hounded you recently, that you have read quite a few items on the Internet regarding collectors. The problem is, the "helpful" articles do not really explain how to sue a debt collector. Most of them are inaccurate regurgitations of general information on what a debt collector can and cannot do to you. I will list many of the most common illegal and abusive tactics used by many debt collectors, and go into detail on how to use this to file your own lawsuit against them. Some of the information you may have read before, however I am quite sure you are going to learn new ways to combat illegal collections of which you may not be previously aware.

What Debt Collectors Cannot Do

Harassment. Debt collectors may not harass, oppress, or abuse you or any third parties they contact. For example, they may not:

- Use threats of violence or harm;
- Publish a list of names of people who refuse to pay their debts (but they can give this information to the credit reporting companies);
- Use obscene or profane language
- Repeatedly use the phone to annoy someone.
- Use false statements. Debt collectors may not lie when they are trying to collect a debt. For example, they may not:
    - falsely claim that they are attorneys or government representatives;
    - falsely claim that you have committed a crime;
    - falsely represent that they operate or work for a credit reporting company;
    - misrepresent the amount you owe;
    - indicate that papers they send you are legal forms if they aren't; or
    - indicate that papers they send to you aren't legal forms if they are.

Debt collectors also are prohibited from saying that

- you will be arrested if you don't pay your debt;
- they'll seize, garnish, attach, or sell your property or wages unless they are permitted by law to take the action and intend to do so; or
- legal action will be taken against you, if doing so would be illegal or if they don't intend to take the action.

Debt collectors may not

- Give false credit information about you to anyone, including a credit reporting company;
- Send you anything that looks like an official document from a court or government agency if it isn't; or
- Use a false company name.

Unfair practices. Debt collectors may not engage in unfair practices when they try to collect a debt. For example, they may not:

- Try to collect any interest, fee, or other charge on top of the amount you owe unless the contract that created your debt – or your state law – allows the charge;
- Deposit a post-dated check early; take or threaten to take your property unless it can be done legally; or contact you by postcard.
- In addition, a debt collector cannot represent that they are attorneys if they are not, or imply that communications are from an attorney. 15 U.S.C. 1692e(3).

The first thing you need to do is identify whether or not the collector is the original creditor or a third party, such as junk debt collector or assignee of the original creditors. Original creditor collections are exempt from the fair debt collections practices act, however they are bound by the Fair Credit Reporting Act (FCRA), the Truth in Lending Act (TILA), and possibly by the Telephone Consumer Protection Act (TCPA). In other words, if an original creditor's collector misbehaves, we have actionable avenues in which to pursue them in court, just as we do with third party collection assignees and junk buyers and collectors.

This chapter is long, as it covers a lot of information that you must be aware of before we can begin the process of catching collectors in illegal activities and suing them for it.

I will start with third party collection assignee and junk debt buyers/collectors and finish up with original creditor collections. I am doing so, as more often than not, the third party and junk collectors are the most likely to use illegal collection tactics than original creditors. A third party assignee collector is a third party attempting to collect a debt on behalf of the original creditor, as opposed to a junk debt buyer/collector that purchased a debt that was charged off and sold at a steep discount and are trying to recoup their money and profits from a consumer.

The debt collection industry as a whole is a huge interwoven mass of companies that often work together, or hide behind the scenes and hire other collection companies to do their dirty work. Often times a consumer is confused as to who owns the debt or whom they should pay in the event they decide to settle the debt.

I will share several methods on how to find out exactly whom the debt was sold to, as we can use this against many debt collectors in lawsuits. These methods do not work one hundred percent of the time, and if they don't we have other avenues to pursue after filing a lawsuit, such as discovery. I will explain them throughout this book.

We will start with what you should and should not do when dealing with debt collectors. The first portion of this is also included in my book "Stick it to Sue Happy Debt Collectors" as every consumer should be aware of the information.

Never become emotional when talking to a debt collector on the phone. Debt collectors will attempt to evoke strong emotion from you (anger, outrage, frustration, guilt, fear etc.). Many collectors use this method in an attempt to cause you to think irrationally. Their hope is to make you very emotional, so that they can get you to agree to something you most likely would never have agreed to had you not been in a state of mental distress. Do not trust them, they will do anything (lie, slander, threaten legal action, etc.) to be paid.

This tactic works well and they WILL use it, so do not fall for it. Always remain calm when dealing with a collector on the phone.

If they become abusive, calmly state that you are not going to discuss the matter further until they calm down, tell them that if they continue, you will hang up. Chances are they will yell and scream more. When they do start yelling or abuse you, simply hang up. They will undoubtedly call you back. If they become abusive or start yelling, remain calm and repeat that you will not discuss the matter until they calm down, if they don't calm down then hang up again. Repeat this as often as necessary.

Never under any circumstance give a debt collector or collection agency your bank account information, checking account number, or debit card number to draft your account. Always pay by money order or cashier's check. Many times the collection agency will draft your account for more than the agreed upon amount, thus over drafting your account. They may also draft your account multiple times. You would not give a total stranger walking down the street your bank account information, so do not give a debt collector your banking information. Often the collector will say they must have your payment by the end of the day and moan and groan. Tell them you will send them a cashier's check or money order. They WILL object, tell them if they want to be paid they will accept a check or money order. If you remain firm, they will accept this.

ALWAYS record the telephone conversation; even they are calling from a two party consent state, record the conversation. If they are calling from a one party state, you DO NOT have to tell them you are recording the conversation. If they are being abusive, tell them you are recording the conversation. They will either change their tone or hang up on you.

Several states require the consent of both parties of a telephone conversion in order to allow the call to be recorded. Thirty-seven states allow the consent of just ONE party (i.e. You do not have to disclose that you are recording the conversation). If you are at work, neither you nor they have any reasonable expectancy of privacy, so if a collector calls you at work you still may be able to record the conversation without violating any state or federal law

IMPORTANT

A recent Federal court ruling (2nd U.S. Circuit Court of Appeals) trumps state laws regarding two party consent (both parties must agree to record the conversation.

"Plaintiff-Appellant Marshall Caro filed a complaint in the United States District Court for the District of Connecticut (Dorsey, J.) alleging, inter alia, a civil cause of action under Title III of the Omnibus Crime Control and Safe Streets Act of 1968, codified at 18 U.S.C. §§ 2510-21 ("Title III" or the "Wiretap Act"). The district court dismissed Caro's complaint. We affirm, and, in so doing, hold that the exception to the one-party consent provision of 18 U.S.C. § 2511(2)(d) requires that a communication be intercepted for the purpose of a tortious or criminal act that is independent of the intentional act of recording." ~ CARO v. WEINTRAUB LLP, Marshall CARO, Plaintiff-Appellant, v. Eric WEINTRAUB, David H. Weintraub, Glenn William Dowd, and Day Pitney LLP, Defendants-Appellees. Docket No. 09-3685-cv. Argued: April 19, 2010. -- August 13, 2010

"The defendant must have the intent to use the illicit recording to commit a tort of crime beyond the act of recording itself,"

The decision is a win for consumers that reside in a two party consent state as the decision states that one party can record another party without consent as long as the recording is not being used to commit a crime, such as extortion or blackmail.

Since consumers are recording telephone conversations with collection agencies to prove that the collectors are breaking the law, consumers now have a federal court decision to ensure they are in the clear no matter what their particulars states laws are regarding consent to record a telephone conversions. Of course this might not stop a debt collection from claiming there was no proper consent, however consumers have a court US district court ruling in which to defend themselves in the event that it is needed/

You can also use the sneaky and legal method to record a debt collector's conversation. Use their own methods against them, especially if the debt collector is calling from a two party consent* state. When they read off their script, "this call may be recorded for", say (in a humorous and joking way) "I am recording this call for customer service reasons", they won't think about it and probably think you are joking, however by them not saying "NO" they are giving consent for you to record the conversation.

NOTE: If the debt collectors phone number does not show up on the caller ID or displays "unknown", you then you have every right to assume that they are calling from a one party state, because they are attempting to hide their location. A Federal Trade Commission staff attorney disclosed this to me.

REMEMBER

Always keep a record of every phone call and postal mail contact from all collection agencies. Be sure to write down the time, date, the name of person that contacted you, the company and any phone numbers. Always remain calm when talking with a debt collector on the phone.

As I mentioned earlier original creditors themselves and their in-house collection department are exempt from the Fair Debt Collection Practices Act (FDCPA). Third party debt collectors (junk debt collectors or assignees of the original creditor) and collection law firms are bound by the FDCPA, the Telephone Consumer Protection Act (TCPA) as well as both the Fair Credit Reporting Act. I will go into more detail on each throughout this book.

First, we will look at the Fair Debt Collection Practices Act (FDCPA) as this is the Federal statute that most abusive debt collectors violate.

Fair Debt Collection Practices Act (FDCPA)

If debt collectors are ringing your phone off the hook, there are several things you can do to lessen and even stop it. If they do not, you can sue and receive monetary compensation for your troubles. With that said, most FDCPA lawsuit settlements are under five thousand dollars ($5,000.00). There are several exceptions to this rule. However, you will most likely receive anywhere from one thousand dollars and up, per legitimate lawsuit you file. I am speaking from experience here as I have sued a good many debt collectors and collection law firms and to date I have never collected more than five thousand dollars from a single lawsuit.

Of course, settlement amounts depend on the type of harassment you have endured. Several consumers have won hundreds of thousands to more than a million dollars for the anguish caused by collectors.

I am not sure why debt collectors believe that abusive tactics will help them collect debts. Increasingly, consumers are taking matters into their own hands and filing suit against collectors that break the law. Many times collectors will attempt to make you upset, guilty or angry because you are more likely to pay them something to shut them up. Do not fall for it. All they want is to be paid and will often do anything they can, to get you to pay. They are not your friends or family. Do not listen to them.

Rule Number One

Record all phone calls from debt collectors. Many answering machines have a record function on them. Use it.

Rule Number Two

If a collector gets abusive or starts yelling, tell them that if they continue with that behavior you will hang up, if they continue then hang up. They will call back, if they do remain calm and answer the phone (or let it go to the answering machine), if you choose to answer the phone and they again become abusive or start yelling, calmly tells them that until they calm down and stop misbehaving you are not going to talk to them and hang up. You take their "power" away from them when you remain calm and tell them you aren't going to discuss anything until they calm down. *(See Rule Number One)*

If they are calling your place of employment, you can write them a cease and desist calling letter, be sure to send it certified mail with return receipt so you know they got it (this may come in handy if they violate the cease and desist letter). As soon as the first call hits where I work, I write up a simple cease and desist letter (see example below) and send it certified mail. More than 95% of the collectors will stop calling after receiving such a letter. A collector can call once after receiving such a letter but that's it, if they call more than that they are in violation of the Fair Debt Collections Practices Act (FDCPA) and of course sue them for the violation(s). (*See Rule Number One)*

I have had collectors violate the FDCPA by calling repeatedly after receiving my cease and desist letter. One collector recently settled with me out of court for violating the FDCPA because they violated my cease calling demand. Several others have done the same and subsequently I filed suit against them. I kept all of the recorded phone conversations (*see rule number one*), photos of the caller ID and the return receipt card they signed when they received my certified cease and desist calling letter. There are 37 states allow one party (one-person) consent to record a telephone call. Additionally if they are calling your employer, and you record it you may be okay, as at your place of employment you have no reasonable expectancy of privacy, it would hold up in court even if the person calling you is in a two party consent state. Also, see the recent appellate court decision *CARO v. WEINTRAUB LLP* earlier in this chapter regarding consumers being able to record conversations. If a collector that you are suing makes a claim that the call you recorded should not be allowed because your state is a two-party state, you have a higher court ruling to use to trump their claim. Since it is a higher court ruling, a judge has almost no choice but to allow the evidence.

Rule Number Three

Write down each time a collector calls and keep track of this, keep all of the return receipts from your cease and desist letters, save those phone recordings, you never know when you will need them.

You can send a letter to cease and desist ALL telephone calls. However, this could trigger them filing a lawsuit (not likely though on debts under $2000.00). This is a judgment call on your part. If the collector is very abusive then this may be an avenue you want to take. A cease calling letter should be sent certified / return receipt requested as this is one of the tools we will use in the next chapter to catch collectors violating the law.

SAMPLE CEASE CALLING LETTER

[DATE]

[YOUR NAME AND ADDRESS]

[DEBT COLLECTORS NAME AND ADDRESS]

RE: Regarding calls to employer [ADD ANY REFERENCE NUMBERS FROM DEBT COLLECTOR HERE]

Dear [INSERT DEBT COLLECTION COMPANY NAME HERE],

I am writing to formally request that your firm (or any agency hired by your firm) no longer contact me at my place of employment, [INSERT YOUR EMPLOYER HERE AND PHONE NUMBER(S)].

My employer requests that calls such as yours must cease, under the terms of the 1977 Federal Fair Debt Collection Practices Act, I formally demand all such calls to my place of employment cease. You will take note that this letter was mailed certified mail, so I have proof that you are in receipt of this letter should legal action against you become necessary on this matter.

Please give this matter the attention that it deserves.

Sincerely,
[SIGN HERE]

END OF SAMPLE CEASE CALLING LETTER

Remember to send the cease calling letter via certified postal mail, return receipt requested. You need a record of when they received the letter so that you can begin documenting any future FDCPA violations.

Fair Credit Reporting Act (FCRA)

Did a third party debt collection law firm pull your credit report? You may have a case against them for violating the Fair Credit Reporting Act (FCRA).

Litigation is not permissible use of a consumer's credit report as litigation is not a business to consumer transaction and thus violates the FCRA.

"In the 1990 Commentary on the FCRA, the Federal Trade Commission ("Commission") stated that "[t]he possibility that a party may be involved in litigation involving a consumer does not provide a permissible purpose for that party to receive a consumer report on such consumer . . . because litigation is not a 'business transaction' involving the consumer." 16 C.F.R. § 600 App., 55 Fed. Reg. 18804, 18816 (May 4, 1990). This statement extends to all aspects of litigation, including the pre-litigation discussions and settlement preparations that you describe, and was not altered by the recent amendments to the statute." – FTC Opinion Bureau of Consumer Protection

If you are being sued (or being threatened with such) it might be a good idea to pull your own credit reports and see if the law firm did a soft or hard inquiry of your credit. If so, you may be eligible for damages under the Fair Credit Reporting Act.

This exact scenario happened to me, Macey, Wilensky, Kessler and Hennings a debt collection law firm in Atlanta pulled my credit report three times in a very short period of time. The third one was in the same month they filed civil litigation naming American Express (AMEX) as the plaintiff. What's even funnier I filed a complaint with the FDIC (American Express is now a Bank) and I received a letter from American Express stating that they assigned the debt to Nationwide Credit (also violated the FDCPA numerous times) and not Macey, Wilensky, Hennings and Kessler. After discovering that the law firm did not directly represent American Express I filed a motion to dismiss and won.

I suggest that if you are having creditor problems that you freeze all three credit reports (Equifax, TrasnUnion and Experian). For most consumers it is only $3.00 to freeze your credit with each reporting agency.

While the FDCPA does prohibit collectors from giving false information to consumer reporting agencies, the Fair Credit Reporting Act (FCRA) specifies in certain language what they cannot do in regards to your credit reports. Debt collectors must conduct a reasonable investigation if a consumer disputes information contained in their credit reports (they often do not). The FCRA also prohibits accessing a consumers reports without permissible or under false pretenses. Many times debt collection companies, especially junk debt buyers/collectors post negative items, when in fact they may have no legal right to do so. If they add false information to your credit report, you can add it to your list of allegations when you file suit against the collector.

Permissible Uses of Consumers Credit Reports

The FCRA limits the use of the credit report to certain purposes. They are:

- Applications for credit, insurance, and rentals for personal, family or household purposes.
- Employment, which includes hiring, promotion, reassignment or retention. A CRA may not release a credit report for employment decisions without consent.
- Court orders, including grand jury subpoenas.
- "Legitimate" business needs in transactions initiated by the consumer for personal, family, or household purposes. (litigation is not legitimate by 3rd parties)
- Account review. Periodically, banks and other companies review credit files to determine whether they wish to retain the individual as a customer.
- Licensing (professional).
- Child support payment determinations.
- Law enforcement access: Government agencies with authority to investigate terrorism and counterintelligence have secret access to credit reports.

Telephone Consumer Protection Act (TCPA)

Chances are if debt collectors are calling your cell phone (or any other phone) they are using software known as a predictive dialer. It's an automated program that dials thousands of phone numbers in a single day. You can generally tell when you answer if there is several seconds of silence before their representative comes onto the line.

Guess what? Using automated software such as a predictive dialer without your express prior permission is against the law and is covered under the Telephone Consumer Protection Act (TCPA) and you can get money from debt collectors who violate this law by using a predictive dialer to call your cell phone.

First, never answer toll-free numbers, blocked numbers, or strange numbers (such as 000-000-0000 and 999-999-9999) that call your phone if you believe it may be a collection agency. If you call back, their predictive dialing software will track it and they will continuously harass you.

If it is too late and they are calling your cell phone with automated dialers or using pre-recorded messages then under the TCPA you could be entitled to $500.00 per call.

A while back I had a collector call my cell phone, so I "Googled" the number and found their compliance officer's name and phone number. I called them and they even admitted that somehow my number was stuck in their "dialer". Subsequently they tried to settle with me. I turned them down and filed a civil lawsuit against them. I got a nice check from them for my troubles. I cover cell phone abuse in the next chapter (Catching them in the Act).

3

CATCH THEM IN THE ACT

Diligence and documentation are the "keys" that will help ensure that the collection company will pay up when sued. Without proper evidence, it may become difficult to prove your case and will delay possible settlements. With proper documentation most collection companies will settle, rather than taking a chance on a higher judgment amount at trial.

In most cases, consumers do not have to set a trap to catch debt collectors breaking the law, more often than not the collectors trip over their own feet and give consumers the evidence they need to sue. With that being said, there are tactics that a consumer can use to catch collectors violating the law. In this chapter, I will outline the most common ways that debt collectors will hand you what you need to take them to court. It is almost akin to shooting fish in a barrel (seriously).

You have one year from the date of abuse to file a Fair Debt Collections Practices Act (FDCPA) suit against a collector. However, if it is continuing harassment and abuse, you could argue that since it was all part of the same illegal activity that all allegations should be considered as a whole. I have filed FDPCA lawsuits that contained allegations that occurred over a period of more than two years. This is where patience and diligence pays off.

Gathering Evidence

"The warning, which states, "This is an attempt to collect a debt...," is one that debt collectors must give at the beginning of each communication, whether by voice or in print.

In an earlier case, *Foti v. Davis*, the automated voice system left a message on Paul S. Foti's answering machine that said the collector was calling *"requiring a personal business matter that requires your immediate attention...."*. The message was deemed to be a violation of Fair Debt Collection Practices Act (FDCPA) Section 1692e (11) because the simple identification of the caller at the beginning of the message "did not adequately disclose that the caller was attempting to collect the debt."

Many unscrupulous debt collectors violate the Fair Debt Collection Practices Act (FDCPA) every day. Violations include calling your neighbors and telling them you are a dead beat, telling you they are sending the police to put you in jail, or that they have a fraud complaint in their office (while claiming to be an attorney).

By law they cannot do either of these nor can they use underhanded collection tactics (lying to you, abuse you, etc.).

Before I go any further, you need to do several things:

1. Get caller ID on your phone (it's going to be your best friend)
2. Document every call made to you by a debt collector
3. Save all answering machine messages (especially the ones that lie about sending you to jail, etc.)

Lack of Proper Disclosure

A 'third party debt collector' must make certain statements during their initial contact (verbal or written) and other information is not required until any subsequent contact (or follow-up). In general, original creditors are exempt from this and the fair debt collection practices act.

The 'Mini-Miranda' (as some call it), falls under the following FDCPA statutes:

§ 807. False or misleading representations [15 USC 1692e]
A debt collector may not use any false, deceptive, or misleading representation or means in connection with the collection of any debt. Without limiting the general application of the foregoing, the following conduct is a violation of this section:

(11) The failure to disclose in the initial written communication with the consumer and, in addition, if the initial communication with the consumer is oral, in that initial oral communication, that the debt collector is attempting to collect a debt and that any information obtained will be used for that purpose, and the failure to disclose in subsequent communica-

tions that the communication is from a debt collector, except that this paragraph shall not apply to a formal pleading made in connection with a legal action.

The lack of proper disclosure, *i.e. mini-Miranda*, in written and oral telephone communications by debt collectors to consumers is a violation of the FDCPA. Debt collectors frequently do not properly disclose whom they are in telephone conversations or in voice mails left on consumers' answering machines. A debt collector must abide by certain federal regulations concerning the collection of debts. However, many times debt collectors will refrain from disclosing exactly whom they are in order to entice (or scare), a consumer into calling back and this sort of behavior is illegal and actionable in a court of law (you can sue them for it).

One of my most recent encounters with the lack of proper disclosure revolves around a debt collection company, Phillips & Cohen Associates LTD (sounds like a law firm name, right? They are not, and through my research, I found several federal cases where Phillips & Cohen lost their motions regarding proper disclosures, among others). Below is a court decision that outlines the fact that a lack of disclosure, whether in writing or oral, is a violation of the fair debt collection practices act.

SPARKS v. PHILLIPS & COHEN ASSOCIATES, LTD.

ASHLEY SPARKS, et al., Plaintiffs, v. PHILLIPS & COHEN ASSOCIATES, LTD., Defendant.

Civil Action 07-0477-WS-C.

United States District Court, S.D. Alabama, Northern Division.

June 20, 2008.

As noted supra, Ashley's § 1692d claim proceeds under subsection (6)'s prohibition on the placement of telephone calls by a debt collector in connection with the collection of a debt without meaningful disclosure of the caller's identity. Pursuant to the plain language of § 1692d(6), a debt collector's failure to identify herself as such in communications relating to the collection of a debt has been held to be a per se violation of the FDCPA. See Masciarelli v. Richard J. Boudreau & Associates, LLC, 529 F. Supp.2d 183, 185 (D. Mass. 2007) (defendant's failure to identify himself as a debt collector in voice-mail message to debtor violates the FDCPA as a matter of law). Ashley has unequivocally averred that, with reference to the January 24, 2007 call, "[t]he female never identified herself." (A. Sparks Aff., ¶ 3.) This testimony, if believed by a jury, would establish a violation of §

1692d(6). Defendant's Rule 56 Motion is therefore denied as to this claim.[19] (Defendant Phillips & Cohen, is denied (lost the motion).

in addition the defendant also violated section § 1692e (and lost the motion)

Plaintiffs also seek to travel under § 1692e, which proscribes debt collectors from the use of "any false, deceptive, or misleading representation or means in connection with the collection of any debt." 15 U.S.C. § 1692e. The gist of § 1692e is that "where some aspect of a debt collector's communication — whether explicit or implied — has the purpose or effect of making a debtor more likely to respond, the FDCPA requires that it be true." Campuzano-Burgos v. Midland Credit Management, 497 F. Supp.2d 660, 665 (E.D. Pa. 2007). For purposes of a § 1692e claim, "[t]he question is not whether [plaintiff] was deceived, but whether the 'least sophisticated consumer' would have been deceived." Jeter, 760 F.2d at 1177 n.11. "A debt collection practice may violate the FDCPA even if it does not fall within any of the enumerated circumstances set forth in Section 1692e." Larsen v. JBC Legal Group, P.C., 533 F. Supp.2d 290, 299 (E.D.N.Y. 2008). Plaintiffs contend that defendant violated § 1692e in three specific respects.

First, Sparks asserts a claim under § 1692e(10), which enumerates as conduct violative of this section "[t]he use of any false representation or deceptive means to collect or attempt to collect any debt." Under § 1692e(10), "mere deception, intentional or unintentional, to collect or attempt to collect any debt ... is sufficient to constitute a violation." Cambron, 379 B.R. at 379 (citation omitted). Sparks contends that defendant violated § 1692e(10) when Strine told her that "we've investigated you already," that Ashley "pretended to be" Sparks, and that Peoples was screening defendant's calls. (Plaintiffs' Brief, at 15-16.)[22] Clearly, there are jury questions as to the veracity of these statements. Defendant's sole basis for seeking summary judgment on this claim is that plaintiffs have no evidence that Strine's allegedly false representations to Sparks were made in connection with the collection of a debt. The Court having already found to the contrary in Section III.A.1., supra, there is no need to re-plow this ground here. Defendant's Motions for Summary Judgment are denied as to Sparks' FDCPA claims under § 1692e(10).

Furthermore

The "Mini-Miranda" Warning: The FDCPA requires that a debt collector, in its initial communication (oral and written) with a consumer, state that the "debt collector is attempting to collect a debt and that any information obtained will be used for that purpose." 15 U.S.C. § 1692e(11). Every communication that follows must state that the communication is from a debt collector. - Must be done in first communication regardless of whether oral or written. Id. FDCPA exempts "formal pleadings" from the requirement, but does not define "formal pleading." Id. "Least Sophisticated" Consumer: Debt collectors must assume that they are communicating with the least sophisticated consumer when collecting debts. All determinations as to whether conduct violates the FDCPA are made from the perspective of whether the "least sophisticated consumer" would have been deceived, misled or harassed by the conduct. Jeter v. Credit Bureau, Inc., 760 F.2d 1168, 1172-75 (11th Cir. 1985); Brown v. Card Serv. Ctr., 464 F.3d 450, 453 (3d Cir. 2006). Generally, a debt collector cannot use a false representation or deceptive means to collect a debt or to obtain information concerning a consumer. 15 U.S.C. § 1692e(10); Tsenes v. Trans-Continental Credit & Collection Corp., 892 F. Supp. 461 (E.D.N.Y. 1995).

In chapter seven, you will find more legal decisions and citations regarding violations of the FDCPA.

Initial Written Communications (Dunning Letter / Validation Notice)

The following must be included in the notice:

- The amount of the debt.
- The name of the creditor.
- A statement to the effect that unless the consumer, within 30 days of the receipt of the notice, disputes the validity of the debt or any portion of it, the debt will be assumed to be valid by the debt collector.
- A statement to the effect notifies the debt collector within a 30-day period that the debt or any portion of it is disputed, the debt collector will obtain verification of the debt or a copy of the judgment against the consumer, and a copy of verification or judgment will be mailed to the consumer.
- A statement to the effect that, on the consumer's written request within the 30-day period, the debt collector will provide the consumer with the name and address of the original creditor, if different from the current creditor.

The dunning letter / validation notice should include the "Mini-Miranda" as well.

Cease Communication Letters Can Be Your Best Friend

I love it when debt collectors continue to call me after I have sent them a cease and desist telephone communication notification via certified mail. Collection agencies large and small tend to violate the law and continue to call. You can sue collection agencies for ongoing harassment. While the FDCPA states that an oral notification to cease calling is sufficient, it is best to put it in writing, send the cease communications letter via certified mail, and return receipt requested. It is much easier to prove they violated the FDCPA if you have a signed confirmation such as a certified letter return receipt.

I have had several collection agencies call repeatedly after receiving one or more cease communications letters. In two cases, they both settled with me after I filed suit against them for the violations.

To keep track collectors and potential harassment, I use a legal pad with columns drawn on them (date, caller, time, and other info). I enter the date that is stamped on the certified mail return receipt and wait for them to call again. When they do I log the information, take a picture (digital camera) of the caller ID and if they left a voice mail, I transfer the message to my computer (and later make a DVD copy of the calls).

You can use a simple microphone plugged into your computer and any audio recording software. Most operating systems have some sort of audio recording utility installed by default. Of course, it requires a bit of patience on your part, however more often than not the collection agency will call again and most likely more than once.

The now defunct Mann Bracken law firm called me more than twelve times after receiving two cease communications letters, and after responding to the Better Business Bureau Complaint (BBB) I filed. Shortly after I filed suit against Mann Bracken they went into receivership (bankruptcy). While I never was paid for my troubles, I am now a creditor of the company since they went bankrupt while owing me money. Now that is what I call irony.

In another case that I filed against a collection company for violating my cease communications letter, they settled out of court. I cannot disclose the amount or details as I and the defendant signed a non-disclosure agreement. However, I was paid for my troubles. It also exposed who was behind the collections. Because of this, I started to see how many in the collection worked together to collect debts. I can now show long-term abuse originating from the actual company pursuing the debt.

False Statements and Fraudulent Collection Practices

Besides using lack of disclosure against abusive collectors, false statements and fraudulent practices are the second most common violations of state and federal law that a consumer can file suit on. This section may help you collect a lot more than four or five thousand dollars in court.

I have had collectors claim to be an officer (including stating their "badge" number), claim they had papers on the desk of the local district attorney (DA's only handle criminal cases and credit card debts are civil cases), call my neighbors and/or harass family members, just to name a few of the harassments I have endured.

A collector cannot threaten that you will go to jail, that they take away your children or anything of similar nature. They cannot use foul language, demean or humiliate you on the phone or in written communications. They cannot state that they are going to take certain actions, such as put a lien on your home or take you to court, unless they actually do so. These are the things that you can sue a collector for and force them to pay you.

I have been hounded by some of the worst (and most aggressive) debt collection companies on the planet. Believe me when I say I have heard it all. Their behavior is the reason I started suing collection companies and law firms. To date, not one of them have collected a penny from me, however I have been paid for their abusive collection tactics.

Cell Phones

Illegal collection calls are not only protected by the Fair Debt Collection Practices Act (FDCPA) but also the Telephone Consumer Protection Act (TCPA). The TCPA has higher penalties for violations than does the FDCPA. Where violations of the FDCPA limits damages to $1,000.00 per violation, the TCPA typical allows for $500.00 to $1500.00 "per call". The amount of damages can pile up quickly for TCPA violators.

Automated dialer (predictive dialer) calls to cell phones by debt collectors is in most cases illegal. It is easy to identify these calls as when you answer you hear only silence (dead air), or an automated attendant will ask you to hold for a representative. Some automated dialers will ask you if you are a certain person (your name) to press a number on the keypad or ask you to call a phone number back. The use of automated dialers burn up minutes and costs a consumer money.

If you think you may have given permission for a collector to call you, you can revoke that permission. I do recommend you put it in writing and send it certified mail. That way you have a record (just like the cease calling letter) of it for future use in court.

Bone Fide Error Defense For Collectors Is No Good In Most Cases

Another consumer win is a recent U.S. Supreme Court ruling regarding Debt Collectors and collection law firms misusing the "Bone Fide Error" defense. Previously many collectors and collection law firms would depend on the "we did not mean to do that" defense (Bone Fide Error). With the Supreme Court ruling, they cannot use it as a defense.

Jerman v. CARLISLE, McNELLIE, RINI, KRAMER, 130 S. Ct. 1605 - Supreme Court 2010

On a related note, this Court observes that the Supreme Court recently held that the "bona fide error" defense does not apply to "a violation resulting from a debt collector's mistaken interpretation of the legal requirements of the FDCPA." - in Bradshaw v. HILCO RECEIVABLES, LLC, 2010

In other words, a debt collector's conduct may be intentional even if he lacked the actual knowledge that his conduct violated the FDCPA. - in Bassett v. IC System, Inc., 2010

The bona fide defense may only be used in circumstances where a violation results from other causes, such as a clerical or factual mistake. - in Bradshaw v. HILCO RECEIVABLES, LLC, 2010

This case does not involve statutory regulation of the activity of various market players, say, for example, of lawyers functioning as debt collectors. - in THE REAL ESTATE BAR v. NATIONAL REAL ESTATE INFO., 2010

The full decision and citations can be found in chapter seven.

IMPORTANT

When you do file a civil complaint against a collector alleging FDCPA violations, keep a close eye on your credit reports. If you see that the collection company has accessed your credit report after the date that they received your summons then they may be in violation of the Fair Credit Reporting Act. Civil litigation is not a permissible use of consumers' credit report, as it is not a business to consumer transaction as outlined in the FCRA.

4

PREPARING YOUR CASE

Preparing for and filing a lawsuit is about eighty percent research and about twenty percent paperwork. After filing suit, it is mostly paperwork. I would venture to guess that in ninety-five percent or more cases, the plaintiff (i.e. you) will never see a courtroom or a judge. It is important to include the proper items in a civil complaint to ensure that a collection company will settle early on in the suit.

Who Is Behind the Collections?

Depending on if it is a credit card company or a bank (in my case American Express is a bank) file a FDIC complaint (governs banks) or a Comptroller of the Currency (governs credit card companies).

Filing a complaint with the comptroller of the currency is a good way to find out if a credit card company actually sold the debt and if the debt collector / attorneys are suing under false pretenses, have perjured themselves in court, etc.

You can search to see if the financial institution is governed by the FDIC or Comptroller of the currency.

http://www.ffiec.gov/consumercenter/

Contact information for Comptroller of the Currency

http://www.occ.treas.gov/customer.htm

File a complaint with the Comptroller of the Currency

https://appsec.helpwithmybank.gov/olcc_form/
(you'll need to search to find exactly who regulates them, sometimes they are regulated by the Federal Reserve).

File a FDIC complaint at
https://www2.fdic.gov/starsmail/index.asp

If you can't get any information through filing a FDIC or Comptroller of the Currency complaint then you may have to file discovery during your case and expose the law firm that way.

You don't need an attorney to start a FDCPA lawsuit. You can always get one involved once it gets on the court docket.

Backgrounder

#1 - Log everything like debt collector calls, demand letters, etc. Date/time and who it is. Be vigilant.

#2 - Take pictures of the Caller ID display (if you don't have it get it), save and print these out and put them in a file. I keep one on each debt collector that has or is contacting me so I can keep it organized.

#3 - Record all telephone conversations. If you live in a one-party state (such as Georgia) and the debt collector is calling from a one-party consent state, you don't have to advise them that you are recording the call. An easy way to get around two-party consent state calls is once the debt collector tells you that they call is being recording, jokingly say yes I am too (do it in a humorous or off-hand way), if they don't object you are good to go.

Save the phone calls and burn them to a disc or discs; I save them until I file suit.

#4 - When you get the initial written communication from the debt collector, send them a certified letter disputing the debt and request validation of the debt. This is the point most often where the debt collector will screw up, especially those that bought the debt from the original creditor or from another debt buyer that sold the account to them. They cannot continue to collect until they satisfy your request for validation. If they do then you have at least one FDCPA violation and could ultimately get a case thrown out if they choose to sue you.

#5 - Publicize the debt collectors bad behavior. Let other consumers in on information and more importantly, let the debt collection company know that you don't have a problem telling the world what they are doing. Blog about it, post on consumer complaint forums, contact sites such as Consumerist.com, call your local newspaper or other large newspapers and TV news in your area or state. Let them feel some of the same "heat" they are putting on you.

#6 - If the debt collector is calling your cell phone, and you answer, if you hear a moment of dead silence then they are using an automated dialer and that is a violation of the TCPA (Telephone Consumer Protection Act) in addition to the possibility of them violating the FDCPA.

When I send a dispute/validation request I also demand they Cease and Desist all telephone communications. 99.9% of the time they will violate it and you have a FDCPA violation to sue them for. Send your dispute, validation, cease telephone communications letter via certified mail so you have a record that they received it.

#7 - Always file a FDCPA violation complaint against the Debt Collector for each violation with the Federal Trade Commission (www.ftc.gov). You never know when the FTC might actually begin an investigation, so do it.

Initial Steps in filing FDCPA lawsuits

#1 - Read the Fair Debt Collections Practices Act and familiarize yourself with the sections and chapters that cover debt collector violations (1692a-k). While you are working on this, I suggest you locate and employ a consumer protection or consumer law attorney; you can find one in your state at www.naca.net and www.martindale.com. Consumer protection attorneys generally don't charge any upfront fees and only are paid when you win your case against the debt collector. I have included a copy of the U.S. Code that pertains to the FDCPA in chapter seven.

#2 - The Fair Debt Collection Practices Act allows you to file suit in just about any court in the US, such as small claims court, state court and of course federal court. I generally start at the state court level and let the debt-collecting defendant remove it to federal court if they want. More than likely, they will, so they can invoke an "Offer of Compromise". That is a good thing, when they move it to federal court you can bet the Federal Trade Commission can gain access to more evidence of their bad behavior when they decide to investigate the debt collector. Of course, the Federal Trade Commission seems to move at glacier speed when taking bad debt collectors to task for abusing consumers (maybe this will change one day). You can file a FDCPA suit in the county you live in, even though the defendant is not located in your county or state.

#3 - Check your states procedures on serving a company, most states' laws (code) are online and will give you the information on properly serving them.

For instance, in the State of Georgia, proper service of a foreign corporation is as follows:

O.C.G.A. § 14-2-1510 Foreign Corporations - service.

(a) The registered agent of a foreign corporation authorized to transact business in this state is the corporation's agent for service of process, notice, or demand required or permitted by law to be served on the foreign corporation.

(b) If a foreign corporation has no registered agent or its registered agent cannot with reasonable diligence be served, the corporation may be served by registered or certified mail or statutory overnight delivery, return receipt requested, addressed to the chief executive officer, chief financial officer, or secretary of the foreign corporation, or a person holding a position comparable to any of the foregoing, at its principal office shown in the later of its application for a certificate of authority or its most recent annual registration. Any party that serves a foreign corporation in accordance with this subsection shall also serve a copy of the process upon the Secretary of State and shall pay a $10.00 filing fee.

(c) Service is perfected under subsection (b) of this Code section at the earliest of:

(1) The date the foreign corporation receives the mail;

(2) The date shown on the return receipt, if signed on behalf of the foreign corporation; or

(3) Five days after its deposit in the United States mail, as evidenced by the postmark, if mailed postpaid and correctly addressed.

(d) This Code section does not prescribe the only means, or necessarily the required means, of serving a foreign corporation.

Also see O.C.G.A. § 14-9-902.1

You can search your state's Secretary of State website, or contact them to find the registered agent. Of course this is mainly for out of state defendants, however if you are filing against a debt collector in your state you will still need to serve the corporation's registered agent.

Each state has different rules and regulations on proper service so be sure to check with your state laws to ensure you don't serve it incorrectly.

In State Lawsuits

Once you know who the registered agent is, it will display the county in which they are located. Make a note of it, as you will need this when filing/serving.

Search the Sheriff's office website (for the county the registered agents is located in) and find the civil service section (or call them if they don't have one). Find out what you need to send to them for serving the registered agent. Usually it is a copy of the suit (sometimes they require two original copies) (aka process to serve), a check made out to them for the service fee (money orders are generally acceptable), a Sheriff's Entry of Service (get it from your court clerk's office when filing) and a self-addressed self-stamped envelope (SASE) so you can get your copies back). Remember once you get your copies back you'll need to file one with your court clerk's office and then the 30 day clock starts ticking for the defendant to reply with an answer to you suit.

Draft your FDCPA violations civil complaint, and my advice is to print six original copies and get them all notarized as required by law. Take them to the court clerk's office along with the filing fee. Once it is filed, ask the court clerk for a couple of "Sheriff's Entry of Service" forms (one for each defendant and extras in case you make a typo). I recommend when filing the complaint to demand a jury trial, juries *LOVE* awarding big damages in FDCPA lawsuits.

Then follow the directions for serving the registered agent in the county they reside in.

*If you start stressing or feel like you are over your head when things start heating up in court, get a consumer protection advocate (generally free) or a consumer law attorney involved. You can do this at *any* time during the suing process.*

About ninety-five percent of the time, the debt collector will attempt to settle with you before the case goes to trial. Demand everything they wish to settle in writing, if they won't give it you in writing, politely tell them "we will just have to see each other in court".

NOTE #1

After they answer (if they do), you may receive a "notice of removal". This just means they are moving the case to a higher court, most likely U.S. Federal District Court. I like federal court better than state court, because the rules of procedure are clearer and easier for "non lawyer types" like me to understand.

Just remember you have rights as a consumer and as a human being, don't let *anyone* abuse those rights. Put those corrupt debt collectors where they belong, behind the defendants table in court. It's time to fight back against abusive and illegal debt collection tactics. The more consumers who do this, the less likely these companies will continue their abusive behavior.

NOTE #2

If you are dealing with a third party debt collector or debt buyer, just remember all evidence they provide or testimony they give is hundred percent hearsay.

Court Procedures – Rules of Civil Procedure

Every court in the United States has rules of procedure, which are often referred to as "Rules of Civil Procedure". These "rules" are nothing more than instructions on how to do things such as filing a suit or discovery, when and how motions or briefs should be filed, etc.

Throughout this and other upcoming chapters, I will explain what each is and how to use them.

You can find most court rules online and it is in your best interest to print them out or save them for future reference. The rules are simple and straightforward. For example, in the State of Georgia nearly all courts follow the state's rules of civil procedure found in O.C.G.A Title 9 Civil Practice, Chapter 11 Civil Practices Act.

Luckily, at the time of the writing of this book Lexis-Nexis has the Official Code of Georgia (O.C.G.A) available as free access.

ww.lexis-nexis.com/hottopics/gacode/

It may be that all states offer access to their state laws in the same or similar manner. You will need to check or search online. Many states have their state laws on their website so be sure to check there first.

In most states when you file a lawsuit, you must file a copy with the court clerk's office, along with verification and a certificate of service. I provide and explain examples of each.

In the state of Georgia, when serving a company or their registered agent (out of state corporations), you must serve a summons and order of entry with the lawsuit. The court clerk's office should be able to provide you with the summons and order of entry. Of course, other states and courts may be different, so consult your local court rules regarding how to serve the defendant.

Generally, if you are filing it in a state court, your state's laws should have a title and section concerning serving a defendant. Most states have their laws online and it is relatively easy to find the information you need.

For instance in the state of Georgia serving a corporation is referred to a "Service of Process" and is covered un OCGA Title 14 Corporations, Partnerships, and Associations, Article 5 Office and Agent), part 1 Registered Agents and Service of Process, specifically OCGA § 14-2-504. Service on corporation.

When you serve a corporation you must serve the registered agent of the corporation if they have one in your state; if they don't, your state's laws (as in the example above) will outline how to properly serve the defendant. For a lawsuit to be valid, it must be served properly. Federal court lawsuits are a bit different as you can generally serve a summons via registered mail (or FedEx) on a defendant. Be sure you are clear on how to file and serve the defendant before you move forward with your suit.

If in doubt, you might want to contact a civil attorney and pay for an hour or two and have them outline the proper process. I have done so in the past to ensure that I filed everything properly. Many attorneys will be happy to talk to you.

As I mentioned earlier, every state has different laws regarding proper service and summons. In my state, we have to perform three tasks in order to serve a defendant (or registered agent).

In the next chapter, I will explain and illustrate each procedure from filing the initial lawsuit all the way through procedures if the case actually goes to trial. Ninety-nine percent of the time the collection agency will make an offer to settle, so don't get to "caught up" with discovery, motions, briefs, etc. unless you need to.

From my own personal experiences and from performing thousands of hours of research on debt collection FDCPA lawsuits, more often than not the company or law firm will offer a settlement to keep the case from going forward in court.

If you have recorded conversations or voicemails of any harassment, you have a nearly one hundred percent chance of receiving a settlement offer. When you do receive a settlement offer make sure you aren't sacrificing anything beyond keeping the details of the settlement secret and that you won't file a future lawsuit for the same allegations. Force them to remove any language that may limit your right to sue them again in the future for other violations, or anything else you feel shouldn't be part of the settlement.

I have had collection companies draw up settlement agreements that contained language that shouldn't be part of the agreement, so I made them take it out. If they don't, they risk going to trial as you are not obligated to take the settlement, and it is in their best interest to settle with you. If the settlement agreement confuses you, then consult with an attorney. An hour or two of an attorney's time may save you from forfeiting rights you need not give up.

5

FILING SUIT

In this chapter, I am going to cover how to draft a civil complaint. Each of the FDCPA violations in the example complaint below is covered by a different section of law and I will attempt to explain what to include in a complaint and why it is being used.

I recommend that you read this entire chapter before drafting your complaint, so you have a better understanding of the filing and process of service procedure.

NOTE: See the pro se legal resources chapter for legal decisions, citations, and the full US code for FDCPA, FCRA, and TCPA laws. I have attempted to put the information in this chapter in the logical order that you would use it to file your lawsuit.

Under the Fair Debt Collection Practices Act (FDCPA), it states that a civil action for violations of the act can be filed in any court of competent jurisdiction. This means you don't have to file the suit in Federal court. You may file it small claims, state, superior court, etc.

15 USC 1692k § 813 (d)

(d) An action to enforce any liability created by this title may be brought in any appropriate United States district court without regard to the amount in controversy, or in any other court of competent jurisdiction, within one year from the date on which the violation occurs.

I always file my debt collector lawsuits in state court. It is less expensive than filing in US District (Federal) court. In the event that the collector moves it (notice of removal), they must pay the costs to move it. It will save you about three hundred dollars by filing at the state level versus the federal level. Even better that the defendant has to pay the costs, not you.

Although I will go into more detail about a lawsuit being removed from a lower court to US District court later in the chapter, it is a good indication that that collector will make an offer of settlement (Federal Rule 408) shortly after it is removed and accepted by the higher court. See further on in this chapter regarding a Notice of Removal and also Chapter Six as I cover settling the suit or continuing forward with your lawsuit.

Be sure to follow your courts rules of procedure or rules of civil procedure, as I mentioned in the previous chapter.

You can include any state laws that may have been violated as well. Since there are fifty states, I can't go into detail on all of them, so I will leave this option for you to decide or include in your complaint. I have included violations of the Georgia Business Practices Act in my civil filing because I live in the state of Georgia and several sections of the State code (laws) did apply.

The next step is to draft a civil complaint and begin the process of filing and serving the complaint.

NOTE: If you really want to drive the collection company crazy and encourage a quick settlement attach a CDROM of your telephone calls/voicemails evidence to the complaint. I do it on all of my complaints or send them separately via email or postal mail, then truly know I have them in a corner. You might as well put a good scare into them at the same time. This tactic has worked very well for me in the past and can work for you.

Filing the Complaint

The example on the following page can be used in Federal U.S. District Court and in most state courts.

In the example complaint below you will notice that it contains five sections. The first section is a brief introduction of what the complaint contains, the second section covers jurisdiction and venue (where a trial should be held), the third section outlines the parties (plaintiff and defendant), the fourth section contains the allegations (why we are filing the lawsuit) and lastly in section five covers the claims for relief (what you want from the defendant).

You will note in the example that I do not include any specific monetary amounts in the claim for relief. I want a judge or jury to decide what "relief" I should get if the case did go to trial. If you include specific amounts in the complaint for damages, you may limit yourself in regards to monetary awards.

IMPORTANT: You can ask an attorney to get involved at any time during the lawsuit if you feel overwhelmed. If you file the suit as the example is outlined it will help an attorney, should you hire one, to move the case forward. I personally prefer to go all the way on my own (pro se).

A civil filing is drafted and filed in what is commonly referred to a "pleading form" and these forms are uniform no matter what court you are filing the suit in. The example below will work in U.S. District court, most, if not all state courts, as well as lower court.

In chapter seven, I have included the full, title 15 U.S.C. 1692, Fair Debt Collection Practices Act for easy reference while you draft your civil complaint. The example complaint covers the most common FDCPA violations. When drafting your complaint, if you are in doubt just leave it out. You can amend your complaint after it is filed, if necessary.

A civil complaint should be concise and to the point, no need to add personal opinions or legal citations to it. That is what "briefs" and "motions" are for, chances are you won't need them to extract a settlement from the collection company.

BEGIN EXAMPLE COMPLAINT

IN THE STATE COURT OF [YOUR COUNTY] COUNTY
STATE OF [YOUR STATE]

[YOUR NAME],	)	
Plaintiff,	)	Case No.:
vs.	)	
[PLAINTIFFS NAME HERE]	)	
Defendant	)	

COMPLAINT AND DEMAND FOR JURY TRIAL

I. INTRODUCTION

This is an action for damages brought by an individual consumer for Defendant's violations of the Fair Debt Collection Practices Act, 15 U.S.C. § 1692, et seq. (hereinafter ''FDCPA''), which prohibit debt collectors from engaging in abusive, deceptive, and unfair practices.

II. JURISDICTION AND VENUE

Jurisdiction of this Court arises under 15 U.S.C. § 1692k(d) and 28 U.S.C. § 1337. Declaratory relief is available pursuant to 28 U.S.C. §§ 2201 and 2202 Venue in this District is proper in that the defendants transact business here and the conduct complained of occurred here.

III. PARTIES

Plaintiff, [YOUR NAME], is a natural person residing in the state of [YOUR STATE]. Defendant, [PLAINTIFF NAME], is a corporation engaged in the business of collecting debts in this state with its principal place of business located at [PLAINTIFF FULL MAILING ADDRESS]. The principal purpose of Defendant is the collection of debts using the mails and telephone, and Defendant regularly attempts to collect debts alleged to be due another.

Defendant, John Doe, is a natural person employed by Defendant as a collector at all times relevant to this complaint. Defendants are ''debt collectors'' as defined by the FDCPA, 15 U.S.C. § 1692a(6).

IV. FACTUAL ALLEGATIONS

[This paragraph below is for illustration only to give you an idea how to word the complaint, replace the information to suit your own needs]

On or about November 4, 2008, Defendant, while employed as a collector by Defendant, contacted Plaintiff's employer, and requested Plaintiff's employer to speak to Plaintiff regarding the importance of paying alleged debts. Plaintiff's employer informed Plaintiff of this contact. On or about July 29, 2008 Plaintiff wrote requesting Defendants not to contact Plaintiff's employer or otherwise contact Plaintiff via telephone communications. On or about November 19, 2008 Plaintiff filed a complaint with the Better Business Bureau requesting Defendants not to contact Plaintiff's employer. As a result of the acts alleged above, Plaintiff suffered headaches, nausea, embarrassment, mental depression and emotional distress, lost weight, interruption of work, lost time, and expenses.

V. CLAIM FOR RELIEF

Plaintiff repeats and realleges and incorporates by reference paragraphs one through four above. Defendants violated the FDCPA. Defendants' violations include, but are not limited to, the following: (a) The Defendants violated 15 U.S.C. § 1692c(b) by contacting a third party, the Plaintiff's employer, without the Plaintiff's prior consent. (b) The Defendants violated 15 U.S.C. § 1692c(c) by contacting the Plaintiff after the Plaintiff had requested the Defendants cease communication with the Plaintiff. (c) The Defendants violated 15 U.S.C. § 1692g(b) by failing to provide verification of the debt and continuing its debt collection efforts after the plaintiff had disputed the debt in writing within thirty days of receiving notice of the 15 U.S.C. § 1692g debt validation rights. As a result of the above violations of the FDCPA, the Defendants are liable to the Plaintiff for declaratory judgment that defendants' conduct violated the FDCPA, injunctive relief, and Plaintiff's actual damages, statutory damages, and costs and attorney's fees.

WHEREFORE, Plaintiff respectfully prays that judgment be entered against the Defendant for the following:

A. Declaratory judgment that defendants' conduct violated the FDCPA and injunctive relief for the defendants' violations;

B. Actual damages;

C. Statutory damages pursuant to 15 U.S.C. § 1692k.;

D. Costs and reasonable attorney's fees pursuant to 15 U.S.C. § 1692k.;

E. For such other and further relief as may be just and proper.

DEMAND FOR JURY TRIAL

Please take notice that Plaintiff demands trial by jury in this action.

____

Plaintiff
Dated this April 1, 2009

VERIFICATION

I [YOUR NAME] hereby certify that the facts contained in the foregoing Complaint are true and correct to the best of my knowledge, information and belief.

____

[YOURNAME] – *pro se*

[NOTARY PUBLIC]

END OF EXAMPLE COMPLAINT

REMEMBER: in most states, you will need to obtain and order of entry and a summons from the court clerk that must be served upon the defendant along with the complaint. If the defendant is a corporation (i.e. a law firm), you will need to check with your secretary of state's office to find out who their registered agent is. You must serve the registered agent of the law firm/company. All court filings, certificates of service, and verification must be notarized. A copy of anything you file must be sent to the opposing attorney or defendant(s) along with a certificate of service.

Verification

"Verification" is a simple notarized affidavit that states that all of the facts in your complaint are true and correct to the best of your knowledge. It can be typed or printed on a single piece of paper and no special formatting is necessary.

Begin Example Verification

VERIFICATION

I [YOUR NAME HERE] hereby certify that the facts contained in the foregoing Complaint are true and correct to the best of my knowledge, information and belief.

____

[YOURNAME HERE] – pro se
[CURRENT MONTH DAY, YEAR]

End Example Verification

Be sure to have this notarized and file it along with the complaint. Make sure you keep an original copy for yourself and include an original copy with the complaint that you serve on the defendant or defendants registered agent.

Certificate of Service

A certificate of service is a document that you file with the court clerk. Keep an original copy for yourself and include a copy with the complaint you serve on the defendant. It must be notarized.

In the example, you will need to change the heading to fit your court and county and enter the information relevant to your filing. You must file a certificate of service each time you file a document with the court clerk and an original copy must be sent to the defendant (or their attorney of record).

Begin Sample Certificate of Service

IN THE STATE COURT OF [YOUR COUNTY] COUNTY
STATE OF [YOUR STATE}

[YOUR NAME], Plaintiff	)	
	)	
vs.	)	
	)	Civil Action File No. ____________
[DEFENDANTS NAME] Defendant	)	
	)	
	)	
	)	
	)	

CERTIFICATE OF SERVICE

I hereby certify that I have this day served the foregoing COMPLAINT upon counsel for all parties, by depositing a copy of same in the United States mail in an envelope with sufficient postage thereon addressed as follows:

[DEFENDANTS (or attorney) NAME AND FULL ADDRESS HERE].

This [INSERT DATE HERE, ______ day of Month, Year.

____

Plaintiff
Address: [YOUR ADDRESS HERE]
Phone: [YOUR PHONE NUMBER]

[NOTARY PUBLIC]

Sworn and subscribed before me this ____ day of MONTH, YEAR.

____

Notary Public, State of ______________

End Sample Certificate of Service

Registered Agent (Corporations)

Most companies have a registered agent in each state that they do business in. There are a few exceptions to this rule. You should be able to look up a company's registered agent at the Secretary of State website for the state that you live in. As far as I am aware, all state corporations' registered agent directories are available online. Be sure that you find and serve the proper company and registered agent.

No Registered Agent?

Some companies may not have a presence in your state even though they are collecting debts in it. Several states do not require debt collectors to hold state licenses or maintain a presence in the state. If this were the case, you would need to check your state's laws regarding serving a business entity (corporation) if they do not have a registered agent or presence in the state.

For instance, in the state of Georgia there are several methods of serving an out of state (foreign) corporation that doesn't maintain a registered agent in the state. One of which is serving an officer of the corporation (CEO, CFO, Secretary of the corporation) via registered or certified mail and also serving a copy of the process on the Secretary of State (Georgia). Because each state may have different methods of serving an out of state defendant, be sure to find this information.

I prefer to sue out of state corporations, especially if they don't have registered agents in the state. It will cost them more money to respond to the suit and chances are they will have the case moved from where I file it to U.S. District court. This of course means they will most likely make an offer of settlement shortly after the case is removed from the lower court.

Serving the Complaint, Order of Entry and Summons

Each state has its own rules (laws) on how to serve a complaint. Most the time the procedure is similar regardless of what state you reside in. I do recommend that you look up your state's laws on service of a complaint. If not done properly you may have to re-file your complaint. Defects in a complaint will cost you time and money, so prepare in advance for filing.

In the state of Georgia, you must file the complaint and 'serve' the complaint upon the defendant via the county Sheriff's office for in-state lawsuits. If the defendant doesn't have a registered agent and is a foreign entity (out of state companies), there are alternative methods of serving them.

In most states, you must send an officer of the company the complaint and summons as well as serve your state's secretary of state if they do not maintain a business presence in your state or have a registered agent.

Order of Entry and Summons documents can be obtained from the local court clerk's office.

In the event that you are filing suit (in-state) and the company you are suing lives in a different county, you will need to contact the sheriff's office in the other county to find out how much (generally ten to twenty dollars) the cost is to serve the company's registered agent. Once that information is obtained, you would then fill out the summons and order of entry and send them along with the complaint to the other county's sheriff's department.

In many states, you may be able to utilize an independent process server. Be sure to check your states laws regarding service. The whole process of serving the defendant is primarily paperwork and waiting for service to be perfected (defendant served).

The day the defendant is served, the clock starts in regards to them responding to (answering) the complaint. If by chance, they fail to answer in the proper period, you would then be able to file a motion for default judgment (entry of default). Surprisingly, this happens quite often and the plaintiff (you) could then begin judgment proceedings and collect money via the legal system.

6

SETTLE OR MOVE FORWARD?

A large number of collectors will attempt to offer a monetary settlement rather than go to trial, especially out of state collectors.

In most cases, a collection company will make an offer of compromise, which is a settlement. If both parties agree to discuss such an offer, nothing discussed may be used against the other party in the even the settlement talks breakdown and the case moves back to the courtroom.

Federal Rule 408. Compromise and Offers to Compromise

a) Prohibited uses.—Evidence of the following is not admissible on behalf of any party, when offered to prove liability for, invalidity of, or amount of a claim that was disputed as to validity or amount, or to impeach through a prior inconsistent statement or contradiction:

(1) furnishing or offering or promising to furnish or accepting or offering or promising to accept a valuable consideration in compromising or attempting to compromise the claim ; and

(2) conduct or statements made in compromise negotiations regarding the claim, except when offered in a criminal case and the negotiations related to a claim by a public office or agency in the exercise of regulatory, investigative, or enforcement authority.

Permitted uses. This rule does not require exclusion if the evidence is offered for purposes not prohibited by subdivision (a). Examples of permissible purposes include proving a witness's bias or prejudice; negating a contention of undue delay; and proving an effort to obstruct a criminal investigation or prosecution.

I have performed extensive research on suits brought against collection companies, from the federal filings I have reviewed; the companies will settle a case about ninety-eight percent of the time. This is the collection industry "Achilles Heel". I imagine they prefer that consumers did not know that there is an extremely high rate of settlements in cases filed.

I cannot cover all aspects or language of a settlement agreement in this book as they vary widely. I do suggest that once an initial agreement is set, carefully read the agreement and not agree to anything you feel that would bind you from pursuing future abuse against the company. If you are unsure about the agreement language, most attorneys will review documents for a small hourly fee.

In the event that you do not agree to the terms of a settlement agreement, attempt to have them remove the offending language. It never hurts and I personally have had collection companies remove language or conditions from a settlement agreement that I felt had no place in it.

7

LEGAL PRECEDENTS AND RESOURCES

In this chapter I have included legal citations (court decisions), the full US code (laws) for the Fair Debt Collection Practices Act (FDCPA), Fair Credit Reporting Act (FCRA), and the Telephone Consumer Protection Act (TCPA). I have marked the relevant sections of each that I use in the book for your convenience. The reason why I included the full text is so that you have full access to these resources in one convenient location.

Important Legal Decisions and Citations Regarding Fair Debt Collection Practices Act Violations

FOTI v. NCO FINANCIAL SYSTEMS, INC.

[424 F.Supp.2d 643, 653]

II. Discussion

A. The FDCPA

The FDCPA was enacted "to eliminate abusive debt collection practices by debt collectors, to insure those debt collectors who refrain from using abusive debt collection practices are not competitively disadvantaged, and to promote consistent State action to protect consumers against debt collection abuses." 15 U.S.C. § 1692e. Congress found such abuses by debt collectors to be "serious and widespread." Russell v. Equifax A.R.S., 74 F.3d 30, 33 (2d Cir.1996).

"The FDCPA establishes a civil cause of action against `any debt collector who fails to comply with any provision of this subchapter with respect to any person.'" Sakrani v. Koenig, No. Civ. A 05-1192, 2006 WL 20514, at *2 (D.N.J. Jan. 3, 2006) (quoting 15 U.S.C. § 1692k(a)). Specifically, the FDCPA "prohibits unfair or unconscionable collection methods, conduct which harasses, oppresses or abuses any debtor, and the making of any false, misleading, or deceptive statements in connection with a debt, and it requires that collectors make certain disclosures." Acosta v. Campbell No. 6:04 Civ. 761, 2006 WL 146208, at *12 (M.D.Fla. Jan. 18, 2006) (citing 15 U.S.C. §§ 1692d, 1692e, 1692f). The Act also requires debt collectors to notify debtors about their ability to challenge the validity of a debt and to provide other basic information. See 15 U.S.C. § 1692g.

B. Standard of Review

NCO seeks to dismiss the Amended Complaint, pursuant to Fed.R.Civ.P. 12(c). While the Motion is styled as being brought pursuant to Rule 12(c), because the Motion was filed prior to the filing of an answer to the Amended Complaint, it is more properly construed as a Motion made pursuant to Fed.R.Civ.P. 12(b)(6). Cf. Harris v. City of New York, 186 F.3d 243, 249 (2d Cir.1999) ("[W]e look to the allegations in [the amended complaint], which is the legally effective pleading for Rule 12(b)(6) purposes."); Shields v. Citytrust Bancorp, Inc., 25 F.3d 1124, 1128 (2d Cir. 1994) ("It is well established that an amended complaint ordinarily supersedes the original, and renders it of no legal effect.'"), superseded by statute on other grounds, Private Securities Litigation Reform Act, 15 U.S.C. § 78u-4, as recognized in In re Paracelsus Corp. Sec. Litig., 61 F.Supp.2d 591, 595 (S.D.Tex.1998) (quoting Int'l Controls Corp. v. Vesco, 556 F.2d 665, 668 (2d Cir.1977)). Even if, however, this Court were to consider the Motion as one made pursuant to Rule 12(c), the standard under Rule 12(c) is substantively identical to that under 12(b)(6). See Ziemba v. Wezner, 366 F.3d 161, 163 (2d Cir.2004) ("In deciding a Rule 12(c) motion, we apply the same standard as that applicable to a motion under Rule 12(b)(6), accepting the allegations contained in the complaint as true and drawing all reasonable inferences in favor of the nonmoving party.'") (quoting Burnette v. Carothers, 192 F.3d 52, 56 (2d Cir.1999)).

In examining a motion to dismiss, the Court must "accept as true the factual allegations made in the complaint and draw all inferences in favor of the plaintiffs." Grandon v. Merrill Lynch & Co., Inc., 147 F.3d 184, 188 (2d Cir.1998). "The court's function on a Rule 12(b)(6) motion is not to weigh the evidence that might be presented at a trial but merely to determine whether the complaint itself is legally

[424 F.Supp.2d 643, 654]

sufficient." Goldman v. Belden, 754 F.2d 1059, 1067 (2d Cir.1985). Dismissal is appropriate "only if there are no legal grounds upon which relief may be granted." Virgilio v. City of New York, 407 F.3d 105, 111 (2d Cir.2005).

C. Whether NCO Sent "Communications" to Plaintiffs

In order to be subject to some of the protections of the FDCPA, correspondence must be a "communication" within the meaning of the Act. There is no dispute that the January 26 Conversation constitutes a "communication."[18] Moreover, there is no suggestion that telephone communications, in contrast to written communications, are not protected by the FDCPA.

NCO argues, however, that the January 18 Pre-Recorded Message is not a "communication" within the meaning of the FDCPA because it "does not convey any information regarding a debt, but instead simply requests a return call regarding an important business matter." (NCO Mem. 4) NCO suggests that to the extent the message is not a "communication," Plaintiffs' § 1692g and § 1692e(10) claims (in Count One), and

Plaintiffs' § 1692e(11) claims (in Count Two) should be dismissed with respect to the January 18 Pre-Recorded Message.

While it is clear that the message must be a "communication" to be protected by § 1692e(11) (requiring disclosure in "subsequent communications") (emphasis added), correspondence does not necessarily need to be a "communication" in order to be subject to Plaintiffs' § 1692g claims in Count One. Rather, the § 1692g claim, discussed below, addresses whether the January 18 Pre-Recorded Message "overshadowed" the otherwise valid initial communication, the January 1 Letter. Resolution of that claim, however, does not depend on whether the January 18 Pre-Recorded Message is a "communication" under the Act. 15 U.S.C. § 1692a(2) ("The term `communication' means the conveying of information regarding a debt directly or indirectly to any person through any medium."). Additionally, the § 1692e(10) claim (in Count One) hinges on whether the debt collector made "use of any false representation or deceptive means to collect or attempt to collect any debt. . . ." 15 U.S.C. § 1692e(10). This claim also does not depend on a finding that an allegedly false representation was in the form of a "communication" under the Act. Thus, even if NCO prevails in establishing that the January 18 Pre-Recorded Message does not constitute a "communication," this would only implicate the § 1692e(11) claim in Count Two.

In any event, NCO's Memorandum of Law in support of its Motion failed to cite one case in support of its position that the January 18 Pre-Recorded Message is not a communication, and pointed to only one case at oral argument.[19] (Tr. 7) Given this paucity of authority, the Court has little

[424 F.Supp.2d 643, 655]

difficulty in rejecting NCO's narrow interpretation of the word "communication," and concludes that the January 18 Pre-Recorded Message is protected as a "communication" under the FDCPA.

"The FDCPA defines `communication' very broadly as the conveying of information regarding a debt directly or indirectly to any person through any medium.'" Romea v. Heiberger & Assocs., 163 F.3d 111, 114 n. 2 (2d Cir.1998) (quoting 15 U.S.C. § 1692(a)(2)) (holding that notice demanding payment of rent arrearage or surrender of rented premises to landlord was a "communication" within the meaning of the FDCPA). While the Second Circuit has not precisely defined the scope of the term "communication," it has suggested in other contexts that, consistent with Congress's intent in enacting the FDCPA, the statute should be broadly construed. See Pipiles v. Credit Bureau of Lockport, Inc., 886 F.2d 22, 27 (2d Cir.1989) Mt is apparent that the prescribed requirement can further the Congressional purpose in enacting the FDCPA in 1977, which was to prevent `abusive, deceptive, and unfair debt collection practices.'") (citations omitted) (holding that under the pre-amended version of § 1692e(11), disclosure is required in all communications);[20] see also Cavallaro v. Law Office of Shapiro & Kreisman, 933 F.Supp. 1148, 1153 (E.D.N.Y.1996) ("The Second Circuit also has warned debt collectors against loosely interpreting the FDCPA.") (citing Russell, 74 F.3d at 35); accord Blair v. Sherman Acquisition, No. 04 Civ. 4718, 2004 WL 2870080, at *2 (N.D.Ill. Dec. 13, 2004) ("Because it is designed to protect consumers, the FDCPA is, in general, liberally construed in favor of consumers to effect its purpose.").

Outside the Second Circuit, at least one court has rejected the very claim made by Defendant. In Hosseinzadeh v. M.R.S. Assocs., Inc., 387 F.Supp.2d 1104 (C.D.Cal. 2005), the debt collector argued that its standard voicemail messages to debtors were not "communications" under the FDCPA because "they did not convey[information regarding a debt directly or indirectly to any person."[21] Id. at 1115 (omitting quotations) (brackets in original). In rejecting the argument, the court held:

While the messages may not technically mention specific information about a debt or the nature of the call, § 1692a(2) applies to information conveyed "directly or indirectly." Defendant conveyed information to plaintiff, including the fact that there was an important matter that she should attend to and instructions on how to do so.

Id. at 1116. Further, as is evident from Plaintiffs' allegations in this case, the Hosseinzadeh court found it significant that the voicemails "were merely the first step in a process designed to communicate with plaintiff about her alleged debt." Id.

Hosseinzadeh is on all-fours with this case. Defendant's voicemail message, while devoid of any specific information about any particular debt, clearly provided some information, even if indirectly, to the intended recipient of the message. Specifically,
[424 F.Supp.2d 643, 656]

the message advised the debtor that the matter required immediate attention, and provided a specific number to call to discuss the matter. Given that the obvious purpose of the message was to provide the debtor with enough information to entice a return call, it is difficult to imagine how the voicemail message is not a communication under the FDCPA.[22]

The scope of the term "communication" has been addressed in other contexts as well, including under § 1692c(b), which regulates communications between debt collectors and third parties (people other than the debtor).[23] Two cases have suggested that correspondence is not a "communication" where it does not convey any specific information about the debt being collected. See Horkey v. J.V.D.B. & Assocs., Inc., 179 F.Supp.2d 861, 868 (N.D.Ill. 2002) ("The Court agrees with Defendant and finds that there is no evidence that [defendant's employee] in communicating with [p]laintiff's co-worker . . . discussed [p]laintiff's debt. Rather, [the] conversation with [plaintiffs co-worker] was merely limited to inquiring as to [p]laintiff's whereabouts. . . ."), aff'd on other grounds, 333 F.3d 769 (7th Cir.2003); Fava, 1997 WL 205336, at *6 ("The March 12th fax does not convey any information regarding the [plaintiffs'] debt and therefore is not a communication within the meaning of the Act.").

However, in West v. Nationwide Credit, 998 F.Supp. 642, 644 (W.D.N.C.1998), the court rejected a narrow interpretation of the word "communication," similar to that advanced by NCO in this case. The plaintiff in West alleged that defendants violated §

1692c(b) by contacting plaintiffs neighbor. Defendants argued that a debt collector's phone call informing a neighbor that he had a "very important" matter to discuss did not violate § 1692c(b) because no information was actually conveyed about plaintiffs debt. The West court rejected this narrow interpretation of "communication" in favor of a broader interpretation. Id. at 644. In reaching this conclusion, the West court noted that "[i]n interpreting the meaning of a statute, it is well settled that `[t]he "plain meaning" of statutory language controls its construction,'" and went on to examine the dictionary definitions of "regarding." Id. (quoting

[424 F.Supp.2d 643, 657]

Summit Inv. & Dev. Corp. v. Leroux, 69 F.3d 608, 610 (1st Cir.1995)). In particular, the court noted: "Webster's Ninth New Collegiate Dictionary (1st ed.1983) defines the term `regard' as, inter alia, `to relate to,' while it provides the following definition of the term `regarding': `with respect to: concerning.'" Id. "Based on these definitions, the court believes the ordinary meaning of the term `regarding' is consistent with the broader interpretation advocated by Plaintiff." Id.

This conclusion has been embraced by other courts as well in the context of applying § 1692c(b). See, e.g., Henderson, 2001 WL 969105, at *2 (rejecting defendant's argument that letter sent to employer seeking information about whether plaintiff was employed, her wage scale, her type of employment, the full name of her employer, and if terminated, the name of her present employer, did not violate § 1692c(b) because it did not suggest a debt collection purpose).[24]

Thus, given the choice of language by Congress, the FDCPA should be interpreted to cover communications that convey, directly or indirectly, any information relating to a debt, and not just when the debt collector discloses specific information about the particular debt being collected. Indeed, a narrow reading of the term "communication" to exclude instances such as the present case where no specific information about a debt is explicitly conveyed could create a significant loophole in the FDCPA, allowing debtors to circumvent the § 1692e(11) disclosure requirement, and other provisions of the FDCPA that have a threshold "communication" requirement, merely by not conveying specific information about the debt. In fact, under Defendant's interpretation of "communication," a debt collector could call regularly after the thirty-day validation notice is sent, and not be subject to § 1692e(11)'s requirement so long as the message did not convey specific information about the debt.[25] Such a reading is inconsistent with

[424 F.Supp.2d 643, 658]

Congress's intent to protect consumers from "serious and widespread" debt collection abuses.

The term "communication," of course, is limited to those situations involving the "conveying of information regarding a debt directly or indirectly." 15 U.S.C. § 1692(a)(2). A phone call by a debt collector that in no way regards, or relates to, an outstanding debt would not violate the Act. See Bailey, 154 F.3d at 388-89. Here, however, there appears to be no question that the call related to the collection of a debt—when Foti returned the call he was explicitly told that it was in connection with the collection of a debt. Moreover, even under a more narrow reading of the term "communication," requiring specific information about the debt to be conveyed, the January 18 Pre-Recorded Message arguably satisfies that standard. The message indicates that it is a call from NCO Financial Systems—such identification could suggest to a listener who is familiar with the fact that NCO Financial Systems is a debt collector—and that the call is about a debt, and thus may indirectly convey information about the debt. This conclusion is not inconsistent with the Court's rejection, below, of NCO's argument that Count Two should be dismissed as to the January 18 Pre-Recorded Message. Arguably, the message sufficiently conveys information about a debt to be deemed a "communication," particularly given the Second Circuit's suggestion that the Act should be broadly construed, despite the fact the Court concludes that it fails to comply with § 1692e(11)'s disclosure requirement under the "least sophisticated consumer" standard.

Finally, Defendant suggests that its interpretation of "communication" is necessary to avoid placing debt collectors in a virtual "Hobson's choice"—debt collectors must disclose their identity as a debt collector to comply with § 1692e(11)'s requirements, but are prohibited from leaving a message identifying themselves as such by § 1692c(b)'s prohibition on communications to third parties. (NCO Mem. 7) Thus, Defendant argues that "[t]he safest thing to do is to recognize what it is. It is not a communication. Once you recognize that it is not a communication, then there is no obligation to identify that you are a debt collector." (Tr. 8) This argument is unconvincing.

The fact that FDCPA provisions affect the means by which NCO wishes to collect the debt during the thirty-day validation period does not warrant disregarding Congress's clear intent to combat widespread abuse in debt collection practices. NCO's argument is essentially based on the assumption that it is somehow entitled to leave pre-recorded messages. It is true that the FDCPA does not prevent all conduct by the debt collector during the thirty-day validation period. See Orenbuch v. Computer Credit, Inc., No. 01 Civ. 9338, 2002 WL 1918222, at *2 (S.D.N.Y. Aug. 19, 2002) ("[N]othing in the FDCPA prevents a debt collector that has not received a request for validation or other reply from a consumer from continuing to attempt to collect the debt during the 30-day validation

[424 F.Supp.2d 643, 659]

period, provided that, in so doing, it does not create the impression that the consumer has less than 30 days in which to dispute the debt.") (citing Smith v. Computer Credit, Inc., 167 F.3d 1052, 1054-55 (6th Cir.1999)); Kramsky v. Trans-Cont'l Credit & Collection Corp., 166 F.Supp.2d 908, 912 (S.D.N.Y.2001) ("The FDCPA does not prohibit debt collectors from encouraging consumers to pay their debts. It was created to protect consumers from harassing and unscrupulous practices of debt collectors, including misleading representations.").

However, just because a debt collector is permitted to continue to attempt to collect the debt does not entitle the collector to use any means, even if those means are the most economical or efficient. See Clomon v. Jackson, 988 F.2d 1314, 1321 (2d Cir.1993) ("It is apparent that mass mailing may sometimes be the only feasible means of contacting a large number of delinquent debtors, particularly when many of those debtors owe relatively small sums. But it is also true that the FDCPA sets boundaries within which debt collectors must operate."). In this case, the fact that NCO may not be able to leave a pre-recorded message that complies with both § 1692e(11) and § 1692c(b) of the Act in no way warrants a conclusion that "communication" should be narrowly interpreted. Rather, it merely suggests that a debt collector is not permitted to leave a prerecorded message in violation of the FDCPA. Debt collectors, however, could continue to use other means to collect, including calling and directly speaking with the consumer or sending appropriate letters. Thus, the alleged "Hobson's Choice" in this case is self-imposed by NCO. It is only because of the method of debt collection selected—calling and leaving the type of pre-recorded messages— that NCO is faced with this potential dilemma. "As the Supreme Court has held in the general context of consumer protection—of which the Fair Debt Collection Practices Act is a part—`it does not seem unfair to require that one who goes deliberately close to an area of proscribed conduct shall take the risk that he may cross the line.'"[26] Russell, 74 F.3d at 35 (quoting

[424 F.Supp.2d 643, 660]

FTC v. Colgate-Palmolive Co., 380 U.S. 374, 393, 85 S.Ct. 1035, 13 L.Ed.2d 904 (1965)) (additional quotations omitted).

In sum, the January 18 Pre-Recorded Message is properly deemed a "communication" under the FDCPA.

D. Whether NCO Violated the FDCPA By "Overshadowing" the Validation Notice

The next question is whether the two subsequent communications—(1) the January 18 Pre-Recorded Message and (2) the January 26 Conversation—violated the FDCPA by "overshadow[ing] [the January 1 Letter's proper validation notice] in such a way as to create confusion as to Plaintiffs' rights, and thereby illegally shorten the 30 day period in which a debtor may request verification of the alleged debt." Orenbuch, 2002 WL 1918222, at *1. This is a question of law, and is therefore properly considered on a motion to dismiss. See Russell, 74 F.3d at 33; accord Wilson v. Quadramed Corp., 225 F.3d 350, 353 n. 2 (3d Cir.2000) ("[T]he Seventh Circuit is the only court of appeals to have held that whether an unsophisticated consumer would be confused by allegedly contradictory or overshadowing language is a question of fact which precludes dismissal under Fed.R.Civ.P. 12(b)(6).") (citing, inter alia, Russell).

1. Applicable Legal Standards

The FDCPA mandates that debt collectors provide debtors with a written validation notice, informing debtors of their rights under § 1692g, including, among other things, the right to dispute the validity of the debt in question within thirty days of receiving the notice[27] See Bartlett v. Heibl, 128 F.3d 497, 498-99 (7th Cir.1997); see also Wilson, 225 F.3d at 354 ("[T]he debt validation provisions of section 1692g were included by Congress to guarantee that consumers would receive adequate notice of their rights under the law."); Johnson v. Equifax Risk Mgmt. Servs., No. 00 Civ. 7836, 2004 WL 540459, at *4 (S.D.N.Y. Mar. 17, 2004) ("In short, . . . § 1692g requires the debt collector to inform the consumer of his right to dispute and demand verification of the debt."). Upon the expiration of the thirty-day validation period, the debt collector may presume the validity of the debt. Id. at 498. "This validation period, however, is not a grace period: a debt collector is `perfectly free' to demand payment and pursue collection efforts, including an appropriate lawsuit against the debtor, within the validation period." Durkin v. Equifax Check Servs., 406 F.3d 410, 416 (7th Cir.2005) (quoting Bartlett, 128 F.3d at 500-01). "Thus, during the validation period, the debtor's right to dispute coexists with the debt collector's right to collect." Durkin, 406 F.3d at 416.

Even when the initial validation notice is adequate, a defendant "may still be liable under § 1692g and § 1692e(10) if it sends a subsequent communication within the validation period that `overshadows or contradicts' such notice." Barrientos v. Law Offices of Mark L. Nichter, 76

[424 F.Supp.2d 643, 661]

F.Supp.2d 510, 513 (S.D.N.Y.1999) (citing Russell, 74 F.3d at 34-35). That is, "[e]ven if a debt collector conveys the required information, the collector nonetheless violates the Act if it conveys that information in a confusing or contradictory fashion so as to cloud the required message with uncertainty. Thus, a debt collector violates the Act if its communication is `reasonably susceptible to an inaccurate reading' of the required message." De-Santis v. Computer Credit Inc., 269 F.3d 159, 161 (2d Cir.2001) (quoting Russell, 74 F.3d at 35); see also Savino v. Computer Credit, Inc., 164 F.3d 81, 85 (2d Cir.1998) ("A debt collection notice is overshadowing or contradictory if it fails to convey the validation information clearly and effectively and thereby makes the least sophisticated consumer uncertain as to her rights."). Moreover, the Second Circuit has explicitly held that, in establishing whether language contained in a notice overshadowed or contradicted the mandatory validation notice, "[i]t is unnecessary to prove the contradiction is threatening." Russell, 74 F.3d at 35; see also Desantis v. Roz-Ber, Inc., 51 F.Supp.2d 244, 249 (E.D.N.Y.1999).

"The FDCPA establishes a strict liability standard; a consumer need not show intentional violation of the Act by a debt collector to be entitled to damages."[28] Castro v. ARS Nat'l Servs., Inc., No. 99 Civ. 4596, 2000 WL 264310, at *2 (S.D.N.Y. Mar. 8, 2000) (citing Russell, 74 F.3d at 33). A single violation of the Act is sufficient to subject a debt collector to liability under the Act. Id.

The Second Circuit has explained that "[w]hen determining whether § 1692g has been violated, an objective standard, measured by how the `least sophisticated consumer' would interpret the notice received from the debt collector, is applied." Russell 74 F.3d at 34 (citing Clomon, 988 F.2d at 1318) (additional citations omitted); see also Greco v. Trauner, Cohen & Thomas, L.L.P., 412 F.3d 360, 363 (2d Cir.2005); Miller v. Wolpoff & Abramson, L.L.P., 321 F.3d 292, 309 (2d Cir.2003); McStay v. I.C. Sys., Inc., 308 F.3d 188, 190 (2d Cir.2002). That is, "the test is how the least sophisticated consumer—one not having the astuteness of a `Philadelphia lawyer' or even the sophistication of the average, everyday, common consumer—understands the notice he or she receives." Russell, 74 F.3d at 34.

"The basic purpose of the least-sophisticated-consumer standard is to ensure that the FDCPA protects all consumers, the gullible as well as the shrewd." Clomon, 988 F.2d at 1318. At the same time, courts have been conscious of countervailing interests: "It should be emphasized that in crafting a norm that protects the naive and the credulous the courts have carefully preserved the concept of reasonableness. Indeed, courts have consistently applied the least-sophisticated consumer standard in a manner that protects debt collectors against liability for unreasonable misinterpretations of collection notices." Id. at 1319 (internal citations omitted); see also Acheampongtieku, 2005 WL 2036153, at *3 ("[T]he least sophisticated consumer standard serves the FDCPA's dual purpose: to protect the consumer from unscrupulous collection

[424 F.Supp.2d 643, 662]

practices and save debt collectors from liability for unreasonable misrepresentations of collection notices.") (omitting quotations).

With this standard in mind, the Court considers the two communications at issue.

2. The January 18 Pre-Recorded Message

The January 18 Pre-Recorded Message is comprised of approximately thirty words. After greeting the listener ("Good day"), the message: (i) identifies the caller as NCO Financial Systems; (ii) states that the call is about a personal business matter; (iii) which requires immediate attention; and (iv) ends by asking the recipient of the message to "please call back," providing a toll-free number. (Am. Compl. ¶ 27, Ex. B) The question, therefore, is whether this message confuses or overshadows the initial validation notice in the eyes of the reasonable, least sophisticated consumer, and, therefore, violates § 1692g.

Plaintiffs claim that this message does in fact violate § 1692g by overshadowing the initial validation notice. Plaintiffs' main argument is that the message emphasized that the matter requires "immediate attention," and, accordingly, might suggest to the least sophisticated consumer that s/he is not entitled to a thirty-day validation period. Indeed, a number of cases have found violations of the FDCPA where a written notice includes the words "immediate attention" or similar language suggesting an urgency to resolution of the debt, even without demanding immediate payment.[29] See, e.g., Roz-Ber, 51 F.Supp.2d at 246, 250 (finding violation where notice read, in pertinent part: "Your account has been placed in our hands by the above named client with full authority to demand payment. You may not have intentionally neglected this obligation, but it is seriously past due and demands your IMMEDIATE ATTENTION! If you would like our cooperation then: 1. Remit payment in full to this office or, 2. Contact the undersigned in person or by telephone and arrange settlement."); Flowers v. Accelerated

[424 F.Supp.2d 643, 663]

Bureau of Collections, No. 96 Civ. 4003, 1997 WL 224987, at *2 n. 2 (N.D.Ill. April 30, 1997) (finding violation where second notice read: "PLEASE BE ADVISED: You were previously notified and given ample opportunity to resolve this matter, and you have failed to do so. If you feel you have some legitimate reason for failing to respond, NOW is your opportunity to bring it to my attention. Telephone me immediately or write me today! We will discuss your delinquent account and help you come to a reasonable conclusion. THIS IS MY NOTIFICATION TO YOU."); cf. McNab v. Statewide Recovery Servs., No. Civ. A. 99-1571 R., 2000 WL 135839, at *1, *4 (E.D.La. Feb. 4, 2000) (rejecting defendant's motion for summary judgment and finding that "a reasonable jury could determine that the language in the letter would lead the least sophisticated consumer to believe that she had to waive her statutory right to contest the debt within thirty days" where letter read, in pertinent part: "We bring to your attention the above account which has been handed to us for immediate collection, and hereby request your prompt remittance to pay this long standing account. Failure to respond to this request for payment will leave us no alternative but to proceed against you within state and federal regulations to collect your past due account. Please give this your immediate attention. Do not simply ignore this notice!").

These cases, however, are distinguishable from the present circumstances. Those decisions have focused less on the words "immediate attention" as constituting a per se violation of the FDCPA, and more on whether the overall tenor of the notice creates an impression of dire urgency that might confuse the least sophisticated consumer about his/her validation rights. For example, in Roz-Ber, the court focused on the overall sense of urgency conveyed in the notice:

Specifically, the words "IMMEDIATE ATTENTION," followed by an exclamation mark raises significant concern. Moreover, the contested language implicitly threatens the debtor that if he does not either "(1) remit payment in full to this office or, (2) Contact the undersigned in person or by telephone and arrange settlement" he will not receive "cooperation" from the collection agency. Although . . . a threat is not required for the contested language to overshadow or contradict the validation notice, the Court is of the view that the debt collection letter at issue is in fact threatening in nature. Indeed, who would not want the "cooperation" of a collection agency attempting to collect a debt? Recognizing this undeniable fact, the defendant has cleverly attempted to push the boundaries of a lawful collection letter, by using implicit, rather than explicit threats, by couching what is in essence a demand for immediate payment, with language that the defendant argues does not overshadow the debtor's rights under section 1692g.

[51 F.Supp.2d. at 250].

Flowers also is different in that the follow-up letter was specifically phrased in a manner that suggested that the validation period had expired by referencing the fact that "[y]ou were previously notified and given ample opportunity to resolve this matter, and you have failed to do so."[30]

[424 F.Supp.2d 643, 664]

Flowers, 1997 WL 224987, at *2 n. 2 (emphasis added); see id. at *2 ("When coupled with Defendants' statement that the consumer has been `given ample opportunity to resolve this matter,' Plaintiffs argue, the second notice leads an unsophisticated consumer to believe that the period to dispute the validity of the debt has expired.").

In this case, the January 18 Pre-Recorded Message simply indicated that the call was "regarding a personal business matter that requires your immediate attention." (Am.Compl. ¶ 27, Ex. B) There is no suggestion that the thirty-day validation period should be disregarded, or that immediate payment is required. Nor is there an implicit suggestion that failure to cooperate immediately could jeopardize resolution of the debt. On the contrary, the message merely asks the consumer for a return call ("please call back").

As noted above, "nothing in the FDCPA prevents a debt collector that has not received a request for validation or other reply from a consumer from continuing to attempt to collect the debt during the 30 day validation period, provided that, in so doing, it does not create the impression that the consumer has less than 30 days in which to dispute the debt." Orenbuch, 2002 WL 1918222, at *2. Thus, Plaintiffs' argument essentially boils down to the claim that the mere use of the phrase "immediate attention" constitutes an overshadowing of a validation notice. There is little, if any, support in the caselaw for this proposition.

First, a number of cases within the Second Circuit have distinguished between merely contacting the debtor (as happened here), and demanding or urging immediate payment of the debt (which did not happen here).[31] See, e.g., Acheampongtieku, 2005 WL 2036153, at *4 (noting that a follow-up letter from a debt collector did not violate § 1692g, in part, because "there is no indication that repayment, and repayment only, would resolve the dispute"); Spira, 358 F.Supp.2d at 159 ("Plaintiff's argument misses the mark because unlike the letter in Savino, the Follow-up Letter did not state or imply that payment was due immediately."); Barrientos, 76 F.Supp.2d at 515 ("Defendants cite a number of cases for the well-settled proposition that a debt collector may contact the debtor within the thirty-day validation period so long as the communication does not demand or urge immediate payment of the debt. . . . But demanding immediate payment is precisely what Defendants did . . .") (internal quotations and citations omitted).

Moreover, a great number of courts have rejected the argument that the urgency conveyed by phrases such as "immediate

[424 F.Supp.2d 643, 665]

attention" by themselves overshadow an otherwise sufficient validation notice. See, e.g., Peter v. GC Servs. L.P., 310 F.3d 344, 349-50 (5th Cir.2002) ("[S]tatements that request payment or other actions with no time period specified have been found not to contradict § 1692g notice."); Spira, 358 F.Supp.2d at 159 ("Plaintiff's argument that the Follow-up Letter overshadows the validation notice because Defendant will use `every means available' to collect the debt, and Plaintiff should send payment in full or `call . . . at once,' is unpersuasive.") (ellipses in original); Keen v. Omnibus Int'l, Inc., No. 98 Civ. 3947, 1998 WL 485682, at *4 (N.D.Ill. Aug. 12, 1998) (rejecting claim that language in letter stating that "you should notify us in writing immediately" overshadowed validation notice); Gammon v. Belzer, P.A., No. 96 Civ. 5936, 1997 WL 189291, at *3 (N.D.Ill. Apr. 11, 1997) (rejecting argument that validation notice is rendered ineffective by virtue of language that "Your immediate attention to this matter is in your best interest"); Vasquez, 987 F.Supp. at 657 (holding that asking for payment without "further delay" did not contravene § 1692g).

Thus, for example, notices from debt collectors seeking contact from the debtor, even if requested immediately or urgently, are regularly found to be consistent with § 1692g. As the court noted in Lerner v. Forster, 240 F.Supp.2d 233, 238 (E.D.N.Y. 2003): "It does not follow that simply because a collection letter instructs a consumer to contact a debt collector that the validation notice is necessarily overshadowed or contradicted." Instead, the "request for the consumer to contact [the debt collector] . merely `encourages the debtor to communicate with the debt collection agency. . . ." Madonna v. Acad. Collection Serv., Inc., No. 3 95 Civ. 000875, 1997 WL 530101, at *5 (D.Conn. Aug. 12, 1997) (quoting Terran v. Kaplan, 109 F.3d 1428, 1430 (9th Cir.1997)). This sentiment has been echoed by other courts in rejecting claims similar to those made by Plaintiffs here. See, e.g., Terran, 109 F.3d at 1434 ("Here, the request that the alleged debtor immediately telephone a collection assistant does not overshadow the language in the notice that the alleged debtor has thirty days in which to dispute the debt."); Acheampongtieku, 2005 WL 2036153, at *4 (noting that "the Collection Letter simply requests that the debtor contact Allied"); Spira, 358 F.Supp.2d at 159 ("[T]he fact that the Follow-up Letter `instructed' Plaintiff `to pay in full or call at once, even though the thirty day validation period was still in effect,' did not limit her rights under the Act. . . . ").[32]

In this case, the Court concludes that the language of the January 18 Pre-Recorded Message could not reasonably confuse even the least sophisticated consumer.

[424 F.Supp.2d 643, 666]

A debt collector is entitled to follow-up on debt collection during the thirty-day period, and the mere expression of some time sensitivity and a request to return a call does not suggest to the least sophisticated consumer that s/he is no longer entitled to a thirty-day validation period. Notably, this message was devoid of any suggestion that the time to dispute the debt had passed, and it did not cause any confusion about the time remaining to dispute the debt. Nor did the message otherwise contain misleading or inaccurate information. See Durkin, 406 F.3d at 417-18 (noting that follow-up message from debt collector which did not "indicate that the time for disputing the debt had passed," or "cloud the amount of time remaining to dispute the debt," or otherwise "contain any overt misinformation, apparent contradiction, or noticeable lack of clarity concerning the validation period" was lawful). While certain communications, even those not explicitly demanding payment, could rise to the level of overshadowing, here the mere use of the phrase "immediate attention" accompanying a request for a return call, in the context of the entire message, does not overshadow. Therefore, Defendant's Motion as to the January 18 Pre—Recorded Message is granted.

3. The January 26 Conversation

In contrast, to the extent NCO's argument for dismissal can even be construed to encompass the January 26 Conversation, the Court concludes that dismissal of that claim is inappropriate. The January 26 Conversation repeatedly demands payment, and threatens continuous demands for payment absent immediate remittance, all before the thirty-day validation period had expired. (Am. Compl. ¶ 31, Ex. C) ("Q: So what do you need me to do today? A: Pay the account.") (emphasis added) Such a conversation is likely to confuse the least sophisticated consumer as to whether s/he continues to enjoy the protections of the thirty-day validation period. See Savino, 164 F.3d at 86 (noting that debt collector's "violation of the Act consisted of its decision to ask for immediate payment without also explaining that its demand did not override the consumer's rights under Section 1692g to seek validation of the debt").

In sum, the Motion to Dismiss Count One is granted to the extent that it challenges the sufficiency of the Amended Complaint's allegations relating to the January 18 Pre-Recorded Message. However, NCO's challenge to Count One as it relates to the January 26 Conversation is denied.

4. The § 1692e(10) Claims

NCO also seeks to dismiss the claims brought pursuant to § 1692e(10) in Count One. NCO argues that "[s]ince the prerecorded message did not violate § 1692g, it cannot be `false or deceptive' as contemplated by § 1692e(10)." (NCO Mem. 5) Section 1692e(10) prohibits "[t]he use of any false representation or deceptive means to collect or attempt to collect any debt or to obtain information concerning a consumer." 15 U.S.C. § 1692e(10). The Second Circuit has explained that "a collection notice is deceptive when it can be reasonably read to have two or more different meanings, one of which is inaccurate. The fact that the notice's terminology was vague or uncertain will not prevent it from being held deceptive under § 1692e(10) of the Act." Russell, 74 F.3d at 35 (internal citations omitted).

The standard for determining a violation of § 1692e(10) is essentially the same as that for § 1692g. See id. ("Because the initial collection notice in the instant case was reasonably susceptible to

[424 F.Supp.2d 643, 667]

an inaccurate reading, it was also deceptive within the meaning of the Act."); Vera v. Trans-Cont'l Credit and Collection Corp., No. 98 Civ. 1866, 1999 WL 163162, at *4 (S.D.N.Y. Mar. 24, 1999) ("For essentially the same reasons that I conclude that the debt validation notice violates § 1692g(a)(3), I also conclude that the notice violates § 1692e(10)."); Tipping-Lipshie v. Riddle, No. 99 Civ. 4646, 2000 WL 33963916, at *4 (E.D.N.Y. Mar. 2, 2000) (citing Vera for the proposition that a "misleading validation notice violates both sections 1692g and 1692e(10)"). Moreover, Plaintiffs advance no independent argument in support of the § 1692e(10) claim.

Accordingly, for the reasons stated above, the Court grants the Motion to Dismiss the § 1692e(10) claim (in Count One) as to the January 18 Pre-Recorded Message, and denies the Motion to Dismiss the § 1692e(10) claim (also in Count One) as to the January 26 Conversation.

5. The § 1692f Claims

NCO also argues that "[s]ince both the §§ 1692g and 1692e(10) claims are unsupportable, the ancillary § 1692f claim fails." (NCO Mem. 6) Section 1692f generally prohibits a debt collector from employing "unfair or unconscionable means to collect" a debt. 15 U.S.C. § 1692f. Eight subsections list certain practices that violate the section, however, "conduct that may be deemed `unfair or unconscionable' is not limited to the acts enumerated in subsections (1) through (8)." Bryant v. Bonded Account Service/Check Recovery, Inc., 208 F.R.D. 251, 258 (D.Minn.2000). Instead, § 1692f "allows the court to sanction improper conduct that the FDCPA fails to address specifically." Adams v. Law Offices of Stuckert & Yates, 926 F.Supp. 521, 528 (E.D.Pa.1996).

Here, Plaintiff does not allege any improper acts listed within Section 1692f. This alone, of course, is not fatal as § 1692f may provide a cause of action for conduct that is not specifically listed in that section or any other provision of FDCPA. However, Plaintiffs' Complaint is deficient in that it does not identify any misconduct beyond that which Plaintiffs assert violate other provisions of the FDCPA. See Tsenes v. Trans-Cont'l Credit and Collection Corp., 892 F.Supp. 461, 466 (E.D.N.Y.1995) ("[T]he Complaint is devoid of support for the contention that the defendant engaged in practices that were `unfair' or `unconscionable' within the meaning of the section; all the allegations in the Complaint support claims asserted under either §§ 1692g or 1692e."). "As such, [Plaintiffs have] failed to state a cause of action under § 1692f, and the [D]efendant's motion should be granted to that extent."[33] Id.

E. Whether NCO Complied With the § 1692e(11) Requirements

NCO also seeks dismissal of Count Two, alleging violations of § 1692e(11). "[Section] 1692e provides a broad prohibition on false or misleading statements. . . . The section lists a variety of misleading tactics, but notes that the list is not exhaustive." Forman v. Acad. Collection Serv., Inc., 388 F.Supp.2d 199, 203 (S.D.N.Y.2005). At issue in this case is the specific provision requiring a debt collector to disclose certain information:

The failure to disclose in the initial written communication with the consumer and, in addition, if the initial communication with the consumer is oral, in that initial oral communication, that the debt

[424 F.Supp.2d 643, 668]

collector is attempting to collect a debt and that any information obtained will be used for that purpose, and the failure to disclose in subsequent communications that the communication is from a debt collector, except that this paragraph shall not apply to a formal pleading made in connection with a legal action.

15 U.S.C. § 1692e(11). Here, the allegations in the Amended Complaint are limited to the "subsequent communications" (Am.Compl. ¶ 80)—that is, communications after the initial January 1 Letter. As the plain language of the statute makes clear, § 1692e(11), provides that "in subsequent communications with the consumer the debt collector need only state that the communication is from a debt collector.[34] Lewis v. ACB Bus. Servs., Inc., 135 F.3d 389, 400 n. 9 (6th Cir.1998).

The Second Circuit has held that "there simply is no requirement that the letter quote verbatim the language of the statute." Emanuel v. Am. Credit Exch., 870 F.2d 805, 808 (2d Cir.1989); see also Forman, at 205 ("While [the] letter does not track the language of the statute verbatim, it is not required to as long as the warning comes across."); Cavallaro, 933 F.Supp. at 1156 ("In order to comport with the FDCPA, the notice does not have to quote verbatim the language of § 1692e(11).") (citing Emanuel, 870 F.2d at 808). In fact, even Plaintiffs' counsel acknowledges that "I don't believe that there are magic words that you are absolutely, unequivocally obligated to say." (Tr. 37)

In determining whether there is a violation of § 1692e, courts apply the least sophisticated consumer test. Clomon, 988 F.2d at 1318; see also Forman, at 203, 205 (applying least sophisticated consumer test to issue of whether violation of § 1692e(11) occurred). However, the courts appear to agree that to comply with § 1692e(11), the debt collector must "clearly" be identified in the communication to the debtor. See Epps, 1998 WL 851488, at *8 ("[A] debt collector satisfies subsection 11's notice requirement as long as it is clear from the subsequent letter that the sender is a debt collector.").

NCO seeks to dismiss Count Two with respect to both the (1) January 18 Pre-Recorded Message and the (2) January 26 Conversation. The Court concludes that dismissal is appropriate as to the January

[424 F.Supp.2d 643, 669]

26 Conversation, but not as to the January 18 Pre-Recorded Message.

1. January 18 Pre-Recorded Message

Apart from arguing that the January 18 Pre-Recorded Message is not a "communication," NCO's brief does not advance any argument in support of the claim that the January 18 Pre-Recorded Message complies with the disclosure requirements in § 1692e(11). (NCO Mem. 6-7) The Court concludes above that the January 18 Pre-Recorded Message is properly considered a "communication" within the meaning of the FDCPA. Moreover, to the extent NCO's argument can be construed as maintaining that the January 18 Pre-Recorded Message complied with the disclosure requirements, the Court rejects this argument.

The issue is whether the identification of the debt collection agency by name— "NCO Financial Systems"—is sufficient to fulfill the requirement of disclosure that "the communication is from a debt collector." 15 U.S.C. § 1692e(11). The Court notes that, other than the name "NCO Financial Systems," the January 18 Pre-Recorded Message contains no other suggestion or clue that the correspondence is from a debt collector. Put another way, this is not a case where the fact that the communication is from a debt collector would be apparent even to the least sophisticated consumer. Compare Epps, 1998 WL 851488, at *9 (holding that where letter indicated "this is an attempt to collect a debt and any information obtained will be used for that purpose," and that "it is imperative that you immediately forward the past due balance," the letter would not confuse an unsophisticated consumer about the author's status as a debt collector); Ross v. Commercial Fin. Servs., Inc., 31 F.Supp.2d 1077, 1079-80 (N.D.Ill.1999) (holding that letter, which disclosed that debt collector was a "different kind of debt collection company," satisfied § 1692e(11), even though it did not use exact term "debt collector").

Rather, there is nothing in the context of the January 18 Pre-Recorded Message that would clearly inform a consumer that s/he is speaking to a debt collector, or, for that matter, that the subject of the "business matter" requiring "immediate attention" is a debt. Instead, a consumer would have to, upon hearing the message, recall that it previously received mail from a debt collection agency by the name of "NCO Financial Systems."[35] Such a burden on the consumer is unreasonable. The least sophisticated consumer, who may receive voluminous messages and calls, could easily be confused about the identify of "NCO Financial Systems," particularly given the vague reference in the message to "a personal business matter that requires your immediate attention." See Irwin v. Mascott, 112 F.Supp.2d 937, 954 (N.D.Cal.2000) (holding that subsequent letter from debt collector violated § 1692e(11) because the "text advises ambiguously, `This may have been sent to you by a collection agency'"). An alternative view of § 1692e(11) would eviscerate the statute's protections in subsequent communications, placing the burden on the consumer to recall the first communication and draw the connection to the second communication. Accordingly, the Court denies the Motion to Dismiss Count Two as to the January 18 Pre-Recorded Message.

CITATIONS

—dismissing Section 1692f claim where plaintiff failed to plead misconduct other than that asserted to violate other FDCPA provisions - in Baker v. Allstate Financial Services, Inc., 2008

—finding a "communication" under § 1692e (b) includes contacts that do not convey specific information about the debt; citing cases - in Thomas v. Consumer Adjustment Co., Inc., 2008

—rejecting a debt collector's assertion that its voicemail message was not a communication because it did not contain information regarding a debt - in Mark v. JC CHRISTENSEN & ASSOCIATES, INC., 2009

Namely, Elizabeth, the caller, failed to state her messages were from a debt collector and in regards to the debt owed on plaintiff's NextCard account. - in Costa v. National Action Financial Services, 2007

As such, the call is "in connection with the collection of any debt," within the meaning of 15 USC § 1692c. - in Thomas v. Consumer Adjustment Co., Inc., 2008

—a case also involving Defendant NCO, where the court held that a pre-recorded message left on a debtor's voicemail was a "communication" under the FDCPA. - in Inman v. NCO FINANCIAL SYSTEMS, INC., 2009

The Taylor case cited by UCB appears to reflect a growing consensus, at least among district courts, that a claim under § 1692f must be based on conduct either within the listed provisions, or be based on conduct which falls outside of those provisions, but which does not violate another provision of the FDCPA. - in Winberry v. UNITED COLLECTION BUREAU, INC., 2010

The provisions of the FDCPA are clear that in initial or subsequent communications, it must be disclosed that the communication is from a debt collector. - in DROSSIN v. NATIONAL ACTION FINANCIAL SERVICES INC., 2009

—holding that a phone message that "advised the debtor that the matter required immediate attention, and provided a specific number to call to discuss the matter" was a communication, "given the obvious purpose of the message was to provide the debtor with enough information to entice a return call - in Ramirez v. APEX FINANCIAL MANAGEMENT, LLC,, 2008

The Court has no authority to carve an exception out of the statute just so CCS may use the technology they have deemed most efficient. - in Edward s v. Niagara Credit Solutions, Inc., 2008

INMAN v. NCO FINANCIAL SYSTEMS, INC.

Furthermore, the Court will resolve one legal issue as to whether the pre-recorded messages, which Defendant generated to the Plaintiff, constitute a "communication" as defined by the statute. The Court will adopt the decision set forth in Foti v. NCO Financial Systems, Inc., 424 F.Supp. 2d 643 (S.D.N.Y. 2006), a case also involving Defendant NCO, where the court held that a pre-recorded message left on a debtor's voicemail was a "communication" under the FDCPA.

In Foti, a debtor brought a class action against NCO alleging that NCO violated the FDCPA based on two communications, one of which was a pre-recorded message left on the debtor's home voicemail. That message went as follows:

Good day, we are calling from NCO Financial Systems regarding a personal business matter that requires your immediate attention. Please call back 1-866-701-1275 once again please call back, toll-free, 1-866-701-1275, this is not a solicitation.

Id. at 648. NCO argued that the pre-recorded message was not a "communication" within the meaning of the FDCPA because the message did not "convey any information regarding a debt, but instead simply request[ed] a return call regarding an important business matter." Id. at 654. The court disagreed, holding that the pre-recorded message was properly deemed a "communication" under the FDCPA. Id. at 660.

Judge Karas began his analysis by noting that the FDCPA defines "communication" very broadly as "the conveying of information regarding a debt directly or indirectly to any person through any medium." Id. at 655 (quoting 15 U.S.C. § 1692a(2)). Regarding the specific voicemail message left by NCO, the court stated:

[NCO]'s voicemail message, while devoid of any specific information about any particular debt, clearly provided some information, even if indirectly, to the intended recipient of the message. Specifically, the message advised the debtor that the matter required immediate attention, and provided a specific number to call to discuss the matter. Given that the obvious purpose of the message was to provide the debtor with enough information to entice a return call, it is difficult to imagine how the voicemail message is not a communication under the FDCPA."

Id. at 655-56 (emphasis added). The court further noted that NCO failed to cite in its brief any case supporting its position that the pre-recorded message was not a communication, and only pointed to one "unhelpful" case at oral argument. Id. at 654. The court held that "[g]iven this paucity of authority, the Court has little difficulty in rejecting NCO's narrow interpretation of the word `communication,' and concludes that the . . . Pre-Recorded Message is protected as a `communication' under the FDCPA." Id. at 654-55.

This Court finds the Foti decision to be highly instructive, and therefore adopts its reasoning in holding that the messages left by Defendant NCO on Plaintiff Inman's voicemail system are "communications" under the FDCPA. First, the messages here are very similar in content to the message left in the Foti case.[1] Second, the obvious purpose of Defendant NCO's voicemail message was to provide the listener with enough information to entice a return call. Third, the voicemail messages, while devoid of any specific information about the particular debt,[2] clearly provided some information to Plaintiff. Fourth, Defendant NCO has failed to cite to any authority supporting its position that these specific messages in this case do not constitute "communications" under the FDCPA.

At Oral Argument, Defendant argued that the messages left on Plaintiff's voicemail were not "communications" under the FDCPA because Defendant did not intend to leave such messages on Plaintiff's voicemail for Plaintiff to hear. Further, Defendant argued that its messages should not — or could not — have been left on Plaintiff's voicemail system.

The Court concludes that Defendant's subjective intent has no bearing on whether these messages are "communications" under the FDCPA. Whether the messages were intended to be left on Plaintiff's voicemail relates to the broad technological and factual disagreements between the parties — significant issues which preclude the Court from granting summary judgment at this time. What is clear at this juncture is that the messages were left on Plaintiff Inman's voicemail; they relate to a debt Plaintiff owes, and to NCO's efforts to collect; they provide a Reference ID number which relates to a business record of an American Express account in Plaintiff Inman's name that was placed with NCO for collection; and they provide a telephone number for the debtor, Plaintiff Inman, to return the call.

For a "communication" to fall under the FDCPA's "broadly defined" statutory definition, it must "convey information `regarding a debt directly or indirectly to any person through any medium.'" Coll v. Toll, 2007 WL 4105382, at *5 (E.D. Pa. Nov. 16, 2007)

(Buckwalter, J.) (emphasis added) (quoting 15 U.S.C.A. § 1692(a)). Simply stated, the messages left by Defendant NCO on Plaintiff's voicemail conveyed information regarding a debt to a debtor through messages left on the debtor's voicemail. The Court therefore finds that the messages left by Defendant NCO on Plaintiff's voicemail system constitute "communications" under the FDCPA.

MASCIARELLI V. RICHARD J. BOUDREAU & ASSOCIATES, LLC, 529 F. SUPP.2D 183, 185 (D. MASS. 2007)

Count I- Violation of the Fair Debt Collection Protection Act

In light of the admitted conduct, a reasonable jury could not return a verdict in Case favor of Boudreau. Count I asserts claims under 15 U.S.C. § 1692 et seq., the Fair Debt Collection Practices Act ("FDCPA"). The FDCPA prohibits unfair or unconscionable collection methods, including the making of any false, misleading, or deceptive statements in connection with a debt, and requires that debt collectors make certain disclosures, including a disclosure of their identity as a debt collector. Id. See also Acosta v. Campbell, No. 6:04 Civ. 761, 2006 WL 146208, at *12 (M.D. Fla. Jan 18, 2006); Lewis v. ACB Bus. Servs., Inc., 135 F.3d 389, 400 n. 9 (6th Cir. 1998). Here, Boudreau has admits to leaving a message on Masciarelli's voice-mail that, though in connection with the collection of a debt, failed to disclose Boudreau's identity as a debt collector in violation of the FDCPA. Accordingly, Boudreau's message violated the FDCPA as a matter of law. See Hosseinzadch v. M.R.S. Assoc., Inc., 387 F. Supp. 2d 1104, 1116 (C.D. Cal. 2005) (defendant's messages failed to convey its status as a debt collector, in violation of FDCPA).

Additionally, the FDCPA imposes strict liability on debt collectors who violate

2. "A debt collector may not use any false, deceptive, or misleading representation or means in connection with the collection of any debt. Without limiting the general application of the foregoing, the following conduct is a violation of this section:

(5)The threat to take any action that cannot legally be taken or that is not intended to be taken. (10) The use of any false representation or deceptive means to collect or attempt to collect any debt or to obtain information concerning a consumer." 15 U.S.C. Section 1692e(5), (10) (extraneous text omitted). its provisions. Harrington v. CACV of Colo., LLC, No. 06 Civ. 11216, 2007 WL 2452891, at *3 (D. Mass. Aug. 30, 2007); see also Picht v. John R. Hawks, Ltd., 236 F.3d 446, 451 (8th Cir. 2001). Thus, Boudreau's rationale behind the violation of provisions under the FDCPA is of little concern. Lastly, Boudreau's false threats to contact Masciarelli's employer and garnish his wages also violated the FDCPA. See 15 U.S.C. § 1692e(5), 1692e(10).2 Accordingly, Boudreau violated the FDCPA as a matter of law and Masciarelli's motion for partial summary judgment as to Count I is hereby GRANTED.

CITATIONS

—defendant's failure to identify himself as a debt collector in voice-mail message to debtor violates the FDCPA as a matter of law - in Sparks v. Phillips & Cohen Associates, Ltd., 2008

The First Circuit, however, as well as many district courts, have held that violations of the FDCPA are per se violations of ch. 93A, and have not dismissed such claims on preemption grounds. - in Som v. Daniels Law Offices, PC, 2008

The majority of courts that have addressed this issue have concluded that messages from a debt collector left on a consumer's voicemail or answering machine requesting that the consumer call a phone number regarding an "important matter" (or similar such language) may be considered "communications" under the FDCPA because the debt is referenced indirectly if … - in Edwards v. Niagara Credit Solutions, Inc., 2008

Accordingly, because it is undisputed that the messages failed to identify the callers as being employed by or associated with Niagara in any way, the Court finds that Defendant violated 15 USC § 1692d (6) by placing telephone calls to Plaintiff without making any meaningful disclosure of the identity of the caller. - in Edwards v. Niagara Credit Solutions, Inc., 2008

Although there is no Third Circuit case law dealing with the appropriateness of identification of a debt-collector in a voicemail or answering machine message, numerous district courts have been faced with the issue and determined that the debt-collector's failure to identify itself as a debt-collector when leaving messages violates the FDCPA. - in GRYZBOWSKI v. IC System, Inc., 2010

Pursuant to the plain language of § 1692d (6), a debt collector's failure to identify herself as such in communications relating to the collection of a debt has been held to be a per se violation of the FDCPA. - in Sparks v. Phillips & Cohen Associates, Ltd., 2008

Because the FDCPA imposes strict liability on debt collectors who violate its provisions, and Defendant admits to failing to identify itself, Defendant violated section 1692d (6). - in GRYZBOWSKI v. IC System, Inc., 2010

This restriction has caused problems for debt collectors that leave messages for consumers on recording machines - in THE ROLE OF VALIDATION AND COMMUNICATION IN THE DEBT COLLECTION PROCESS

Given the clear and unambiguous language of 15 USC Section 1692 et seq., a collection agent must follow the disclosure requirement of identifying himself as a debt collector in all communications. Where, as here, the disclosure was not provided, summary judgment is appropriate - in Edwards v. Niagara Credit Solutions, Inc., 2008

Although Defendant believed that the number was that of her employer, its subjective belief is irrelevant as the FDCPA is a strict liability statute. - in GRYZBOWSKI v. IC System, Inc., 2010

CAMPUZANO-BURGOS V. MIDLAND CREDIT MANAGEMENT, 497 F. SUPP.2D 660, 665 (E.D. PA. 2007)

MEMORANDUM

DALZELL, District Judge.

In this putative class action under the Fair Debt Collection Practices Act ("FDCPA"), we address the question of whether an officer of the debt collector who signs a dunning letter must have any involvement with the collection of the debt in question. Although courts have examined related questions in some depth, it appears that this is a question of first impression and so we treat it in some detail.

Facts[1] and Procedural History

Named plaintiffs Lisa Campuzano-Burgos, Charmaine Angus, and Tiaisha Hall each received a debt collection letter from defendant Midland Credit Management ("MCM") between March and August of 2006. Each of the letters was signed[2] by 662*662 either J. Brandon Black, President of MCM or Ron Eckhardt, Executive Vice President and General Manager of Consumer Debt. The letters include Black's and Eckhardt's titles below their names at the bottom of the letter. Neither Black nor Eckhardt had any role in the collection of these particular debts nor were they aware that collection letters were being sent to these particular debtors. They are, however, real people and they hold the positions shown on the letters.

On January 22, 2007, plaintiffs filed an amended class action complaint alleging violations of the FDCPA on behalf of themselves and all other Pennsylvania residents who had received similar letters from MCM on or after January 22, 2006.[3] At the Rule 16 conference on April 9, 2007, the parties agreed to brief the question of statutory liability before addressing any class certification issues. Accordingly, they filed a joint statement of stipulated facts and cross-motions for summary judgment, which were limited to the question of whether these facts represented an actionable FDCPA violation.[4] It is these motions that we address here.

Analysis

The FDCPA says that "[a] debt collector may not use any false, deceptive, or misleading representation or means in connection with the collection of any debt." 15 U.S.C. § 1692e. Without limiting that broad statement, the statute then goes on to list sixteen specific prohibited practices. Of those, the only one that plaintiffs claim applies here is "[t]he use or distribution of any written communication which simulates or is falsely represented to be a document authorized, issued, or approved by any court, official, or agency of the United States or any State, or which creates a false impression as to its source, authorization, or approval." 15 U.S.C. § 1692e(9).

Our Court of Appeals has directed us to construe the language of the FDCPA broadly and to analyze letters such as these "from the perspective of the least sophisticated debtor." Brown v. Card Serv. Ctr., 464 F.3d 450, 453 (3d Cir.2006) (internal quotation omitted). Although our analysis is from the perspective of the least sophisticated debtor, we must avoid "bizarre or idiosyncratic interpretations of collection notices by preserving a quotient[5] of reasonableness and presuming a basic level of understanding and willingness to read with care." Wilson v. Quadramed Corp., 225 F.3d 350, 354 (3d Cir. 2000). By presuming that the debtor, however unsophisticated, reads the notice with care, we ensure that we consider the letter as a whole and that we understand the debt collector's statements in their proper context. See Rosenau v. Unifund Corp., 2007 WL 1892888 (E.D.Pa. June 28, 2007).

"The basic purpose of the least-sophisticated consumer standard is to ensure that the FDCPA protects all consumers, the gullible as well as the shrewd." 663*663 Brown, 464 F.3d at 453 (quoting Clomon v. Jackson, 988 F.2d 1314, 1318 (2d Cir. 1993)). Applying this standard, a letter "is deceptive when it can be reasonably read to have two or more different meanings, one of which is inaccurate." Wilson, 225 F.3d at 354 (quoting Russell v. Equifax A.R.S., 74 F.3d 30, 35 (2d Cir.1996)).

Plaintiffs allege that the signatures on the letters are false, deceptive, or misleading because they give the impression that these individual debts are being pursued by high-ranking officers of the company. In addition to violating the general prohibition against deceptive and misleading practices, they claim that this "creates a false impression" as to the letters' "source, authorization, or approval" in violation of 15 U.S.C. § 1692e(9).

Although this case presents a question of first impression,[6] there are several authorities that have addressed related issues that can guide us. The most significant of these are the cases dealing with the use of attorneys in debt collection.

The FDCPA specifically bars "[t]he false representation or implication that any individual is an attorney or that any communication is from an attorney." 15 U.S.C. § 1692e(3). This prohibition acknowledges the special authority that a letter from an attorney connotes. As Judge Evans pungently put it for the Seventh Circuit, "[a]n unsophisticated consumer, getting a letter from an `attorney,' knows the price of poker has just gone up." Avila v. Rubin, 84 F.3d 222, 229 (7th Cir.1996). Because attorneys have special status, letters "purporting to be written by attorneys have a greater weight than those written by laymen." Id. (quoting American Bar Assoc., Formal Opinion 68 (1932)).

Courts have also found that communications are false or misleading when, although they come from a licensed attorney, the lawyer has no involvement with the debt. Here again the concern is that debt collectors seek to trade on the attorney's status and authority when "the dunning campaign escalates from the collection agency, which might not strike fear in the heart of the consumer, to the attorney, who is better positioned to get the debtor's knees knocking." Id. Because any other finding would be detrimental to professional standards and would allow attorneys to sell their names (and authority) to debt collectors, "if a debt collector (attorney or otherwise) wants to take advantage of the special connotation of the word `attorney' in the minds of delinquent consumer debtors to better effect collection of the debt, the debt collector should at least ensure that an attorney has become professionally involved in the debtor's file." Id.

But a lawyer is not the only figure who can get the debtor's knees knocking. An escalation from a lowly collection agent to a senior executive of the company could similarly demonstrate to a consumer that the debt collector means business. It is, of course, no accident that MCM used the names and titles of its executives on the collection letters at issue here. They expect, either based on research they may have conducted or just as a matter of common sense, that a title such as "President" or "Executive Vice President" connotes authority and is more likely to generate a response.

Although Clomon dealt with facts similar to Avila, its reasoning focused not on the attorney's professional obligations but on the additional authority his signature 664*664 connoted. A debt collector may use that authority to prod a recalcitrant debtor to pay up, but only if the attorney is directly involved in the collection process. "[T]he use of an attorney's signature on a collection letter implies that the letter is `from' the attorney who signed it; it implies, in other words, that the attorney directly controlled or supervised the process through which the letter was sent." Clomon, 988 F.2d at 1321. Similarly, "the use of an attorney's signature implies — at least in the absence of language to the contrary — that the attorney signing the letter formed an opinion about how to manage the case of the debtor to whom the letter was sent." Id.

Though its facts deal with an attorney, Clomon (and to a lesser degree Avila) expresses a general concern with debt collectors' practice of falsely implying that someone in a position of real authority is supervising the collection of this debt.[7] These concerns readily generalize to other situations, like ours, where debt collectors attempt to goad a debtor into paying by using a signatory who has no involvement in the handling of the debtor's case as a signal that the collection process has escalated to a graver level or, to extend Judge Evans's imagery, to convey that a high-roller has entered the game.

The next line of cases that are relevant to our analysis are those dealing with the use of so-called "desk names", that is, false names that debt collection employees adopt to protect their own privacy. The courts that have considered this issue have found that, so long as the desk name identifies a particular person, it is immaterial whether it is his or her actual name or a name adopted for professional purposes. See, e.g., Youngblood v. GC Svcs. Ltd. P'ship, 186 F.Supp.2d 695, 700 (W.D.Tex. 2002); Johnson v. NCB Collection Svcs., 799 F.Supp. 1298, 1304 (D.Conn.1992). Although an assumed name gives a false impression as to who created the letter, if that name would have no meaning for the debtor, there is no danger that the debtor will react differently than if the letter were signed with the employee's real name. As Youngblood observed, "[n]ames are arbitrary labels used to identify one person from another. They can be changed for any number of reasons. . . . The given name of the employee from whose desk the letter was sent is immaterial, and the use of a professional name or desk name, when used properly, is no violation of § 1692e." 186 F.Supp.2d at 700. Or, put another way, one dandelion is as unwanted as another. Thus, where a desk name identifies a unique employee of the debt collector, the name signed to the letter cannot be fairly regarded as being used to further the collection of the debt and so is not assumed for a fraudulent purpose.

We next consider the Federal Trade Commission's 1988 commentary on the FDCPA, 53 Fed.Reg. 50097. Because the FDCPA does not give the FTC rule-making authority in this area, the commentary does not have the force of law and is not entitled to deference. Dutton v. Wolpoff & Abramson, 5 F.3d 649, 654 (3d Cir.1993). We may, however, consider it as persuasive authority, and courts of appeals, including our own, have on occasion done so. See Brown, 464 F.3d at 455-56; 665*665 Kaltenbach v. Richards, 464 F.3d 524, 528 (5th Cir.2006).[8] The commentary says that § 1692e(9) "covers documents that fraudulently appear to be official government documents, or otherwise mislead the recipient as to their authorship." 53 Fed. Reg. at 50106. An unsophisticated consumer, receiving a letter signed by the president of a corporation, will likely read that letter as having been written, if not personally by the signatory, at least at his or her specific behest. Although the courts that have addressed the question have found that the word "source" in § 1692e(9) refers to the company seeking to collect the debt, see, e.g., Youngblood, 186 F.Supp.2d at 700; Johnson, 799 F.Supp. at 1304, the words "authorization" and "approval" can be interpreted more broadly[9] so as to encompass the individual employee who reviewed the debtor's file and caused the letter to be sent.

Considering these authorities together, we find that where some aspect of a debt collector's communication — whether explicit or implied — has the purpose or effect of making a debtor more likely to respond, the FDCPA requires that it be true. Thus, because a debtor is more likely to respond to a letter from an attorney and is likely to assume that the attorney is familiar with his or her case, a dunning letter that a lawyer signs must have actually been reviewed by that attorney. Conversely, because the use of a desk name does not and cannot have the purpose or effect of making a debtor more likely to respond, it is not deceptive or misleading even though it is technically untrue. Here, the use of top executives of the company as signatories is likely meant to impress upon debtors the seriousness of the communication and will almost certainly have such an effect on at least some debtors. Because the parties have stipulated that those executives did not review plaintiffs' cases, and because the signature of an executive, no less than the signature of an attorney, conveys that the executive had some actual involvement in the decision to send the letter to a particular debtor, we find that the letters here are deceptive and misleading within the meaning of Section 1692e.[10]

Because the individually numbered subparts of Section 1692e do not limit the overall prohibition against deceptive and misleading statements, we need not directly address the question of whether these statements also violate Section 1692e(9). We will grant plaintiffs' motion (and deny defendants') on the grounds that the challenged statements violate the broad prohibition of Section 1692e itself.

LARSEN V. JBC LEGAL GROUP, P.C., 533 F. SUPP.2D 290, 299 (E.D.N.Y. 2008)

JBC Legal Group, P.C., Jack Boyajian, Mary Brandon, Outsource Recovery Management, Inc., pro se.

MEMORANDUM OPINION AND ORDER

E. THOMAS BOYLE, United States Magistrate Judge.

Plaintiff, Kimberly Larsen ("Larsen"), brings this action' pursuant to the Fair Debt Collection Practices Act ("FDCPA"), 15 U.S.C. § 1692 et seq., seeking statutory damages, attorney's fees and costs. Plaintiff alleges that defendants, JBC Legal Group, P.C., formerly known as JBC & Associates, P.C. ("JBC"), Jack Boyajian ("Boyajian"), Mary Brandon, also known as, Marvin Brandon ("Brandon"), and Outsource Recovery Management, Inc. ("ORM"), violated the FDCPA when they attempted to collect a debt from her in 2003. Before the court is the plaintiff's motion for partial summary judgment against all defendants. For the following reasons, plaintiff's motion is granted in part and denied in part.

PROCEDURAL HISTORY

This action was commenced by the filing of a Complaint against all defendants except ORM on October 13, 2004. An Amended Complaint was then filed on December 7, 2004. All of the then-named defendants submitted an Answer on December 30, 2004.

On August 5, 2005, plaintiff filed a Second Amended Complaint against all of the previously named defendants plus ORM, JBC, Boyajian and Brandon submitted a joint Answer on September 7, 2005. ORM filed its Answer on that same date as well.

Although plaintiff initially sought to bring this action on behalf of all others similarly situated and moved for class certification on December 20, 2006, that motion was subsequently withdrawn, without prejudice, on April 10, 2007, at the request of the plaintiff, and not renewed. Accordingly, the within summary judgment motion is brought solely on behalf of plaintiff.

By Order dated May 3, 2007, the Court directed that any dispositive motions be made on or before July 2, 2007. Any opposition was to be filed by August 31, 2007 and a reply, if any, was to be submitted by September 10, 2007. (Order of Boyle, J., dated May 3, 2007.) After granting plaintiffs requests for extensions 295*295 on two occasions, the within motion was ultimately filed on July 11, 2007. Opposition was received from defendant Brandon, apparently acting pro se, on September 4, 2007, which the Court notes is four days beyond the deadline for submitting any opposition and is deficient in many respects. Although Brandon submitted what purports to be a Rule 56.1 counterstatement, his submission does not comport with the requirements of the local civil rules.

Local Civil Rule 56.1(c) states that "unless specifically controverted by a correspondingly numbered paragraph in the statement [of material facts] required to be served by the opposing party," the material facts set forth in the moving party's Rule 56.1 statement "will be deemed to be admitted for purposes of the [summary judgment] motion." Local Civ. R. 56.1(c). Moreover, Local Civil Rule 56.1(d) unambiguously requires that "[e]ach statement by the movant or opponent pursuant to Rule 56.1(a) and (b), including each statement controverting any statement of material fact, must be followed by citation to evidence which would be admissible, set forth as required by Federal Rule of Civil Procedure 56(e)." Local Civ. R. 56.1(d). Brandon has failed to comply with either of these requirements. Rather, the majority of Brandon's Rule 56.1 statement simply contains responses that plaintiffs statements of material fact are "[i]rrelevant" and that they "[d]o[] not relate to liability as against Mary Brandon."[1] (Brandon's Rule 56.1 Stmt. ¶¶ 1-8, 11-76.) Nothing in Brandon's Rule 56.1 statement can be construed as a statement of material fact. Moreover, Brandon has failed to include any evidentiary citations in his Rule 56.1 statement, as required by Rule 56.1(d). As a result of this omission, Brandon's Rule 56.1 statement is wholly inadequate and "must be disregarded."[2] Fernandez v. DeLeno, 71 F.Supp.2d 224, 227 (S.D.N.Y.1999); (citing Titan Indent. Co. v. Triborough Bridge & Tunnel Auth., Inc., 135 F.3d 831, 835 (2d Cir.1998)); see also Cooper v. Gottlieb, No. 95 Civ. 10548, 2000 WL 1277593, at *4, 2000 U.S. Dist. LEXIS 12936, at *12-13 (S.D.N.Y. Sept. 4, 2000) (deeming the statements contained invents' Rule 56.1 statement admitted where non-movants failed to cite to nor submit any evidentiary support for the statements in their Rule 56.1 statement in opposition to motion for summary judgment).

With respect to the remaining defendants, no opposition to the within motion has been received whatsoever. Accordingly, since JBC, Boyajian and ORM have failed to file any opposition, and more specifically have failed to comply with Local Civil Rule 56.1(b), which requires the submission of a counter-statement of "material 296*296 facts" in opposition to a motion for summary judgment, see Local Civ. Rule 56.1, all of the facts in plaintiffs Rule 56.1 Statement that pertain to JBC, Boyajian and ORM are deemed admitted. See Giannullo v. City of New York, 322 F.3d 139, 140 (2d Cir.2003) ("If the opposing party . . . fails to controvert a fact so set forth in the moving party's. Rule 56.1 statement, that fact will be deemed admitted.") (citing Local Rule 56.1(c)). "[W]here a party against whom summary judgment is sought fails entirely to respond to the motion, the court need ensure only that the averments in the movant's Rule 56.1 statement are supported by evidence and show an absence of a genuine issue for trial." Morisseau v. Piper, No. 06 Civ. 13255, 532 F.Supp.2d 595, 618, 2008 WL 273410, at *18, 2008 U.S. Dist. LEXIS 4699, at *60 (S.D.N.Y. Jan. 23, 2008) (citing Vermont Teddy Bear Co. v. 1-800 Beargram Co., 373 F.3d 241, 243 (2d Cir.2004)) (additional citation omitted).

FACTS

Plaintiff, Kimberly Larsen, is a consumer within the, meaning of the FDCPA, who allegedly owes a debt that is the subject of collection efforts. (Pl. 56.1 Stmt. ¶ 1; Decl. of Kimberly Larsen, dated July 9, 2007 ("Larsen Decl."), ¶ 1.) Defendant JBC Legal Group, P.C., formerly known as JBC & Associates, P.C.,[3] is a debt collector incorporated in California, with, a place of business located at 2 Broad Street in Bloomfield, New Jersey. (Pl. 56.1 Stmt. ¶¶ 2-3, 21; Reply Decl. of Brian L. Bromberg, dated Sept. 20, 2007 ("Bromberg Reply Decl."), Ex. A.) Defendant' Boyajian, an attorney licensed to practice in' California, was the President and owner of JBC & Associates, P.C.[4] (Id ¶ 50.) Boyajian is also the President and Secretary of JBC Legal Group, P.C. — and, presumably, its owner as well since he owned its predecessor entity — and is, at various times, personally involved in JBC's collection process, including reviewing new claims and cases, establishing procedures for debtor contact and verification, responding to complaints and inquiries, managing litigation brought to collect debts, overseeing and managing the operations of JBC"s Compliance Department, supervising paralegal and office staff and "dealing with unique issues that arise." (Id. ¶ 7-8; Bromberg Reply Decl., Ex. A.) Defendant Brandon is an attorney licensed to practice in New York and New Jersey who was employed by JBC & Associates, P.C. and appears to currently be in business with defendant Boyajian.[5] (Pl. 56.1 Stint ¶¶ 9, 297*297 12; Brandon's 56.1 Stmt. ¶ 9; Decl. of Brian L. Bromberg, dated July 11, 2007 ("Bromberg Decl."), Ex. EE; Bromberg Reply Decl., Ex. A.)

On or about October 24, 2003, defendant JBC Legal. Group, P.C. sent or caused to be sent a letter to plaintiff, seeking to collect a debt alleged to be owed by plaintiff in the amount of $43.87 (the "debt collection notice"). (Pl. 56.1 Stmt., ¶ 21; Compl. ¶ 28; Larsen Decl., ¶ 3 and Ex. A, annexed thereto.) Boyajian was an officer of JBC Legal Group, P.C. at this time. (Pl. 56.1 Stmt. ¶ 6.) The debt collection notice stated that it sought payment for an alleged "bad check," purported to be have been written by plaintiff on a Chase Manhattan checking account on April 14, 1993, in the amount of $23.87.[6] (Larsen Decl., ¶ 3 and Ex. A.) This was the first communication that plaintiff received from JBC.[7] (PI. 56.1 Stmt., ¶ 22; Larsen Decl., ¶ 3.)

The debt reflected in the October 24, 2003 debt collection notice is allegedly due to defendant ORM, which claims to have acquired the debt in or about October 2003. (Pl. 56.1 Stmt. ¶ 33.) The business of ORM is to purchase debts that are in default from other entities. (Id. ¶ 37.) Boyajian is the president and director of ORM and ORM's address is the same as that of JBC Legal Group, P.C. (Id. ¶¶ 34-36.) ORM retained JBC to collect the alleged debt from plaintiff. (Id. ¶ 38.) ORM uses JBC exclusively as the collector on the debts that it purchases. (Id. ¶ 39.)

Although the October 24, 2003 debt collection notice that plaintiff received stated that failure to satisfy the debt may result in legal action being taken against her, no such litigation was in fact commenced. (Larsen Decl., ¶ 7 and Ex. A; Pl. 56.1 Stmt., ¶ 25.) Plaintiff has not paid the amount alleged to be owed by her in the October 24, 2003 letter. (Pl. 56.1 Stmt., ¶ 24.)

Defendant Boyajian is the individual responsible within JBC for reviewing the accounts and deciding whether to send letters such as the October 24, 2003, debt collection notice received by plaintiff. (Id. ¶ 43.) Boyajian is also responsible for determining the amount demanded in these notices, as well as whether or not to institute litigation with respect to a particular debt. (Id. ¶¶ 44-45.) Boyajian reviewed and/or drafted the form of the notices that JBC sent to alleged debtors in connection with its efforts to collect a debt, including the October 24, 2003 debt collection notice sent to plaintiff, and authorized the mailing of such notices.[8] (Id. ¶¶ 46-47.)

298 DISCUSSION

I. Legal Standard for Summary Judgment

Federal Rule of Civil Procedure 56(c) provides that summary judgment "shall be rendered forthwith if the pleadings, depositions, answers to interrogatories, and admissions on file, together with the affidavits, if any, show that there is no genuine issue as to any material fact and that the moving party is entitled to a judgment as a matter of law." Fed.R.Civ.P. 56(c); see also Celotex Corp. v. Catrett, 477 U.S. 317, 322, 106 S.Ct. 2548, 91 L.Ed.2d 265 (1986). The burden is on the moving party to establish the lack of any factual issues. See Celotex, 477 U.S. at 323, 106 S.Ct. 2548. The very language of this standard reveals that an otherwise properly supported motion for summary judgment will not be defeated because of the mere existence of some alleged factual dispute between the parties. See Anderson v. Liberty Lobby, Inc., 477 U.S. 242, 247, 106 S.Ct. 2505, 91 L.Ed.2d 202 (1986). Rather, the requirement is that there be no "genuine issue of material fact." Id. at 248, 106 S.Ct. 2505.

The inferences to be drawn from the underlying facts are to be viewed in the light most favorable to the non-moving party. See Matsushita Elec. Indus. Co. v. Zenith Radio Corp., 475 U.S. 574, 588, 106 S.Ct. 1348, 89 L.Ed.2d 538 (1986). When the moving party has carried its burden, the party opposing summary judgment must do more than simply show that "there is some metaphysical doubt as to the material facts." Id. at 586, 106 S.Ct. 1348. Under Rule 56(e), the party opposing the motion "may not rest upon the mere allegations or denials of his pleadings, but . . . must set forth specific facts showing there is a genuine issue for trial." Anderson, 477 U.S. at 248, 106 S.Ct. 2505.

When considering a motion for summary judgment, the district court "must also be `mindful of the underlying standards and burdens of proof . . . because the evidentiary burdens that the respective parties will bear at trial guide district courts in their determination of summary judgment motions." SEC v. Meltzer, 440 F.Supp.2d 179, 187 (E.D.N.Y.2006) (quoting Brady v. Town of Colchester, 863 F.2d 205, 211 (2d Cir.1988)) (internal citations omitted). "Where the non-moving party would bear the ultimate burden of proof on an issue at trial, the burden on the moving party is satisfied if he can point to an absence of evidence to support an essential element of the non-movant's claim." Meltzer, 440 F.Supp.2d at 187.

Summary judgment should not be regarded as a procedural shortcut, but rather as an integral part of the Federal Rules of Civil Procedure, which are designed to "secure the just, speedy and inexpensive determination of every action." Celotex, 477 U.S. at 827, 106 S.Ct. 2548. Rule 56 must be "construed with due regard not only for the rights of persons asserting claims and defenses that are adequately based in fact to have those claims and defenses tried to a jury," but also for the rights of those persons "opposing such claims and defenses to demonstrate, . . . prior to trial, that the claims and defenses 299*299 have no factual basis." Id. By its terms, Rule 56 does not require that a trial judge make any findings of fact. See Anderson, 477 U.S. at 250, 106 S.Ct. 2505. The only inquiry to be performed is the determination of whether there is a need for trial See id. The court's principal analysis on a motion for summary judgment is to ascertain whether there are any "genuine factual issues that properly can be resolved only by a finder of fact because they may reasonably be resolved in favor of either party." Id.

II. The FDCPA

The FDCPA prohibits the use of "any false, deceptive, or misleading representation or means in connection with the collection of any debt." 15 U.S.C. § 1692e. The sixteen subsections contained in Section 1692e of the Act provide a non-exhaustive list of practices that fall within the FDCPA's ban. See id. A debt collection practice may violate the FDCPA even if it does not fall within any of the enumerated circumstances set forth in

Section 1692e, see Bentley v. Great Lakes Collection Bureau, Inc., 6 F.3d 60, 62 (2d Cir. 1993) (citing Clomon v. Jackson, 988 F.2d 1314, 1318 (2d Cir.1993)), and "[a] single violation of § 1692e is sufficient to establish civil liability under the FDCPA." Clomon, 988 F.2d at 1318 (citation omitted); see also 15 U.S.C. § 1692k (establishing civil liability' for'"any debt collector who fails to comply with any provision of this subchapter").

The test for determining whether a collection notice violates the FDCPA is "an objective standard, measured by how the `least sophisticated consumer' would interpret the notice received from the debt collector." Russell v. Equifax A.R.S., 74 F.3d 30, 34 (2d Cir.1996) (citing Clomon, 988 F.2d at 1318). The "basic purpose" of this standard is to "ensure that the FDCPA protects all consumers, the gullible as well as the shrewd." Id. "This least"sophisticated-consumer standard best effectuates the [FDCPA's] purpose of limiting the `suffering and anguish' often inflicted by independent debt collectors." Russell v. Equifax A.R.S., 74 F.3d at 34 (quoting S.Rep. No. 95-382, 95th Cong., 1st Sess. 3 (1977), reprinted in 1977 U.S.C.C.A.N. 1695, 1696).

A debt collector who is found to have violated the FDCPA is liable for actual damages incurred by the plaintiff, as well as any other damages that the court, in its discretion, may find appropriate, not to exceed $1,000, plus reasonable attorney's fees and costs. See 15 U.S.C. § 1692k(a); Russell, 74 F.3d at 33. Moreover, the FDCPA is a strict liability statute. See Russell, 74 F.3d at 34. Accordingly, "a consumer need not show intentional conduct by the debt collector to be entitled to damages." Id.

III. Plaintiff is Entitled to Partial Summary Judgment Against JBC, Boyajian and ORM[9]

A. Judgment by Default

Pursuant to Federal Rule of Civil Procedure 56(e), if the non-moving party fails to respond to a summary judgment motion, "summary judgment, if appropriate, shall be entered against the adverse party." Fed.R.Civ.P. 56(e). As the Second Circuit has announced:

[L]itigants should be on notice from the very publication of Rule 56(e) that a party faced with a summary judgment motion `may not rest upon the mere allegations or denials' of the party's pleading and that if the party does not respond properly, `summary judgment, 300*300 if appropriate, shall be entered' against him.

Graham v. Lewinski, 848 F.2d 342, 344 (2d Cir.1988) (quoting Fed.R.Civ.P. 56(e)). Furthermore, the local rules of the district courts in the circuit provide notice that action is called for in response to a motion for summary judgment. See id.; see also Local Civ. R. 56.1.

The courts in this circuit routinely grant summary judgment by default where a party fails to respond to the motion in violation of court rules and/or scheduling orders. See, e.g., Canfield v. Van Atta Buick/GMC Truck, Inc., 127 F.3d 248 (2d Cir.1997) (granting summary judgment by default for failure to respond to the motion despite a local court rule that failure to respond to a motion is deemed consent to the motion); In re Towers Fin. Corp. Noteholders Litig., 996 F.Supp. 266 (S.D.N.Y.1998) (granting default judgment against defendants who failed to respond to summary judgment motion by courtordered deadline); Sea-Land Serv., Inc. v. Citihope Ina, Inc., 176 F.R.D. 118, 121 (S.D.N.Y.1997) (granting summary judgment where defendant failed to respond to plaintiffs Rule 56.1 Statement, "a failure that independently results in the facts there set forth being deemed admitted"); Lediju v. New York City Dep't of Sanitation, 173 F.R.D. 105 (S.D.N.Y.1997) (granting summary judgment by default for plaintiffs failure to respond to defendant's summary judgment motion and failure to obey scheduling orders); Modefine S.A. v. Burlington Coat Factory Warehouse Corp., 919 F.Supp. 723 (S.D.N.Y. 1996) (granting default judgment against defendants who failed to respond to summary judgment motion by deadline set by court).

Plaintiff filed her motion for summary judgment in this action seven months ago. JBC, Boyajian and ORM were afforded adequate time to oppose the within motion. No such opposition has been received by the Court. Nor have these defendants communicated with the Court in any way as to their failure to oppose plaintiffs motion. Accordingly, due to the default of JBC, Boyajian and ORM, plaintiff is entitled to have her motion for summary judgment granted as against those defendants.

B. Judgment on the Merits

Even if the Court were to overlook the failure of JBC, Boyajian and ORM to enter any opposition whatsoever to plaintiffs motion, plaintiff is still entitled to summary judgment on the merits of her FDCPA claims.

1. JBC, Boyajian and ORM Qualify as Debt Collectors Under the FDCPA

As a threshold matter, the Court must determine whether JBC, Boyajian and ORM qualify as debt collectors under the FDCPA for purposes of liability. The FDCPA defines a "debt collector" as:

any person who uses any instrumentality of interstate commerce or the mails in any business the principal purpose of which is the collection of any debts, or who regularly collects or attempts to collect, directly or indirectly, debts owed or due or asserted to be owed or due another.

15 U.S.C. § 1692a(6). Specifically excluded from this definition are creditors who seek to collect their own debts. See Kinel v. Sherman Acquisition II LP, No. 05 Civ. 3456, 2006 WL 5157678, at *5-6, 2006 U.S. Dist. LEXIS 97073, at *17 (S.D.N.Y. Feb. 28, 2006) (citations omitted); Shevach v. Am. Fitness Franchise Corp., No. 98 Civ. 2938, 2001 WL 274121, at *3, 2001 U.S. Dist. LEXIS 2899, at *7 (S.D.N.Y. Mar. 14, 2001) (stating that the FDCPA "creates a cause of action against independent debt collectors rather than creditors seeking to enforce collection of their own debts") (citations omit-

ted); 15 U.S.C. 301*301 § 1692a(6)(F). "An assignee of a debt is also excluded, unless the debt sought to be collected was in default at the time it was obtained." Kind, 2006 WL 5157678, at *6, 2006 U.S. Dist. LEXIS 97078, at *18 (citations omitted); 1.5 U.S.C. § 1692a(6)(F)(iii) (excluding from the definition of debt collector "any person collecting or attempting to collect any debt owed . . . or due another to the extent such activity . . . concerns a debt which was, not, in default at the time it was obtained by such person"). "[T]hose who are assigned a defaulted debt are not exempt from the FDCPA if their principal purpose is the collection of debts or if they regularly engage in debt collection." Kinel, 2006 WL 5157678, at *6, 2006 U.S. Dist. LEXIS 97073, at *19 (quotation omitted).

In the instant action, the defendants have admitted that JBC is a debt collector. (Letter from JBC Legal Group, P.C. to plaintiff, dated Jan. 14, 2004, annexed as Ex. B to Larsen Decl. (stating "[t]his is an attempt to collect a debt by a debt collector"); Def. Reap. to Pl. First Set of Discovery Requests, No. 4, annexed as Ex. K to Bromberg Decl. (admitting that JBC Legal Group, P.C. is a "`debt collector' as that term is defined by 15 U.S.C. § 1692a(6)").) Accordingly, there is no dispute with respect to the ability to hold JBC liable for violations of the FDCPA. Although Boyajian and ORM have failed to interpose any opposition to plaintiffs allegations that they are both debt collectors within the meaning of the FDCPA, the Court will nevertheless examine the status of each to ensure that liability may be properly imposed against them.

With respect to Boyajian, a review of the documentary evidence submitted by plaintiff' in connection with this action establishes that Boyajian is undoubtedly a debt collector. Boyajian is the President and Secretary, and presumed owner, of JBC Legal Group, P.C. In deposition testimony provided by Boyajian in January 2004, he testified in Goins v. JBC Assoc., P.C., No. 3:03cv636 (D.Conn.), that in his role as owner and President of JBC & Associates, P.C., the predecessor to JBC Legal Group, P.C., he "provides services to clients who have debts that are with consumers that I am engaged in recovering for." (Boyajian Dep., 25.) Boyajian further stated that he has sole control over the form of the debt collection notice that is sent to a particular debtor and that he "make[s] the final decision on what letters are sent out and what they `contain." (Id., 39-40.) Based on this same deposition testimony, the court in Goins found that Boyajian "undisputedly acted as a debt collector." Goins, 352 F.Supp.2d at 268. That same finding is made here.

With respect to ORM, the Court finds that it, too, is a debt collector within the meaning of the FDCPA. A review of ORM's Answer to the Second Amended Complaint in this action demonstrates that ORM acquired plaintiffs debt in or about October 2003, about the same time that JBC sent its initial debt collection notice to plaintiff. (ORM Ans. ¶ 34.) The business of ORM is to purchase debts that are in default from other entities. (Id. ¶ 15.) ORM retained JBC to collect plaintiffs debt. (Id ¶ 35.) Moreover, ORM uses JBC exclusively' as the collector on the debts that it purchases. (Boyajian Dep., 42.) As stated above, an assignee of a debt that is in default at the time the debt was obtained is considered a debt collector for purposes of the FDCPA. See Kinel, 2006 WL 5157678, at *6, 2006 U.S. Dist. LEXIS 97073, at *18. ORM's business is to purchase debts that' are in default from other entities and ORM purchased plaintiffs debt in October 2003 — more than ten years after the check plaintiff is alleged to have written was dishonored. The debt was undoubtedly in default before JBC 302*302 was retained to collect plaintiffs debt on behalf of ORM, and thus, there can be no doubt that ORM falls within the definition of a debt collector as used in the FDCPA.

Based on the foregoing, the Court finds that JBC, Boyajian and ORM are all "debt collectors" within the meaning of the FDCPA and as such, can be held liable for any violations of the Act.

2. 15 U.S.C. §§ 1692e and 1692f

As stated above, the FDCPA provides that "[a] debt collector may not use any false, deceptive, or misleading representation or means in connection with the collection of any debt." 15 U.S.C. § 1692e. Moreover, Section 1692f of the FDCPA mandates that "[a] debt collector may not use unfair or unconscionable means to collect or attempt to collect any debt." 15 U.S.C. § 1692f. Plaintiff asserts that defendants have violated Sections 1692e and 1692f in the following ways: (1) by threatening a legal action that cannot be taken; and, (2) by attempting to collect an amount or cost that cannot be recovered.

a. Threatening a Legal Action That Cannot be Taken

15 U.S.C. § 1692e(5) specifically prohibits a debt collector from "threat[ening] to take any action that cannot legally be taken or that is not intended to be taken." 15 U.S.C. § 1692e(5). Section 1692e(10) of the FDCPA prohibits the "use of any false representation or deceptive means to collect or attempt to collect any debt. . . ." 15 U.S.C. § 1692e(10). In order to establish a violation of Sections 1692e(5) and e(10), the plaintiff must demonstrate two things: (i) threatened action, (ii) which was not intended to be taken. See Bentley, 6 F.3d at 62; Tsenes v. Trans-Continental Credit & Collection Corp., 892 F.Supp. 461, 465 (E.D.N.Y. 1995). "To determine whether a communication from a debt collector constitutes a threat, the reviewing court should look to the language used as a whole." Baptist v. Global Holding and Investment Co., LLC, No. 04-CV-2365, 2007 WL 1989450, at *2, 2007 U.S. Dist. LEXIS 49476, at *6 (E.D.N.Y. July 9, 2007) (citing Pipiles v. Credit Bureau of Lockport, Inc., 886 F.2d 22, 25-26 (2d Cir.1989)).

Where a communication merely informs the consumer that the debt collector is seeking repayment, Section 1692e will not be found to have been violated. See Baptist, 2007 WL 1989450, at *2-3, 2007 U.S. Dist. LEXIS 49476, at *7 (citing cases). Similarly, if the communication "only advises a debtor that the collection agency has several options with which to pursue the debt," this too will generally be found insufficient to constitute a threat in violation of Section 1692e. Id. (citing Spira v. Ashwood Fin. Inc., 358 F.Supp.2d 150 (E.D.N.Y.2005)). However, "an explicit threat of litigation or an implication that legal action is inevitable, when such is not the case, will violate § 1692e(5)." Baptist, 2007 WL 1989450, at *3, 2007 U.S. Dist. LEXIS 49476, at *7-8 (citing cases).

With respect to the first element, all that is required is that the least sophisticated consumer reasonably interpret the communication as advancing a threat of legal action. Here, the October 24, 2003 debt collection notice explicitly states "Warning: You may be sued 30 days after the date of this notice if you do not make payment." (Larsen Decl., Ex. A.) The letter goes on to state as follows: "If you do not make payment, you may be sued under New York General Obligations Law Section 11-104 to recover payment. (Id.) The letter is signed "JBC & Associates, P.C., Attorneys at Law." (Id.) Moreover, the letter "suggests that the only way to avoid . . . legal action would be to voluntarily pay the debt[]." Baptist, 2007 WL 1989450, at *4, 2007 U.S. Dist. LEXIS 49476, at *12 (citation omitted). A letter 303*303 from an attorney informing the recipient that the failure to pay the debt in question will result in litigation could reasonably be construed by the least sophisticated consumer as advancing a threat. See Bentley, 6 F.3d at 62 (holding that a letter declaring that a consumer's debt has been, referred to an attorney, and that continued failure to pay the debt will result in legal action, could reasonably be interpreted by the least sophisticated consumer to mean that "legal action was authorized, likely and imminent"). Accordingly, plaintiff has satisfied the first prong of a claim pursuant to Sections 1692e(5) and 1692e(10).

Plaintiff next has the burden of demonstrating that the possibility of the threatened lawsuit could be "ruled out," such that defendants had no intention of ever bringing legal action against her, Tsenes, 892 F.Supp. at 465. Plaintiff asserts that the debt for which defendants sought collection was time-barred under New York law and, accordingly, defendants were threatening to "to take . . . action that cannot legally be taken" in violation of Section 1692e(5), which also constitutes a "false representation" in violation of Section 1692e(10). Although it is permissible for a debt collector to seek to collect on a time-barred debt voluntarily, it is prohibited from threatening litigation with respect to such a debt. See Baptist, 2007 WL 1989450, at *4, 2007 U.S. Dist. LEXIS 49476, at *13 (citing Freyermuth v. Credit Bureau Servs., Inc., 248 F.3d 767, 771 (8th Cir.2001)); see also Goins v. JBC & Assoc., P.C., 352 F.Supp.2d 262, 272 (D.Conn.2005) ("[A]s the statute of limitations would be a complete defense . . ., the threat to bring suit under such circumstances can at best be described as a `misleading' representation, in violation of § 1692e.").

Under New York law, the statute of limitations for an action to recover for a fraudulent check is six years. See N.Y.C.P.L.R. 213. At the time that defendants issued the October 24, 2003 debt collection notice to plaintiff, the check referenced in the communication, which was dated April 14, 1993, was more than ten years old. (Larsen Decl., Ex. A.) Accordingly, any action to collect on that debt would have been time-barred. Given the fact that Boyajian, the owner and operator of JBC, as well as the President of ORM, is a licensed attorney, it is certainly reasonable to conclude that defendants were aware that any legal action with respect to plaintiffs purported debt would be fruitless. "To allow a debt collector to threaten a consumer with legal action, even though the statute of limitations would provide the consumer with the ultimate defense, would be to encourage manipulation and misuse of the legal system." Baptist, 2007 WL 1989450, at *5, 2007 U.S. Dist. LEXIS 49476, at *15.

Based on the foregoing, it is clear that the October 24, 2003 debt collection notice sent to plaintiff by JBC threatened legal action that could not be taken, which also constitutes a false representation. By doing so, JBC, Boyajian and ORM violated Sections 1692e(5) and 1692e(10) of the FDCPA and plaintiff is entitled to summary judgment on those claims.

b. Attempting to Collect an Amount That Cannot be Recovered

15 U.S.C. § 1692f(1) prohibits "[t]he collection of any amount (including any interest, fee, charge, or expense incidental to the principal obligation) unless such amount is expressly authorized by the agreement creating the debt or permitted by law." 15 U.S.C. § 1692f(1).

The October 24, 2003 letter sent to plaintiff by JBC states as follows:

If you, do not make payment, you may be sued under New York General Obligations Law Section 11-104 to recover payment. If a judgment is rendered 304*304 against you in court, it may include not only the original face amount of each check and the service charge for each check, but also statutory penalties equal to twice the face amount of each check or Four Hundred Dollars ($400.00) per check, whichever is less.

(Larsen Decl., Ex. A.) Plaintiff asserts that the above-quoted language violates 15 U.S.C. § 1692f(1) because defendants failed to comply with the notice and mailing requirements set forth in New York General Obligations Law § 11-104, which are prerequisites to obtaining the statutory penalties provided for thereunder. As noted above, JBC, Boyajian and ORM have not provided any opposition to plaintiff's assertion.

New York General Obligations Law § 11-104 provides for the recovery of "additional, liquidated damages" in situations where an individual tenders a check that he or she knows or should know will not be honored for payment. N.Y. Gen. Oblig. § 11-104(1). To be entitled to such additional damages, however, the payee must comply with the requirements of Section 11-104(7) of the New York General Obligations Law, which provides that "[t]he first written demand for payment on the dishonored check . . . shall be sent . . . by first class mail and by certified mail return receipt requested with delivery restricted to the drawer . . ." Id. § 11-104(7). The statute further requires that "[t]he second written demand for payment on the dishonored check . . . shall be sent . . . by first class mail on or after the fifteenth day following the date of receipt of the first written demand for payment" Id. The notice language that is required to be employed when sending a "Demand for Payment of Dishonored' Check" under the New York General Obligations Law is set forth in subsection 8 of the statute. See N.Y. Gen. Oblig. § 11-104(8). Finally, the statutory damages recoverable under the New York General Obligations Law for a dishonored cheek are limited to "twice the face amount of the check or four hundred dollars, whichever is less." N.Y. Gen. Oblig. § 11-104(3).

Although plaintiff asserts in her memorandum of law in support of her motion that defendants failed to comply with the notice and mailing requirements of New York General Obligations Law § 11-104, (Pl. Mem. of Law in Supp. of Partial Summ. J., 16-17), no such statement is included in plaintiffs declaration in support of her motion. Nor has plaintiff provided any documentary evidence from which the Court could reasonably conclude that such a failure on defendants' part occurred. However, as stated above, New York General Obligations Law § 11-104(3) limits the amount of "additional, liquidated damages" that a payee may seek to "twice the amount of the check or four hundred dollars, whichever is less." N.Y. Gen. Oblig. § 11-104(3). Here, the communication sent by JBC to plaintiff on October 24, 2003 states that if a judgment were to be rendered against plaintiff under New York General Obligations Law Section 11-104, "it may include not only the original face amount of each check and the service charge for each check, but also statutory penalties equal to twice the amount of each check or Four Hundred Dollars ($400.00) per cheek, whichever is less." (Larsen Decl., Ex. A) (emphasis added). The service charge for each check is plainly not recoverable under New York General Obligations Law § 11-104.

Accordingly, by stating that they would attempt to collect from plaintiff an amount of damages that is not permitted by law, JBC, Boyajian and ORM have violated 15 U.S.C. § 1692f(1) and plaintiff is entitled to summary judgment on that claim.

3. 15 U.S.C. § 1692g

When a debt collector solicits payment from a consumer, it "must — within five 305*305 days, of the initial communication — provide the consumer with a detailed validation notice" that includes the following information:

(1) the amount of the debt;

(2) the name of the creditor to whom the debt is owed;

(3) a statement that unless the consumer, within thirty days, after receipt of the notice, disputes the validity of the debt, or any portion thereof, the debt will be assumed to be valid by, the debt collector;

(4) a statement that if the consumer notifies the debt collector in writing within the thirty-day period that the debt, or any portion thereof, is disputed, the debt collector, will obtain verification of the debt or a copy of a judgment against the consumer and a copy of such verification or judgment will be mailed to the consumer by the debt, collector; and

(5) a statement that, upon the consumer's written request within the thirty-day period, the debt collector will provide the consumer with the name and address of the original creditor, if different from the current creditor.

Savino v. Computer Credit, Inc., 164 F.3d 81, 85 (2d Cir.1998); 15 U.S.C. § 1692g(a). "This information . . . arms the consumer with the facts necessary to challenge the debt allegedly owed prior to submitting payment to the collection agency." Kolganov v. Phillips & Cohen Assoc., Ltd., No. CV-024710, 2004 WL 958028, at *2, 2004 U.S. Dist. LEXIS 7069, at *5-6 (E.D.N.Y. Apr. 8, 2004) (citations omitted). "However, a is not enough for a debt collection agency simply to include the proper debt validation notice in a mailing to a consumer — Congress intended that such notice be clearly conveyed." Rumpler v. Phillips & Cohen Assoc., Ltd., 219 F.Supp.2d 251, 258 (E.D.N.Y.2002) (quoting Russell, 74 F.3d at 35).

Plaintiff asserts that defendants violated 16 U.S.C. § 1692g in two ways: (1) by failing to set forth the amount of the debt owed and (2) by overshadowing and contradicting the validation notice. As with the other provisions of the FDCPA, the "least sophisticated consumer" test is used to determine whether a violation of Section 1692g has occurred. See Russell 74 F.3d at 34.

a. Failing to Set Forth the Amount of the Debt

Plaintiff argues that the debt collection notice sent to her by JBC violates 15 U.S.C. § 1692g(a)(1) because it does not clearly set forth the amount of the debt that she purportedly owes. The October 24, 2003 communication states in two separate places that the amount of the debt owed is $43.87, which includes the "face amount" of the check plus a $20 "return charge" or "service charge." (Larsen Decl., Ex. A.) However, in another, portion of the letter, defendants state that "[f]ull amount of the cheek(s) and a $25.00 service charge for each check listed is now due in our office." (Id.) (emphasis added.) This language would appear to indicate that the debt that plaintiff allegedly owes is actually $48.87, not $43.87, as stated elsewhere in the communication. Then, just above the signature line, the letter states "Please remit $43.87 payable to JBC & Associates, P.C. and mail to the above address." (Id.) The least sophisticated consumer could reasonably conclude that the debt collection notice sets forth two different amounts with respect to the amount of the debt owed and therefore be confused as to which amount they are being instructed to remit to the debt collector.

Accordingly, the failure by JBC to clearly convey the amount of the debt owed in the October 24, 2003 debt collection notice sent to plaintiff violates 15 U.S.C. 306*306 § 1692g(a)(1) and plaintiff is entitled to summary, judgment against JBC, Boyajian and ORM on that claim.

b. Overshadowing and Contradicting the Validation Notice

Where a debt collection notice "contains language that overshadows or contradicts' other language informing a consumer of her rights, it violates the [FDCPA]." Id. (quoting Graziano v. Harrison, 950 F.2d 107, 111 (3d Cir.1991) (stating that "the juxtaposition of two inconsistent statements" renders the debt collection notice invalid under § 1692g). The question, therefore, is "whether, from the perspective of the least sophisticated consumer, language contained in the [debt collection] notice overshadowed or contradicted the mandatory validation notice; if so, then the [FDCPA] is violated." Russell, 74 F.3d at 35. A debt collection notice will be found to be overshadowing or contradictory where "it fails to convey the validation information clearly and effectively and thereby makes the least sophisticated consumer uncertain as to her rights." Savino, 164 F.3d at 85 (citing Russell, 74 F.3d at 35)). "It is unnecessary to prove the contradiction is threatening." Russell, 74 F.3d at 35.

Here, the October 24, 2003 debt collection notice sent to plaintiff by JBC begins with the following language: "Warning: You may be sued 30 days after the date of this notice if you do not make payment." (Larsen Decl., Ex, A.) Plaintiff asserts that this statement violates the FDCPA because it threatens plaintiff with adverse consequences — namely, a lawsuit — if she does not remit payment within thirty days of the date of the notice, rather than within thirty days of her receipt of the notice, as statutorily mandated under 15 U.S.C. § 1692g(a)(3). The letter goes on to state that plaintiff has "thirty (30) days from receipt of this letter to pay the full amount" and the validation notice contained at the bottom of the letter states that plaintiff has thirty days from receipt of the notice to dispute the debt. (Id.) The various statements indicating different times within which plaintiff is required to respond are clearly contradictory.

"By specifying that the debt must: be disputed within thirty days from the date of receipt of the notice, Congress has consciously protected against abusive tactics of debt collectors, such as the backdating of notices or other practices that might shorten debtors time to respond." Cavallaro v. The Law Office of Shapiro & Kreisman, 933 F.Supp. 1148, 1154 (E.D.N.Y. 1996). In the within action, although the FDCPA permits consumers thirty days from the receipt of a debt collection notice to dispute a debt, defendants herein demand that payment be made thirty days from the date of the notice or else litigation against plaintiff may be commenced. Such a demand implies that plaintiff has less than the statutorily required time period provided for under 15 U.S.C. § 1692g(a)(3) to dispute her debt.

Moreover, "[e]ven the least-sophisticated consumer would calculate that payment must be mailed in advance of a deadline in order to be received by that deadline." Swift v. Maximus, Inc., No. 04-CV-216, 2004 WL 1576618, at *4 (E.D.N.Y. July 15, 2004). Accordingly, "the consumer holds a notice that demands payment from less than thirty days from when she received the letter, and she calculates that payment must be mailed several days before the deadline." Id. Under such circumstances, "[t]he letter's demand for payment takes on a quality of `immediateness.'" Id.

Where an immediate demand for payment is included in a debt collection notice, the demand "must be paired with transitional language'" informing the consumer that the demand does not override his ox her rights under Section 1692g to dispute 307*307 or seek validation of the debt. Id. (quoting Swine, 164 F.3d at 86). Although: the Court presumes that the letter is read in its entirety, see McStay v. I.C. Sys., Inc., 308 F.3d 188, 191 (2d Cir.2002), "when the statements are contradictory there is a greater need for clarifying transitional language." Swift, 2004 WL 1576618, a *4 (citing Hillaire v. Delta Funding Corp., 2002 WL 31123860, at *3 (E.D.N.Y. Sept. 26, 2002)). No such clarifying language can be found in the October 24, 2003 debt collection notice sent by JBC to plaintiff.

Based on the foregoing, although the demand for payment, standing alone, does not violate the FDCPA, the October 24, 2003 debt collection notice fails to adequately explain to plaintiff that she retains her rights pursuant to 15 U.S.C. § 1692g. Rather, the demand for payment at the top of the letter overshadows and conflicts with the validation notice found at the bottom of the letter, particularly since it is accompanied by a "warning" in bold letters. Accordingly, the letter violates Section 1692g of the FDCPA and plaintiff is entitled to summary judgment against JBC, Boyajian and ORM on that claim as well.

IV. Defendant Brandon

Brandon is the only defendant herein to submit opposition to plaintiffs motion. Although difficult to understand, it appears that Brandon's opposition asserts that there is a triable issue of fact as to whether he was functioning as a debt collector on behalf of JBC in 2003 or 2004 — the years in which plaintiff was sent debt collection notices — and whether he had any personal involvement with the debt collection notices received by plaintiff. Brandon further asserts that the documentary evidence pertaining to him, which was relied upon and supplied by plaintiff in support of her motion, actually relates to Brandon's involvement with JBC & Associates, Inc., which, according to Brandon, is a wholly separate entity than JBC & Associates, P.C., the predecessor in interest to JBC Legal Group, P.C.

As noted above, in deposition testimony provided by. Boyajian in another action, Goins v. JBC & Assoc., P.C., No. 3:03cv636 (D.Conn.), which plaintiff submitted in support of the within motion, Boyajian states that there is no relationship between "JBC [& Associates], Inc." and "JBC [& Associates], P.C." (Boyajian Dep., at 19, annexed to Bromberg Decl. at Ex. FF.) Boyajian further states that "JBC [& Associates], Inc. is a New Jersey corporation that was engaged in collection activities and no longer is doing so. And JBC [& Associates], PC is a California professional corporation, a law firm." (Id., at 21.) Moreover, when asked whether JBC & Associates, Inc. and JBC & Associates, P.C. were a "singular entity that changed its name from Inc. to PC," Boyajian responded "[n]o." (Id., 19.)

Similarly, in deposition testimony provided by Brandon in connection with the same action, which was also submitted by plaintiff in support of the within motion, Brandon states that "JBC [& Associates], Inc." is "a collection agency," while "JBC & Associates, P.C. is a law firm." (Brandon Dep., at 5.) Brandon further states that he is an employee of JBC & Associates, P.C. and formerly an employee of JBC & Associates, Inc. (Id.)

The Court has reviewed the documents cited by plaintiff as supportive of the facts pertaining to Brandon contained in plaintiffs Rule 56.1 Statement and can find no evidence that conclusively establishes that Brandon was a debt collector on behalf of JBC in 2003 or 2004. Nor is the Court able to conclude from the evidence submitted that Brandon was personally involved in the debt collection process as it pertained to plaintiff. Moreover, although plaintiff alleges that JBC & Associates, 308*308 Inc. is a predecessor in interest to JBC & Associates, P.C. and JBC Legal Group, P.C., the documents provided in connection with the within motion appear to indicate otherwise, as discussed above.

Plaintiffs evidence and the inferences to be drawn therefrom squarely conflict with Brandon's opposition. Accordingly, there exists a genuine issue of material fact as to whether Brandon was involved in the debt collection efforts at issue herein and summary judgment in plaintiffs favor against Brandon would be, inappropriate.

Based on the foregoing, plaintiffs motion for summary judgment as against defendant Brandon is denied.

CONCLUSION

For the foregoing reasons, plaintiff's motion for partial summary judgment is granted as to plaintiffs FDCPA claims against defendants JBC Legal Group, P.C., Jack Boyajian and Outsource Recovery Management, Inc. Plaintiffs motion for partial summary judgment is denied as to plaintiffs FDCPA claims against Marvin Brandon.

SO ORDERED.

[1] All of Brandon's responses are virtually identical with the exception of two numbered paragraphs. With respect to plaintiff's paragraph eleven, Brandon states that the, statement of material fact contained therein is "[v]ague and [a]mbiguous as to whom it applies," (Brandon's Rule 56.1 Stmt. ¶ 11), and Brandon's response to plaintiff's paragraph nine is simply "none," which the Court presumes is meant to imply that Brandon does not dispute this statement of material fact. (Id. ¶ 9.)

[2] Although it appears that Brandon is acting pro se with respect to this motion, the rules afforded pro se litigants are not relaxed when that litigant is also an attorney, as Brandon is. See Leeds v. Meltz, 898 F.Supp. 146, 149 (E.D.N.Y.1995), aff'd, 85 F.3d 51 (2d Cir. 1996) (holding that pro se attorney was not entitled to the liberality normally accorded pro se litigants); Woods v. State, 469 F.Supp. 1127, 1128 n. 1 (S.D.N.Y.1979) ("Although [defendant] appears pro se, he is an attorney and is held to the same standards as other attorneys appearing before the court."); DeFina v. Latimer, 79 F.R.D. 5, 6

(E.D.N.Y.1977) (requiring skillfully drawn pleadings from the pro se plaintiff because she was an attorney).

[3] In August 2005, JBC Legal Group, P.C. apparently changed its name once again to Boyajian & Brandon Legal Group, P.C. (Bromberg Reply Decl., ¶ 6 and Ex. A, annexed thereto.) This amendment was endorsed by the Secretary of State of California on September 15, 2005. (Bromberg Reply Decl., Ex. A.)

[4] Boyajian was also the President of JBC & Associates, Inc., which plaintiff asserts is also a predecessor in interest to JBC Legal Group, P.C. (Pl. 56.1 Stmt. ¶¶ 4, 49.) However, in deposition testimony provided by Boyajian in another action, Goins v. JBC & Assoc, P.C., No. 3:03cv636 (D.Conn.), which plaintiff submitted in support of the within motion, Boyajian states that there is no relationship between "JBC, Inc." and "JBC, P.C." (Dep. of Jack H. Boyajian, dated Jan. 27, 2004 ("Boyajian Dep."), at 19, annexed to Decl. of Brian L. Bromberg, dated July 11, 2007 ("Bromberg Decl.") at Ex. FF.) Boyajian goes on to state that "JBC, Inc. is a New Jersey corporation that was engaged in collection activities and no longer is doing so. And JBC, PC is a California professional corporation, a law firm." (Id., 21.) In addition, when asked whether JBC & Associates, Inc. and JBC & Associates, P.C. were a "singular entity that changed its name from Inc. to PC," Boyajian responded "[n]o." (Id., 19.)

[5] It is unclear what Brandon's role is in relation to JBC Legal Group, P.C. since, although he disputes the plaintiff's allegations that he functioned as a debt collector for JBC Legal Group, P.C., Brandon does not explain what role, if any, he played with respect to that entity. (See generally Brandon's Opp'n to Mot. for Summ. J.) While the documentary evidence submitted by plaintiff establishes that Brandon was a debt collector for JBC & Associates, Inc., Brandon asserts that JBC & Associates, Inc. is a wholly separate organization than JBC & Associates, P.C., which, as stated above, is the predecessor in interest to JBC Legal Group, P.C. (Id.) In Goins, the United States District Court for the District of Connecticut found that Brandon was an employee of JBC & Associates, P.C. See Goins v. JBC & Assoc., P.C., 352 P.Supp.2d 262, 264

(D.Conn.2005). Brandon testified to that effect as well during a deposition taken in connection with that case. (Dep. of Mary Brandon, dated Sept. 5, 2003 ("Brandon Dep."), at 5, annexed to Bromberg Decl. as Ex. EE.)

[6] While the amount of the check written by plaintiff was alleged to be $23.87, the' amount of the debt sought to be collected was $43.87, which included a $20 "return charge" or "service charge." (Larsen Decl., Ex. A.)

[7] Defendants claim to have sent plaintiff a second letter as well, dated January 14, 2004; however, plaintiff has no recollection of receiving a second letter. (Pl. 56.1 Stmt., ¶ 23; Larsen Decl., 8 and Ex. B, annexed thereto.)

[8] It should be noted that the defendants herein have also been sued in other states for sending notices similar to the one received by plaintiff. See, e.g., Abels v. JBC Legal Group, P.C., No. C 04-02345 (N.D.Cal.); Alexander v. JBC Legal Group, P.C., No. CV-05-16-H (D.Mont.); Casden v. JBC Legal Group, P.C., No. 04-60669-Civ (S.D.Fla.); Culver v. JBC Legal Group, P.C., No. 5:04-CV-389 (E.D.N.C.); Defenbaugh v. JBC & Assoc., Inc., No. C-03-0651 (N.D.Cal.); Dunaway v. JBC & Assoc., Inc., No. 03-73597 (E.D.Mich.); Godfredson v. JBC Legal Group, P.C., No. 5:04-CV-390-FL(1) (E.D.N.C.); Goins v. Brandon, No. 3:02CV01537 (D.Conn.); Goins v. JBC & Assoc., P.C., No. 3:03cv636 (D.Conn.); Littledove v. JBC & Assoc., Inc., No. S-00-0586 (E.D.Cal); Martsolf v. JBC Legal Group, P.C., No. 04-CV-1346 (M.D.Pa.); Sewer v. JBC Legal Group, No. C04-2240L (W.D.Wash.); Sullivan v. JBC Legal Group, P.C., No. 04-3752 (E.D.Pa.); Thinesen v. JBC Legal Group, P.C., No. 05-518 (D.Minn.).

[9] Since defendant Brandon submitted opposition to the within motion, his alleged liability will be discussed separately from that of JBC, Boyajian and ORM.

CITATIONS

By Memorandum Opinion and Order dated February 12, 2008, plaintiff was granted summary judgment on her claims against Boyajian and JBC Legal Group, PC and Outsource Recovery Management, Inc. and the issue of damages was reserved for trial. - in Larsen v. JBC Legal Group, PC, 2008

"A debt collection practice may violate the FDCPA even if it does not fall within any of the enumerated circumstances set forth in Section 1692e." - in Sparks v. Phillips & Cohen Associates, Ltd., 2008

—dunning letter stating"[y] ou may be sued 30 days after the date of this notice if you do not make payment" violated FDCPA - in Owens v. Hellmuth & Johnson, PLLC, 2008

An unsophisticated consumer would still read the letter as threatening legal consequences if the consumer did not pay within thirty days of the letter's date - in THE ROLE OF VALIDATION AND COMMUNICATION IN THE DEBT COLLECTION PROCESS

Because plaintiff has not submitted a corresponding Local Rule 56.1 statement, in accordance with Local Rule 56.1 (c), defendants' Local Rule 56.1 Statements are deemed admitted for the purposes of this motion to the extent the allegations of fact recited therein are supported by the record. - in GELFMAN INTERNATIONAL ENTERPRISES v. MIAMI SUN INTERNATIONAL CORP., 2009

Numerous courts have found threatening legal action to collect a debt, which is time-barred, is an abusive debt collection practice - in Castro v. COLLECTO, INC., 2009

Notwithstanding the letter's equivocal language, an unsophisticated consumer reading the letter reasonably would fear additional consequences-namely, the commencement of legal proceedings or the acceleration of the annual assessment-if payment were not made within 30 days of the date of the letter. - in Owens v. Hellmuth & Johnson, PLLC, 2008

A] n explicit threat of litigation or an implication that legal action is inevitable, when such is not the case, will violate [the FDPCA - in Castro v. COLLECTO, INC., 2009 and one similar citation J] Fair Debt Collective Practices Act: 15 USC § 1692e, 1692k [Larsen v. LBC Legal Group, PC (law firm qualified - in CONSUMER LAW 2009 UPDATE]

Merely advising the debtor of the agency's options with which to pursue the debt is the sort of truism that is legally insufficient to violate § 1692e. - in Sparks v. Phillips & Cohen Associates, Ltd., 2008

BROWN V. CARD SERV. CTR., 464 F.3D 450, 453 (3D CIR. 2006)

CITATIONS

In deciding a motion to dismiss pursuant to Rule 12 (b)(6), the court must accept as true the well-pleaded allegations of the complaint and draw all reasonable inferences in the plaintiff's favor. - in McGowan Investors LP v. KEEFE BRUYETTE & WOODS, 2008

"`Lender-debtor communications potentially giving rise to claims under the FDCPA should be analyzed from the perspective of the least sophisticated debtor.'" - in SCIOLI v. GOLDMAN & WARSHAW, 2009

A motion to dismiss should be granted under Rule 12 (b)(6) if the moving party has established that the plaintiff would not be entitled to relief under any reasonable reading of the complaint. - in McCracken v. Ford Motor Co., 2008

"Because the FDCPA is a remedial statute, we construe its language broadly, so as to effect its purpose." - in Campuzano-Burgos v. Midland Credit Management, 2007

Alleged violations of the FDCPA are to be examined from the perspective of the "least sophisticated consumer." - in POPSON v. Galloway, 2010

A communication is deceptive for purposes of the Act if "it can be reasonably read to have two or more different meanings, one of which is inaccurate." - in Campuzano-Burgos v. Midland Credit Management, 2008

We concluded that" it would be deceptive under the FDCPA for [the collection agency] to assert that it could take an action that it had no intention of taking and has never or very rarely taken before." - in Rosenau v. Unifund Corp., 2008

This standard "requires more than `simply examining whether particular language would deceive or mislead a reasonable debtor because a communication that would not deceive or mislead a reasonable debtor might still deceive or mislead the least sophisticated debtor. " - in Smith v. Lyons, 2008

—the Court found it to be a deceptive practice for a collection agency to mention in a letter that an account could be forwarded to an attorney when the agency had never or very rarely done so before. - in Lesher v. Kay, 2010

Plaintiff also argues that the phrase, "subject to your rights below," suggests to the least sophisticated consumer that the "rights" listed were the only legal rights Plaintiff had even though it was not a comprehensive list. - in LeBlanc v. UNIFUND CCR PARTNERS, GP, 2008

TSENES V. TRANS-CONTINENTAL CREDIT & COLLECTION CORP., 892 F. SUPP. 461 (E.D.N.Y. 1995)

II. DISCUSSION

In deciding a motion to dismiss, a district court must accept the facts alleged in the complaint as true. Scheuer v. Rhodes, 416 U.S. 232, 236, 94 S.Ct. 1683, 1686, 40 L.Ed.2d 90 (1974). Generally, the complaint should not be dismissed unless it appears that plaintiff can prove no set of facts that would entitle him to relief. Conley v. Gibson, 355 U.S. 41, 45-46, 78 S.Ct. 99, 101-02, 2 L.Ed.2d 80 (1957).

The Act establishes a general prohibition against the use of "false, deceptive, or misleading representation or means in connection with the collection of any debt." 15 U.S.C. § 1692e. Litigation under the Act typically involves collection letters sent by "debt collectors" to "consumers" on behalf of "creditors." See 15 U.S.C. § 1692a(3), (4), (6) (defining the terms). The test for determining whether a collection letter violates § 1692e is an objective standard based on the "least sophisticated consumer." Clomon v. Jackson, 988 F.2d 1314, 1318 (2d Cir.1993). The sixteen subsections of § 1692e set forth a nonexhaustive list of practices that fall within this ban.[3] The Complaint charges the defendant with violating subsections (4), (5), and (10).

In order to state a claim under § 1692e(5), a consumer must sufficiently allege that a debt collector (1) threatened action, which (2) was "not intended to be taken." 15 U.S.C. § 1692e(5); see Bentley v. Great Lakes Collection Bureau, 6 F.3d 60, 62 (2d Cir.1993). In Pipiles v. Credit Bureau of Lockport, Inc., 886 F.2d 22 (2d. Cir.1989), a debt collector sent a letter, which read: "`Notice Is Hereby Given That This Item Has Already Been Referred for Collection Action;' `We Will At Any Time After 48 Hours Take Action As Necessary And Appropriate To Secure Payment In Full;' and `Pay This Amount Now If Action Is To Be Stopped.'" Id. at 25. The United States 465*465 Court of Appeals for the Second Circuit held that, to the least sophisticated consumer, the language represented a threat to commence legal action. Id. Calling it a close question, the Second Circuit explained that, given its "vagueness," the "[t]he clear import of the language, taken as a whole, is that some type of legal action has already been or is about to be initiated and can be averted from running its course only by payment." Id. at 25-26. Because there was no indication in the record that any legal action was intended, the court determined that violations of § 1692e(5) and (10) had been established. Id. at 26.

In the instant case, the language relevant to the plaintiff's § 1692e(5), (4), and (10) claims is: "to withhold further action, return this statement with payment in full." Although this language imposes no deadline, another portion of the notice requested payment with five days. The language is somewhat less dire than the language in Pipiles, but just as vague. The least sophisticated consumer could construe this language as a threat to commence legal action — legal action which could result in the imposition of provisional remedies. Because the Complaint alleges that the defendant did not have authority to commence legal action, it states claims under § 1692e(5), (4), and (10) sufficient to survive the motion to dismiss. At a later stage in the litigation, the plaintiff will have to substantiate its allegation and affirmatively show that the defendant did not intend to bring legal action. To do this, plaintiff will have to show that the possibility of a lawsuit could be "ruled out" because, for example, "a creditor had a fixed practice of not bringing suits against customers." See Sluys v. Hand, 831 F.Supp. 321, 326-27 (S.D.N.Y. 1993).

The plaintiff also charges the defendant with violating § 1692g(a). Section § 1692(g)(a) provides, in pertinent part, that the debt collector must in its initial communication (or within five days thereafter) provide written notice to the consumer containing:

a statement that unless the consumer, within thirty days after receipt of the notice, disputes the validity of the debt ... the debt will be presumed to be valid by the debt collector[,] 15 U.S.C. § 1692g(a)(3), and

a statement that if the consumer notifies the debt collector in writing within the thirty-day period that the debt ... is disputed, the debt collector will obtain verification of the debt ... and a copy of such verification ... will be mailed to the consumer by the debt collector....
Id. § 1692g(a)(4).

Although the initial letters, standing alone, complied with the mandate of § 1692g — notifying the plaintiff that he had thirty days within which to contest the underlying debt — the follow-up letter rendered the statutory notice problematic. The follow-up letter, allegedly received by the plaintiff between one and two weeks after receipt of the initial letters, threatened action within ten days — action which could "hurt [the plaintiff's] ability to obtain credit for many years." Faced with these inconsistent statements, it is possible that the least sophisticated consumer "would be induced to overlook his statutory right to dispute the debt within thirty days." Graziano v. Harrison, 950 F.2d 107, 111 (3d Cir.1991). As such, the Complaint states a cause of action under § 1692g.

The Court also determines that the Complaint states a cause of action under 15 U.S.C. § 1692e(10) on grounds that the juxtaposition of the inconsistent statements in the initial letters and the follow-up letter constituted a "false representation or deceptive means to collect ... any debt." See Graziano, 950 F.2d at 111.

Finally, the Complaint alleges that the defendant violated § 1692f. The prefatory language of Section 1692f prohibits a debt collector from using "unfair or unconscionable means to collect ... any debt." Eight subsections then list various practices which violate the section. Although the defendant's conduct does not fall into any of the categories identified by the subsections, the plaintiff insists that it amounts to "unfair" means used to collect a debt, and that the prefatory language standing alone provides a cause of action.

466*466 The list of § 1692f violations found in the subsections are nonexhaustive. Indeed, following the prefatory language, the subsections are introduced with the phrase: "[w]ithout limiting the general application of the foregoing, the following conduct is a violation of this section[.]" The plaintiff, therefore, is correct in his view that the prefatory language provides a cause of action. Nonetheless, the Complaint is devoid of support for the contention that the defendant engaged in practices that were "unfair" or "unconscionable" within the meaning of the section; all the allegations in the Complaint support claims asserted under either §§ 1692g or 1692e. As such, the plaintiff has failed to state a cause of action under § 1692f, and the defendant's motion should be granted to that extent. In the event that the omission of support for the § 1692f claim was the result of a drafting oversight, the plaintiff has leave to amend the Complaint within thirty days of the date of this order.

For the above reasons, **defendant's motion** to dismiss the Complaint is granted in part and denied in part. The motion is granted as to the claim alleged pursuant to 15 U.S.C. § 1692f, which is dismissed without prejudice, and **denied as to the claims alleged pursuant to §§ 1692e(5), (4), and (10), and 1692g.**

[1] The Complaint actually alleges that the initial letters were received in the last week of November 1994. (emphasis added). The plaintiff's papers, submitted in opposition to the defendant's motion, indicate that the initial letters were received in the last week of November 1993. The Complaint having been filed prior to November 1994, the Court considers the time period of receipt to be the last week of November 1993.

[2] The Complaint alleges that the follow-up letter was received in the first week of December 1994. Again, the Court disregards the lazy draftsmanship and considers the time period of receipt to be the first week in December 1993.

[3] The statute reads, in relevant part, as follows:
A debt collector may not use any false, deceptive, or misleading representation or means in connection with the collection of any debt. Without limiting the general application of the foregoing, the following conduct is a violation of this section:

(4) The representation or implication that nonpayment of any debt will result in the arrest or imprisonment of any person or the seizure, garnishment, attachment, or sale of any property or wages of any person unless such action is lawful and the debt collector or creditor intends to take such action.

(5) The threat to take any action that cannot legally be taken or that is not intended to be taken.

(10) The use of any false representation or deceptive means to collect or attempt to collect any debt or to obtain information concerning a consumer.

15 U.S.C. § 1692e.

CITATIONS

A complaint will be deemed deficient under this provision, however, if it "does not identify any misconduct beyond that which Plaintiffs assert violate other provisions of the FDCPA." - in Taylor v. HEATH W. WILLIAMS, LLC, 2007

—dismissing Section 1692f claim where plaintiff failed to plead misconduct other than that asserted to violate other FDCPA provisions - in Baker v. Allstate Financial Services, Inc., 2008

In determining whether a collection letter, such as defendants' Dec. 17, 2002 letter, violates § 1692e, courts in this circuit apply the "least sophisticated consumer" test. - in Failla v. Cohen, 2005

This would require him to plead conduct prohibited by Section 1692f that is not already addressed by other FDCPA sections. - in Baker v. Allstate Financial Services, Inc., 2008

—finding that "least sophisticated consumer" could interpret debt collector's statement that if the consumer paid in full it would "withhold further action" as a threat to commence legal action - in Ellis v. COHEN & SLAMOWITZ, LLP, 2010 The Complaint is devoid of support for the contention that the defendant engaged in practices that were unfair or unconscionable within the meaning of the section; all the allegations in the Complaint support claims asserted under either §§ 1692g or 1692e
- in Foti v. NCO Financial Systems, Inc., 2006

The Court notes that the most compelling cases in which "overshadowing" has been found, the debt collector has given the debtor time limitations in which to pay (ie, five days or ten days), which contradicted the required notice that the debtor had thirty days in which to dispute the debt or to request validation of the debt. - in Powell v. Computer Credit, Inc., 1997

—denying motion to dismiss, because the language used in the collection letter: "to withhold further action, return this statement with payment in full," was vague enough for consumer to construe it as a threat of legal action - in Baptist v. GLOBAL HOLDING AND INVESTMENT COMPANY LLC, 2007

Against this showing, plaintiff's unsupported claims that defendant did not intend to file suit against Mr. Ailyarov are not sufficient to defeat defendant's motion for summary judgment. - in Complete Guide to Credit and Collection

Because courts use this type of evaluation, recent cases evaluating claims of ineffective validation notices offer little insight into resolving the problem - in Two Out of Three Ain't Bad: 1997 Update on the Federal Fair Debt Collection

EDWARDS V. NIAGARA CREDIT SOLUTIONS 584 F.3d 1350 (2009)

Before CARNES, FAY and ALARCÓN[*], Circuit Judges.

CARNES, Circuit Judge:

In an oft-repeated statement from the Vietnam War, an unidentified American military officer reputedly said that "we had to destroy the village to save it."[1] That oxymoronic explanation may be apocryphal, but the debt collection agency in this case offers up much the same logic to explain why it violated the Fair Debt Collection Practices Act: it was necessary to violate the Act in order to comply with the Act.

I.

Brenda Edwards owed money to the Consumer Shopping Network. Her past due account was assigned to Niagara Credit Solutions, Inc. for collection. Niagara is a debt collection agency subject to the provisions of the Fair Debt Collection Practices Act, 15 U.S.C. §§ 1692-1692p, et seq. It attempts to collect debts by sending letters and making phone calls to debtors.

As part of its collection efforts, Niagara left over a dozen messages on Edwards' answering machine from July through October 2007. In September 2007, Niagara left a prerecorded message on her machine stating: "This is an important message for Edwards Brenda. [sic] Please return this message at 1-800-381-0416, between the hours of 8 a.m. and 9 p.m. eastern standard time. It is important that you reach our office." The next month Niagara left another message on her answering machine: "This message is intended for Brenda Edwards. Please contact Jennifer [last name not clear] at 1-800-381-0416, my extension is 220. When returning my call have your file number available, it's 1250740."

At the time of those events Niagara had a well-defined policy about messages that it left on debtors' answering machines. That policy was to: leave a message asking the debtor to call back about an important matter; provide Niagara's phone number; supply the real first name of the person calling on behalf of Niagara; and give any reference number assigned to the account. Niagara purposefully left out of the messages any information disclosing that they were from Niagara Credit Solutions, Inc. or a debt collector, or that the call had been made for the purpose of collecting a debt. The Fair Debt Collection Practices Act specifically requires that a debt collector disclose in all communications with a debtor that the message is from a debt collector. See 15 U.S.C. § 1692e(11). Niagara deliberately chose not to comply with that requirement because it feared that doing so would risk violating another provision of the Act, which generally forbids an agency from communicating about the debt with a third party. See 15 U.S.C. § 1692c(b). It was concerned that answering machine messages 1352*1352 might be played by or within the hearing of a family member or roommate, who would then know that a collection agency was calling the debtor.

II.

In September 2007 Edwards filed a complaint against Niagara alleging that the messages it left on her answering machine violated § 1692e(11) of the Fair Debt Collection Practices Act, as well as § 1692d(6) (requiring meaningful disclosure of the caller's identity). She sought an award of statutory damages, costs, and attorney's fees and moved for summary judgment. Niagara asserted a number of defenses, including the bona fide error defense contained in § 1692k(c). The district court granted summary judgment in favor of Edwards after concluding, among other things, that the messages Niagara left violated § 1692d(6) and § 1692e(11) and that the bona fide error defense did not apply. Niagara concedes at this stage that the messages it left violated § 1692e(11) and is only challenging the district court's conclusion that it is not protected by the bona fide error defense.[2] The issue before us is whether a debt collector is entitled to the bona fide error defense when it intentionally violates one provision of the Act in order to avoid the risk of violating another provision.

III.

The Fair Debt Collection Practices Act was enacted by Congress "to eliminate abusive debt collection practices by debt collectors" and "to protect consumers against debt collection abuses." 15 U.S.C. § 1692(e). Congress found abusive practices by debt collectors to be "serious and widespread." Russell v. Equifax A.R.S., 74 F.3d 30, 33 (2d Cir.1996). The Act provides a civil cause of action against any debt collector who fails to comply with the requirements of the Act, including § 1692e(11). See 15 U.S.C. § 1692k(a). A debt collector can be held liable for an individual plaintiff's actual damages, statutory damages up to $1,000, costs, and reasonable attorney's fees. 15 U.S.C. § 1692k(a)(1)-(3).

The Act, however, provides debt collectors with an affirmative defense called the "bona fide error" defense, which insulates them from liability even when they have failed to comply with the Act's requirements. Johnson v. Riddle, 443 F.3d 723, 727 (10th Cir.2006). The defense is found in 15 U.S.C. § 1692k(c), which provides:

A debt collector may not be held liable in any action brought under this subchapter if the debt collector shows by a preponderance of evidence that the violation was not intentional and resulted from a bona fide error notwithstanding the maintenance of procedures reasonably adapted to avoid any such error.

A debt collector asserting the bona fide error defense must show by a preponderance of the evidence that its violation of 1353*1353 the Act: (1) was not intentional; (2) was a bona fide error; and (3) occurred despite the maintenance of procedures reasonably adapted to avoid any such error. Johnson, 443 F.3d at 727-28. The failure to meet any one of those three requirements is fatal to the defense.

Niagara cannot make the first required showing. Section 1692e(11) requires a debt collector "to disclose in subsequent communications that the communication is from a debt collector." 15 U.S.C. § 1692e(11).[3] By its own admission, Niagara deliberately decided not to disclose in the messages it left that the caller was a debt collector. Its failure to disclose was intentional.

Niagara has also failed to meet the second requirement of the bona fide error defense, which is that the violation actually be a "bona fide" error. Taking Niagara at its word, it was concerned that disclosing that the call was from a debt collector could result in a violation of 15 U.S.C. § 1692c(b), which prohibits a debt collector from communicating with third parties about the consumer's debt.[4] Niagara feared that leaving a message on a debtor's machine stating that it was from a debt collector calling to collect a debt might be viewed as a violation of § 1692c(b) if the message were overheard by or played in the presence of someone other than the debtor, such as a family member or roommate. We do not need to decide whether that concern is well-grounded in the law. Even if there would be a violation of § 1692c(b) in those circumstances, involving fewer than all of the messages left on answering machines, Niagara's violation of § 1692e(11) with every message it left cannot be said to be a bona fide error.

As used in the Act "bona fide" means that the error resulting in a violation was "made in good faith; a genuine mistake, as opposed to a contrived mistake." Kort v. Diversified Collection Servs., Inc., 394 F.3d 530, 538 (7th Cir. 2005); see also Black's Law Dictionary 186 (8th ed.2004) (defining "bona fide" as "1. Made in good faith; without fraud or deceit" and "2. Sincere; genuine"); Garcia v. Vanguard Car Rental USA, Inc., 540 F.3d 1242, 1246 (11th Cir.2008) ("When statutory terms are undefined, we typically infer that Congress intended them to have their common and ordinary meaning, unless it is apparent from context that the disputed term is a term of art."). To be considered a bona fide error, the debt collector's mistake must be objectively reasonable. Johnson, 443 F.3d at 729 ("[I]n effect, [the bona fide] component serves to impose an objective standard of reasonableness upon the asserted unintentional violation." (second alteration in original) (internal quotation marks omitted)). Just as it is not reasonable to destroy a village in order to save it, neither is it reasonable to violate an Act in order to comply with it. It was not reasonable for 1354*1354 Niagara to violate § 1692e(11) of the Fair Debt Collection Practices Act with every message it left in order to avoid the possibility that some of those messages might lead to a violation of § 1692c(b).

Niagara complains that if it is not permitted to leave out of its answering machine messages the disclosure required by § 1692e(11), the result will be that it cannot leave any messages on answering machines. That assumes an answering machine message that includes the disclosure required by § 1692e(11), if heard by a third party, would violate § 1692c(b). We have not decided that issue, but even if Niagara's assumption is correct, the answer is that the Act does not guarantee a debt collector the right to leave answering machine messages.

Because Niagara has failed to meet either of the first two requirements of the bona fide error defense of § 1692k(c), we need not decide whether it also has failed to meet the third one, which requires the maintenance of procedures reasonably designed to avoid the violation of the Act. Although the district court's grant of summary judgment to Edwards was based on that ground, we can and do affirm on different grounds. See Cuddeback v. Fla. Bd. of Educ., 381 F.3d 1230, 1235 (11th Cir.2004) ("This court may affirm [summary] judgment on any legal ground, regardless of the grounds ... relied upon by the district court.").

AFFIRMED.

[*] Honorable Arthur L. Alarcón, United States Circuit Judge for the Ninth Circuit, sitting by designation.

[1] See Bruce O. Solheim, The Vietnam War Era: A Personal Journey 80 (2006).

[2] Niagara has waived any argument that the messages did not also violate § 1692d(6). Although it made such an argument in the district court, Niagara failed to include that argument in the initial brief it filed in this Court. Even though Niagara asserted at oral argument that it had not violated § 1692d(6), that assertion comes too late to preserve the issue. See McFarlin v. Conseco Servs., LLC, 381 F.3d 1251, 1263 (11th Cir.2004) ("A party is not allowed to raise at oral argument a new issue for review."); Marek v. Singletary, 62

F.3d 1295, 1298 n. 2 (11th Cir.1995) ("Issues not clearly raised in the briefs are considered abandoned."). Nevertheless, we will not rely on the waiver because Niagara's concession that it violated one provision of the Act is enough; an additional violation does not affect our analysis.

[3] All the communications alleged in this case were "subsequent communications" within the meaning of § 1692e(11).

[4] Section 1692c(b) provides: "Except as provided in section 1692b of this title, without the prior consent of the consumer given directly to the debt collector, or the express permission of a court of competent jurisdiction, or as reasonably necessary to effectuate a postjudgment judicial remedy, a debt collector may not communicate, in connection with the collection of any debt, with any person other than the consumer, his attorney, a consumer reporting agency if otherwise permitted by law, the creditor, the attorney of the creditor, or the attorney of the debt collector."

CITATIONS

The Act, however, provides debt collectors with an affirmative defense called the "bona fide error" defense, which insulates them from liability even when they have failed to comply with the Act's requirements. - in Winberry v. UNITED COLLECTION BUREAU, INC., 2010

A debt collector asserting the bona fide error defense must show by a preponderance of the evidence that its violation of the FDCPA "(1) was not intentional;(2) was a bona fide error; and (3) occurred despite the maintenance of procedures reasonably adapted to avoid any such error." - in BACELLI v. MFP, INC., 2010

—was faced with the issue of "whether a debt collector is entitled to the bona fide error defense when it intentionally violates one provision of the Act in order to avoid the risk of violating another provision." - in GRYZBOWSKI v. IC System, Inc., 2010

Because the court determined that the defendant" had failed to meet either of the first two requirements of the bona fide error defense of ž 1692k (c)," the court affirmed the district court's decision and explained that it need not decide whether the defendant also had failed to meet the third requirement, which mandates the maintenance of procedures reasonably designed - in Trial Practice and Procedure and one similar citation

"The [FDCPA, 15 USC §§ 1692 et seq.] provides a civil cause of action against any debt collector who fails to comply with the requirements of the Act...." - in HEPSEN v. RESURGENT CAPITAL SERVICES, LP, 2010

—we affirmed the district court's grant of summary judgment in favor of Edwards, concluding that Niagara was not protected by the bona fide error defense because its violation of the Act was intentional and did not constitute a bona fide error. - in Edwards v. NIAGARA CREDIT SOLUTIONS, INC., 2009

UCB acknowledges that the Eleventh Circuit has held that a debt collector cannot leave a message without identifying that the message is from a debt collector. - in Winberry v. UNITED COLLECTION BUREAU, INC., 2010

SPARKS v. PHILLIPS & COHEN ASSOCIATES, LTD

CITATIONS

—explaining the "gist of § 1692e" as a requirement that any "aspect of a debt collector's communication-whether explicit or implied-[that] has the purpose or effect of making a debtor more likely to respond..." is, in fact, true - in LeBlanc v. Unifund CCR Partners, 2010

Conduct that has been held to be insufficient to establish an invasion of privacy as a matter of law involved three people and included the debtor calling an unlisted home telephone number on one occasion, conducting one 96-second telephone conversation, having one heated telephone conversation, mailing a statement of claim form, and accusations by the caller. - in Winberry v. UNITED COLLECTION BUREAU, INC., 2010

Without fully developing its argument, Defendant contends that"[s] imply making telephone calls to Plaintiff's residence are not facts that give rise to the tort invasion of privacy."(Dkt. 9, p. 10). - in Oppenheim v. IC System, Inc., 2010

ONE PARTY CONSENT OF RECORDING CONVERSATIONS

CARO V. WEINTRAUB, COURT OF APPEALS, 2ND CIRCUIT 2010

MARSHALL CARO, Plaintiff-Appellant,
v.
ERIC WEINTRAUB, DAVID H. WEINTRAUB, GLENN WILLIAM DOWD, AND DAY PITNEY LLP, Defendants-Appellees.

No. 09-3685-cv.

United States Court of Appeals, Second Circuit.

Argued: April 19, 2010.
Decided: August 13, 2010.
MARSHALL CARO, pro se, Greenwich, CT, for Plaintiff-Appellant.

ALLAN B. TAYLOR, Day Pitney LLP, Hartford, CT (Erik H. Beard, on the brief), for Defendants-Appellees Dowd and Day Pitney LLP.

Before: CABRANES, WESLEY, LIVINGSTON, Circuit Judges.

WESLEY, Circuit Judge:

Plaintiff-Appellant Marshall Caro filed a complaint in the United States District Court for the District of Connecticut (Dorsey, J.) alleging, inter alia, a civil cause of action under Title III of the Omnibus Crime Control and Safe Streets Act of 1968, codified at 18 U.S.C. §§ 2510-21 ("Title III" or the "Wiretap Act"). The district court dismissed Caro's complaint. We affirm, and, in so doing, hold that the exception to the one-party consent provision of 18 U.S.C. § 2511(2)(d) requires that a communication be intercepted for the purpose of a tortious or criminal act that is independent of the intentional act of recording.

I. BACKGROUND

In early February 2008, Elizabeth Caro, who was in the final days of a painful battle with lung cancer, was visited by her sons Eric and David Weintraub, along with their families, and her brother and sister-in-law Thomas and Lynn Corrigan. During the visit, Elizabeth spoke with her sister-in-law, Lynn, in the kitchen about Lynn's desire to have

Elizabeth sign a draft of a will that Thomas had prepared. The draft named Thomas as the executor of Elizabeth's estate and contained provisions to which Elizabeth allegedly objected. Elizabeth's husband, Marshall Caro — the plaintiff-appellant here — informed Lynn that he had already hired an attorney to prepare their wills and that in their meeting with their attorney, Elizabeth had expressed different intentions than those set out in Thomas's draft.

At some point during this conversation, David and Eric Weintraub entered the kitchen. David placed his iPhone on the kitchen table and, unbeknownst to Marshall, used the device to record the conversation.[1] After the recording began, Thomas also entered the kitchen. It appears from Caro's complaint that the conversation at times included Thomas Corrigan and David Weintraub and, in the end, became quite heated between those involved.

Four days later, on February 6, 2008, Elizabeth died without completing a will. Marshall filed Elizabeth's death certificate with the Connecticut Probate Court and filed a Petition for Letters of Administration for Elizabeth's estate. Eric and David Weintraub, represented by attorneys from Day Pitney LLP, filed an Opposition to Marshall Caro's petition.

The Probate Court held a hearing on April 21, 2008. David testified that he had recordings of the kitchen conversation between Marshall and Elizabeth, and his attorney submitted a CD of the recordings.[2]

On February 27, 2009, Marshall Caro filed a complaint in the United States District Court for the District of Connecticut (Dorsey, J.), alleging violations of Title III, along with various Connecticut state law claims.[3] In addition to David and Eric Weintraub, Caro named as defendants Day Pitney LLP and one of its lawyers, Glenn William Dowd. Upon Day Pitney's motion and over Caro's objection, the district court relieved Day Pitney from Connecticut's Local Civil Rule 83.13 and allowed a firm attorney to represent Day Pitney for the purpose of filing a motion to dismiss the complaint.

Defendants[4] moved to dismiss, arguing, inter alia, that the recorded conversations did not qualify as "oral communications" within the scope of Title III because David Weintraub was a party to the conversation and Caro had no reasonable expectation of privacy in the conversation. Caro opposed the motion, arguing that he did not reasonably expect to be recorded and that David was not a party to the conversation. He also requested leave to amend his complaint.

The district court granted the motion to dismiss and denied Caro's motion to amend his complaint. Caro v. Weintraub, No. 3:09 CV 00335, 2009 WL 2358919, at *1 (D. Conn.

July 31, 2009). The district court agreed that the recordings were not "oral communications" under the Wiretap Act because David Weintraub was a party to the conversation and Caro did not have a reasonable expectation that his conversation was private. Id. at *2-3. The district court declined to exercise supplemental jurisdiction over Caro's state law claims. Id. at *3.

Caro appealed.

II. DISCUSSION

We review the dismissal of a complaint de novo, accepting all factual allegations in the complaint as true and drawing all reasonable inferences in favor of the plaintiff. Chambers v. Time Warner, Inc., 282 F.3d 147, 152 (2d Cir. 2002). To survive a motion to dismiss, the complaint must plead sufficient facts to make out a plausible claim to relief. Bell Atl. Corp. v. Twombly, 550 U.S. 544, 570 (2007). When, as here, the complaint is filed by a pro se plaintiff, we construe the complaint liberally, interpreting it "to raise the strongest arguments that [it] suggest[s]." Triestman v. Fed. Bureau of Prisons, 470 F.3d 471, 474 (2d Cir. 2006) (per curiam); accord Harris v. Mills, 572 F.3d 66, 72 (2d Cir. 2009).

In relevant part, the Wiretap Act affords a civil cause of action to an aggrieved individual who has had her oral communications intentionally intercepted by a party to those communications for the purpose of committing a crime or tort. 18 U.S.C. §§ 2520, 2511(1), 2511(2)(d). We hold that David Weintraub was a party to the conversation, but Caro did not allege a tort that could provide the independent tortious intent necessary to bring a civil claim under the Wiretap Act. Thus, it is futile to allow him to amend his complaint.

A. Party to the Conversation

The district court found that David Weintraub was a party to the relevant conversation, and we agree.

Caro argues that David Weintraub was not a party to the conversation because there were actually multiple conversations that occurred in the kitchen, and the participants in the conversations did not invite David to join any of them. Limiting ourselves, as we must, to the facts pled in the complaint, we conclude that David Weintraub was a party to the conversation for purposes of the Wiretap Act.

In the context of the statute, a party to the conversation is one who takes part in the conversation. Caro offers — and we can find — no support for the proposition that one must be invited to a conversation in order to be a party to it. Caro admits in his complaint that David Weintraub was present at the table during the conversation in the kitchen and that David "spoke up a few times urging [Caro] to continue." Those facts are sufficient to establish that David was a party to the conversation.[5]

Concluding that David Weintraub was a party to the conversation is not fatal to Caro's claims. The Wiretap Act forbids someone who is a party to a conversation to record it, if the "oral... communication is intercepted for the purpose of committing any criminal or tortious act." 18 U.S.C. § 2511(2)(d). Invocation of this provision raises the question of what must be alleged to demonstrate tortious intent.

B. Tortious Intent

The statute requires that an oral communication be intercepted "for the purpose of committing any criminal or tortious act." 18 U.S.C. § 2511(2)(d). The district court did not address this issue and the original complaint as filed does not allege a tortious intent behind David Weintraub's recording. Caro requested leave before the district court to amend his complaint. The district court denied Caro's request, a decision that both sides agree was in error under the Federal Rules of Civil Procedure in effect at the time.[6] Caro now argues that if he were permitted to amend the complaint, he would allege that Weintraub recorded his statements with tortious intent, while Weintraub argues that the effort would be futile.

Caro's assertion that he would plead a tortious intent is simply a recitation of the missing element in his claim — an exercise insufficient to rescue the complaint from its deficiencies. See Ashcroft v. Iqbal, 129 S.Ct. 1937, 1949-50 (2009). However, we remain obligated to construe pro se complaints liberally. See Harris v. Mills, 572 F.3d 66, 71-72 (2d Cir. 2009). Because Caro, a pro se plaintiff, should have been afforded leave to amend his complaint, and because he contends that he will address the deficiency, there is a strong argument that we should remand the case to allow him a chance to fix the fault. Fulton v. Goord, 591 F.3d 37, 45 (2d Cir. 2009). But Weintraub's contention is well-taken — we need not remand if the re-pleading effort would be futile. Id.

Determining the futility of an amended pleading turns on whether Title III requires that the claimant assert that the recording occurred with a separate and independent tortious intent, or whether the necessary tortious intent can be inferred from the act of recording itself. In other words, must a plaintiff plead that the defendant had intent to use the illicit recording to commit a tort beyond the act of recording illicitly or may the defendant merely have the intent to record and that alone is sufficient? Several of our sister circuits have tackled the issue, each reaching the conclusion that, under Title III, the defendant must have the intent to use the illicit recording to commit a tort of crime beyond the act of recording itself.

In Desnick v. American Broadcasting Cos., 44 F.3d 1345, 1347-48 (7th Cir. 1995), a producer of the ABC show PrimeTime Live arranged for individuals posing as patients to enter the Desnick Eye Center and to film their encounters using concealed cameras. PrimeTime Live eventually aired a segment on its "undercover investigation," asserting misconduct by Center employees. Id. at 1348. Center employees brought suit, charging in part that ABC had used an illegal wiretap under Title III. Id. at 1353.

The Seventh Circuit upheld the dismissal of the employees' Wiretap Act claims, concluding that ABC did not send the "patients" into the Center in order to commit a crime, tort, or other injurious act. Id. Even if the PrimeTime Live episode that followed the taping was defamatory, there was no evidence that ABC sent the test patients into the Center for the purpose of defaming the Center employees. Id.

In Sussman v. American Broadcasting Cos., 186 F.3d 1200, 1201 (9th Cir. 1999), ABC conducted an undercover investigation of the Psychic Marketing Group using various surveillance devices; two employees of the Group brought suit. The employees did not allege "that the tape was made for the purpose of committing some other subsequent crime or tort," but instead "argue[d] that the taping itself was tortious." Id. at 1202. The Ninth Circuit found that this allegation was insufficient to meet the requirements of the statute. "Where the taping is legal, but is done for the purpose of facilitating some further impropriety, such as blackmail, § 2511 [of Title III] applies. Where the purpose is not illegal or tortious, but the means are, the victims must seek redress elsewhere." Id. at 1202-03 (emphasis added); accord Lucas v. Fox News Network, LLC, 248 F.3d 1180, 2001 WL 100181, at *4 (11th Cir. Jan. 16, 2001) (per curiam); Vazquez-Santos v. El Mundo Broad. Corp., 219 F. Supp. 2d 221, 229-30 (D.P.R. 2002).

The legislative history of the Wiretap Act is also instructive. The Wiretap Act as initially proposed did not prohibit interception where one of the parties to the communication consented, regardless of the parties' intent. See S. Rep. No. 90-1097, at 2182 (1968). Senator Philip A. Hart objected to the broad language, observing that it permitted "surreptitious monitoring of a conversation by a party to the conversation, even though the monitoring may be for insidious purposes such as blackmail, stealing business secrets, or other criminal or tortious acts in violation of Federal or State laws." Id. at 2236. Senator Hart and Senator John L. McClellan proposed an amendment to the bill that would limit the one-party consent rule to "private persons who act in a defensive fashion." 114 Cong. Rec. 14694 (1968). This meant that interceptions by a party to the conversation would be forbidden if they were made "with an unlawful motive," such as "blackmailing the other party, threatening him, or publicly embarrassing him." Id. However, a party to a criminal conversation that recorded the conversation in order to bring evidence to the police or recording "out of a legitimate desire to protect himself and his own conversations from later distortions or other unlawful or injurious uses by the other party" would be protected under the statute. Id. The amendment passed. Id. at 14695. As the Eighth Circuit so aptly observed, it is "apparent from the context in which [Title III] was enacted that the sort of conduct contemplated was an interception by a party to a conversation with an intent to use that interception against the non-consenting party in some harmful way and in a manner in which the offending party had no right to proceed." Meredith v. Gavin, 446 F.2d 794, 799 (8th Cir. 1971).

There is a temporal thread that runs through the fabric of the statute and the case law. At the time of the recording the offender must intend to use the recording to commit a criminal or tortious act. Merely intending to record the plaintiff is not enough. If, at the moment he hits "record," the offender does not intend to use the recording for criminal or tortious purposes, there is no violation. But if, at the time of the recording, the offender plans to use the recording to harm the other party to the conversation, a civil cause of action exists under the Wiretap Act.

Intent may not be inferred simply by demonstrating that the intentional act of recording itself constituted a tort. A simultaneous tort arising from the act of recording itself is insufficient. Congress chose the word "purpose" for a reason. Therefore, the offender must have as her objective a tortious or criminal result. Had Congress intended for the act of recording itself to provide the tortious intent necessary, it could have chosen to define the exception in terms of interception of oral communications resulting in a tortious or criminal act. But Congress limited the cause of action to instances where one party to the conversation deliberately seeks to harm the other participant through the information intercepted.

We join the courts that have considered this question, and hold that a cause of action under § 2511(2)(d) requires that the interceptor intend to commit a crime or tort independent of the act of recording itself. Thus, to survive a motion to dismiss, a plaintiff must plead sufficient facts to support an inference that the offender intercepted the communication for the purpose of a tortious or criminal act that is independent of the intentional act of recording.

The only tort Caro asserts in his complaint that could plausibly provide the intent necessary to bring the recording under the Wiretap Act is invasion of privacy, a tort recognized under Connecticut common law. See Goodrich v. Waterbury Republican-Am., Inc., 188 Conn. 107, 127-28 (1982). Other circuits appear to have implicitly recognized invasion of privacy as a tort that could provide the necessary intent to bring a recording within the purview of the Wiretap Act. See, e.g., Deteresa v. Am. Broad. Cos., 121 F.3d 460, 467 n.4 (9th Cir. 1997); Phillips v. Bell, No. 08-1420, 2010 WL 517629, at *7 (10th Cir. Feb. 12, 2010). But, under Connecticut law, invasion of privacy includes four distinct types of incursion that "otherwise have almost nothing in common except that each represents an interference with the right of the plaintiff to be let alone." Goodrich, 188 Conn. at 127-28 (quoting Prosser, Torts (4th ed. 1971) § 117, p. 804) (quotation marks omitted). The four categories of invasion of privacy are: "(a) unreasonable intrusion upon the seclusion of another; (b) appropriation of the other's name or likeness; (c) unreasonable publicity given to the other's private life; or (d) publicity that unreasonably places the other in a false light before the public." Id. at 128.

Caro specifically pled invasion of privacy by unreasonable intrusion upon the seclusion of another, as opposed to a general claim of invasion of privacy. Connecticut courts have interpreted this version of the tort as the intentional invasion "upon the solitude or seclusion of another or his private affairs or concerns... if the intrusion would be highly offensive to a reasonable person." Bonanno v. Dan Perkins Chevrolet, No. CV 99-066602, 2000 WL 192182, at *1 (Conn. Super. Ct. Feb. 4, 2000) (quoting 3 Restatement (Second) of Torts, § 652B (1977)); accord Birge v. Med. Elec. Distribs., Inc., No. XXXXXXXXX, 2009 WL 1959393, at *3 (Conn. Super. Ct. June 5, 2009); Hellanbrand v. Nat'l Waste Assocs., LLC, No. CV XXXXXXXXX, 2008 WL 442136, at *4 (Conn. Super. Ct. Jan. 31, 2008).

Invasion of privacy through intrusion upon seclusion presents a problem for Caro — it is a tort that occurs through the act of interception itself. "The intrusion itself makes the defendant subject to liability, even though there is no publication or other use of any kind of the... information outlined." Restatement (Second) of Torts § 652B cmt. b (1977).[7] Nothing more is required after the interception is made for liability to attach based on this tort. All that is required is that the tortfeasor intended to commit the act that was the basis for the invasion — as Caro alleges here, setting up the iPhone and hitting "record."

The remaining three categories of invasion of privacy cannot be accomplished simply by intercepting one's communications; the tortfeasor is required to take an affirmative step or steps beyond the recording or the nature of the tort is such that interception would not further it. See Gleason v. Smolinski, No. NNH CV XXXXXXXXXS, 2009 WL 2506607, at *2-7 (Conn. Super. Ct. July 20, 2009) (detailing elements necessary to make out a cause of action under each category of invasion of privacy).

The language and history of the Wiretap Act indicate that Congress authored the exception to the one-party consent rule to prevent abuses stemming from use of the recording not the mere act of recording.[8] Connecticut's tort of invasion of privacy by intrusion upon the seclusion of another occurs through the simple act of the recording itself and therefore cannot satisfy the Wiretap Act's requirement of a separate and independent tortious intent.

Based on the facts alleged in Caro's complaint, intrusion upon the seclusion of another is the only category of invasion of privacy that could have possibly transpired here and Caro did not tell us or the district court if he has another tort in mind. Even if Caro were granted leave to amend his complaint and given the opportunity to allege that Weintraub had the intent to invade his privacy, that intent could only apply to invasion of privacy by intrusion upon the seclusion of another, which we hold cannot serve as the basis for the statutorily required tortious intent. Thus, we need not reach the question of whether any of the other three categories of invasion of privacy could serve as a predicate to the necessary intent. We need only say here that to bring a claim under the Wiretap Act, the offender must intercept with tortious intent that relates to a tort independent from the act of recording itself, and invasion of privacy by intrusion on the seclusion of another cannot serve that purpose.

Because Caro does not allege an independent tort that could provide the basis for the tortious intent necessary to bring a claim under the Wiretap Act, allowing him leave to amend his complaint would be futile.

Conclusion

For the foregoing reasons, the district court's order of August 4, 2009, dismissing Caro's complaint, is hereby AFFIRMED.

[1] David used a program called "Recorder," which allowed his iPhone to operate as a recording device.

[2] According to Caro's complaint, David Weintraub testified at a deposition that he "made at least three separate surreptitious recordings" of the conversation.

[3] To wit, invasion of privacy by intrusion upon seclusion, intentional spoliation of evidence, fraudulent misrepresentation to the Probate Court, negligent misrepresentation to the Probate Court, and intentional violations of the Connecticut Rules of Professional Conduct.

[4] Eric and David Weintraub filed pro se motions to dismiss that adopted by reference Day Pitney's arguments.

[5] We view the discussion in the kitchen as one conversation, instead of a series of separate conversations as Caro contends.

[6] Under the version of Federal Rule of Civil Procedure 15(a) in effect on May 28, 2009, the date of Caro's Opposition to the Motion to Dismiss, Caro had the right to amend his complaint "once as a matter of course... before being served with a responsive pleading." Fed. R. Civ. P. 15(a)(1) (amended 2009).

[7] The Restatement (Second) of Torts is valuable to our analysis as the Connecticut Supreme Court often embraces it when confronting an invasion of privacy claim. See, e.g., Foncello v. Amorossi, 284 Conn. 225, 234 (2007); Goodrich, 188 Conn. at 128.

[8] At first glance, the legislative history suggests that invasion of privacy was a tort Congress intended to reach in the Wiretap Act. When Senator Hart proposed the amendment that forbade interception when one party to the conversation operated with tortious or criminal intent, he noted that the blanket one-party consent rule left "wide open the problem of... many... abuses of the right of privacy." 114 Cong. Rec. 14694 (1968). However, he then went on to distinguish the injuries he wished to avoid through the amendment — "blackmailing the other party, threatening him, or publicly embarrassing him" — from "legitimate" uses like protection from "later distortions or other unlawful or injurious uses by the other party." Id. It was not invasion of the right of privacy per se that Senator Hart wished to avoid through his proposal, but invasions and abuses that would result through use of the interception itself.

Debt Collectors Often Misused Claim Of Bone Fide Error Defense

Jerman v. CARLISLE, McNELLIE, RINI, KRAMER, 130 S. Ct. 1605 - Supreme Court 2010 Decision

Karen L. JERMAN, Petitioner,
v.
CARLISLE, McNELLIE, RINI, KRAMER & ULRICH LPA, et al.
No. 08-1200.
Supreme Court of United States.

Argued January 13, 2010.
Decided April 21, 2010.
1608*1608 Kevin K. Russell, Bethesda, MD, for petitioner, by William M. Jay, for United States as amicus curiae, by special leave of the Court, supporting the petitioner.

George S. Coakley, Cleveland, OH, for respondents.

George S. Coakley, Counsel of Record, Clifford C. Masch, Brian D. Sullivan, Martin T. Galvin, James O'Connor, Reminger Co., L.P.A., Cleveland, OH, for respondents.

Stephen R. Felson, Cincinnati, OH, Edward Icove, Icove Legal Group, Ltd., Cleveland, OH, Kevin K. Russell, Counsel of Record, Amy Howe, Howe & Russell, P.C., Bethesda, MD, Pamela S. Karlan, Jeffrey L. Fisher, Stanford Law School, Supreme Court Litigation Clinic, Stanford, CA, for petitioner.

Justice SOTOMAYOR delivered the opinion of the Court.

The Fair Debt Collection Practices Act (FDCPA or Act) imposes civil liability on "debt collector[s]" for certain prohibited debt collection practices. Section 813(c) of the Act, 15 U.S.C. § 1692k(c), provides that a debt collector is not liable in an action brought under the Act if she can show "the violation was not intentional and resulted from a bona fide error notwithstanding the maintenance of procedures reasonably adapted to avoid any such error." This case presents the question whether the "bona fide error" defense in § 1692k(c) applies to a violation resulting from a debt collector's mistaken interpretation of the legal requirements of the FDCPA. We conclude it does not.

I

A

Congress enacted the FDCPA in 1977, 91 Stat. 874, to eliminate abusive debt collection practices, to ensure that debt collectors who abstain from such practices are not competitively disadvantaged, and to promote consistent state action to protect consumers. 15 U.S.C. § 1692(e). The Act regulates interactions between consumer debtors and "debt collector[s]," defined to include any person who "regularly collects . . . debts owed or due or asserted to be owed or due another." §§ 1692a(5), (6). Among other things, the Act prohibits debt collectors from making false representations as to a debt's character, amount, or legal status, § 1692e(2)(A); communicating with consumers at an "unusual time or place" likely to be inconvenient 1609*1609 to the consumer, § 1692c(a)(1); or using obscene or profane language or violence or the threat thereof, §§ 1692d(1), (2). See generally §§ 1692b-1692j; Heintz v. Jenkins, 514 U.S. 291, 292-293, 115 S.Ct. 1489, 131 L.Ed.2d 395 (1995).

The Act is enforced through administrative action and private lawsuits. With some exceptions not relevant here, violations of the FDCPA are deemed to be unfair or deceptive acts or practices under the Federal Trade Commission Act (FTC Act), 15 U.S.C. § 41 et seq., and are enforced by the Federal Trade Commission (FTC). See § 1692l. As a result, a debt collector who acts with "actual knowledge or knowledge fairly implied on the basis of objective circumstances that such act is [prohibited under the FDCPA]" is subject to civil penalties of up to $16,000 per day. §§ 45(m)(1)(A), (C); 74 Fed.Reg. 858 (2009) (amending 16 CFR § 1.98(d)).

The FDCPA also provides that "any debt collector who fails to comply with any provision of th[e][Act] with respect to any person is liable to such person." 15 U.S.C. § 1692k(a). Successful plaintiffs are entitled to "actual damage[s]," plus costs and "a reasonable attorney's fee as determined by the court." Ibid. A court may also award "additional damages," subject to a statutory cap of $1,000 for individual actions, or, for class actions, "the lesser of $500,000 or 1 per centum of the net worth of the debt collector." § 1692k(a)(2). In awarding additional damages, the court must consider "the frequency and persistence of [the debt collector's] noncompliance," "the nature of such noncompliance," and "the extent to which such noncompliance was intentional." § 1692k(b).

The Act contains two exceptions to provisions imposing liability on debt collectors. Section 1692k(c), at issue here, provides that

"[a] debt collector may not be held liable in any action brought under [the FDCPA] if the debt collector shows by a preponderance of evidence that the violation was not intentional and resulted from a bona fide error notwithstanding the maintenance of procedures reasonably adapted to avoid any such error."

The Act also states that none of its provisions imposing liability shall apply to "any act done or omitted in good faith in conformity with any advisory opinion of the [Federal Trade] Commission." § 1692k(e).

B

Respondents in this case are a law firm, Carlisle, McNellie, Rini, Kramer & Ulrich, L.P.A., and one of its attorneys, Adrienne S. Foster (collectively Carlisle). In April 2006, Carlisle filed a complaint in Ohio state court on behalf of a client, Countrywide Home Loans, Inc. Carlisle sought foreclosure of a mortgage held by Countrywide in real property owned by petitioner Karen L. Jerman. The complaint included a "Notice," later served on Jerman, stating that the mortgage debt would be assumed to be valid unless Jerman disputed it in writing. Jerman's lawyer sent a letter disputing the debt, and Carlisle sought verification from Countrywide. When Countrywide acknowledged that Jerman had, in fact, already paid the debt in full, Carlisle withdrew the foreclosure lawsuit.

Jerman then filed her own lawsuit seeking class certification and damages under the FDCPA, contending that Carlisle violated § 1692g by stating that her debt would be assumed valid unless she disputed it in writing.[1] While acknowledging 1610*1610 a division of authority on the question, the District Court held that Carlisle had violated § 1692g by requiring Jerman to dispute the debt in writing. 464 F.Supp.2d 720, 722-725 (N.D.Ohio 2006).[2] The court ultimately granted summary judgment to Carlisle, however, concluding that § 1692k(c) shielded it from liability because the violation was not intentional, resulted from a bona fide error, and occurred despite the maintenance of procedures reasonably adapted to avoid any such error. 502 F.Supp.2d 686, 695-697 (N.D.Ohio 2007). The Court of Appeals for the Sixth Circuit affirmed. 538 F.3d 469 (2008). Acknowledging that the Courts of Appeals are divided regarding the scope of the bona fide error defense, and that the "majority view is that the defense is available for clerical and factual errors only," the Sixth Circuit nonetheless held that § 1692k(c) extends to "mistakes of law." Id., at 473-476 (internal quotation marks omitted). The Court of Appeals found "nothing unusual" about attorney debt collectors maintaining "procedures" within the meaning of § 1692k(c) to avoid mistakes of law. Id., at 476. Noting that a parallel bona fide error defense in the Truth in Lending Act (TILA), 15 U.S.C. § 1640(c), expressly excludes legal errors, the court observed that Congress has amended the FDCPA several times since 1977 without excluding mistakes of law from § 1692k(c). 538 F.3d, at 476.[3]

We granted certiorari to resolve the conflict of authority as to the scope of the FDCPA's bona fide error defense,[4] 557 1611*1611 U.S. ___, 129 S.Ct. 2863, 174 L.Ed.2d 575 (2009), and now reverse the judgment of the Sixth Circuit.

II

A

The parties disagree about whether a "violation" resulting from a debt collector's misinterpretation of the legal requirements of the FDCPA can ever be "not intentional" under § 1692k(c). Jerman contends that when a debt collector intentionally commits the act giving rise to the violation (here, sending a notice that included the "in writing" language), a misunderstanding about what the Act requires cannot render the violation "not intentional," given the general rule that mistake or ignorance of law is no defense. Carlisle and the dissent, in contrast, argue that nothing in the statutory text excludes legal errors from the category of "bona fide error[s]" covered by § 1692k(c) and note that the Act refers not to an unintentional "act" but rather an unintentional "violation." The latter term, they contend, evinces Congress' intent to impose liability only when a party knows its conduct is unlawful. Carlisle urges us, therefore, to read § 1692k(c) to encompass "all types of error," including mistakes of law. Brief for Respondents 7.

We decline to adopt the expansive reading of § 1692k(c) that Carlisle proposes. We have long recognized the "common maxim, familiar to all minds, that ignorance of the law will not excuse any person, either civilly or criminally." Barlow v. United States, 7 Pet. 404, 411, 8 L.Ed. 728 (1833) (opinion for the Court by Story, J.); see also Cheek v. United States, 498 U.S. 192, 199, 111 S.Ct. 604, 112 L.Ed.2d 617 (1991) ("The general rule that ignorance of the law or a mistake of law is no defense to criminal prosecution is deeply rooted in the American legal system").[5] 1612*1612 Our law is therefore no stranger to the possibility that an act may be "intentional" for purposes of civil liability, even if the actor lacked actual knowledge that her conduct violated the law. In Kolstad v. American Dental Assn., 527 U.S. 526, 119 S.Ct. 2118, 144 L.Ed.2d 494 (1999), for instance, we addressed a provision of the Civil Rights Act of 1991 authorizing compensatory and punitive damages for "intentional discrimination," 42 U.S.C. § 1981a, but limiting punitive damages to conduct undertaken "with malice or with reckless indifference to the federally protected rights of an aggrieved individual," § 1981a(b)(1). We observed that in some circumstances "intentional discrimination" could occur without giving rise to punitive damages liability, such as where an employer is "unaware of the relevant federal prohibition" or acts with the "distinct belief that its discrimination is lawful." 527 U.S., at 536-537, 119 S.Ct. 2118. See also W. Keeton, D. Dobbs, R. Keeton, & D. Owen, Prosser and Keeton on Law of Torts 110 (5th ed. 1984) ("[I]f one intentionally interferes with the interests of others, he is often subject to liability notwithstanding the invasion was made under an erroneous belief as to some . . . legal matter that would have justified the conduct"); Restatement (Second) of Torts § 164, and Comment e (1963-1964) (intentional tort of trespass can be committed despite the actor's mistaken belief that she has a legal right to enter the property).[6]

Likely for this reason, when Congress has intended to provide a mistake-of-law defense to civil liability, it has often done so more explicitly than here. In particular, the FTC Act's administrative-penalty provisions—which, as noted above, Congress expressly incorporated into the FDCPA—apply only when a debt collector acts with "actual knowledge or knowledge fairly implied on the basis of objective circumstances" that its action was "prohibited by [the FDCPA]." 15 U.S.C. §§ 45(m)(1)(A), (C). Given the absence of similar language in § 1692k(c), it is a fair inference that Congress chose to permit injured consumers to recover actual damages, costs, fees, and modest statutory damages for "intentional" conduct, including violations resulting from mistaken interpretation of the FDCPA, while reserving the more onerous penalties of the FTC Act for debt collectors whose intentional actions also reflected "knowledge fairly implied on the basis of objective circumstances" that the conduct was prohibited. Cf. 29 U.S.C. § 260 (authorizing courts to reduce liquidated damages under the Portal-to-Portal Act of 1947 if an employer 1613*1613 demonstrates that "the act or omission giving rise to such action was in good faith and that he had reasonable grounds for believing that his act or omission was not a violation of the Fair Labor Standards Act of 1938"); 17 U.S.C. § 1203(c)(5)(A) (provision of Digital Millennium Copyright Act authorizing court to reduce damages where "the violator was not aware and had no reason to believe that its acts constituted a violation").

Congress also did not confine liability under the FDCPA to "willful" violations, a term more often understood in the civil context to excuse mistakes of law. See, e.g., Trans World Airlines, Inc. v. Thurston, 469 U.S. 111, 125-126, 105 S.Ct. 613, 83 L.Ed.2d 523 (1985) (civil damages for "willful violations" of Age Discrimination in Employment Act of 1967 require a showing that the employer "knew or showed reckless disregard for the matter of whether its conduct was prohibited" (internal quotation marks omitted)); cf. Safeco Ins. Co. of America v. Burr, 551 U.S. 47, 57, 127 S.Ct. 2201, 167 L.Ed.2d 1045 (2007) (although "`willfully'" is a "`word of many meanings'" dependent on context, "we have generally taken it [when used as a statutory condition of civil liability] to cover not only knowing violations of a standard, but reckless ones as well") (quoting Bryan v. United States, 524 U.S. 184, 191, 118 S.Ct. 1939, 141 L.Ed.2d 197 (1998)). For this reason, the dissent missteps in relying on Thurston and McLaughlin v. Richland Shoe Co., 486 U.S. 128, 133, 108 S.Ct. 1677, 100 L.Ed.2d 115 (1988), as both cases involved the statutory phrase "willful violation." Post, at 1629.

The dissent reaches a contrary conclusion based on the interaction of the words "violation" and "not intentional" in § 1692k(c). Post, at 1629-1630. But even in the criminal context, cf. n. 6, supra, reference to a "knowing" or "intentional" "violation" or cognate terms has not necessarily implied a defense for legal errors. See Bryan v. United States, 524 U.S. 184, 192, 118 S.Ct. 1939, 141 L.Ed.2d 197 (1998) ("`[T]he knowledge requisite to knowing violation of a statute is factual knowledge as distinguished from knowledge of the law'") (quoting Boyce Motor Lines, Inc. v. United States, 342 U.S. 337, 345, 72 S.Ct. 329, 96 L.Ed. 367 (1952) (Jackson, J., dissenting)); United States v. International Minerals & Chemical Corp., 402 U.S. 558, 559, 563, 91 S.Ct. 1697, 29 L.Ed.2d 178 (1971) (statute imposing criminal liability on those who "`knowingly violat[e]'" regulations governing transportation of corrosive chemicals does not require "proof of [the defendant's] knowledge of the law"); Ellis v. United States, 206 U.S. 246, 255, 257, 27 S.Ct. 600, 51 L.Ed. 1047 (1907) (rejecting argument that criminal penalty applicable to those who "intentionally violate" a statute "requires knowledge of the law").

The dissent advances a novel interpretative rule under which the combination of a "mens rea requirement" and the word "`violation'" (as opposed to language specifying "the conduct giving rise to the violation") creates a mistake-of-law defense. Post, at 1629-1630. Such a rule would be remarkable in its breadth, applicable to the many scores of civil and criminal provisions throughout the U.S.Code that employ such a combination of terms. The dissent's theory draws no distinction between "knowing," "intentional," or "willful" and would abandon the care we have traditionally taken to construe such words in their particular statutory context. See, e.g., Safeco, supra, at 57, 127 S.Ct. 2201. More fundamentally, the dissent's categorical rule is at odds with precedents such as Bryan, supra, at 192, 118 S.Ct. 1939, and International Minerals, supra, at 559, 563, 91 S.Ct. 1697, in which we rejected a mistake-of-law 1614*1614 defense when a statute imposed liability for a "knowing violation" or on those who "knowingly violat[e]" the law.[7]

The dissent posits that the word "intentional," in the civil context, requires a higher showing of mens rea than "willful" and thus that it should be easier to avoid liability for intentional, rather than willful, violations. Post, at 1630. Even if the dissent is correct that the phrase "intentional violation," standing alone in a civil liability statute, might be read to excuse mistakes of law, the FDCPA juxtaposes the term "not intentional" "violation" in § 1692k(c) with the more specific language of § 45(m)(1)(A), which refers to "actual knowledge or knowledge fairly implied on the basis of objective circumstances" that particular conduct was unlawful. The dissent's reading gives short shrift to that textual distinction.

We draw additional support for the conclusion that bona fide errors in § 1692k(c) do not include mistaken interpretations of the FDCPA, from the requirement that a debt collector maintain "procedures reasonably adapted to avoid any such error." The dictionary defines "procedure" as "a series of steps followed in a regular orderly definite way." Webster's Third New International Dictionary 1807 (1976). In that light, the statutory phrase is more naturally read to apply to processes that have mechanical or other such "regular orderly" steps to avoid mistakes—for instance, the kind of internal controls a debt collector might adopt to ensure its employees do not communicate with consumers at the wrong time of day, § 1692c(a)(1), or make false representations as to the amount of a debt, § 1692e(2). The dissent, like the Court of Appeals, finds nothing unusual in attorney debt collectors maintaining procedures to avoid legal error. Post, at 1637-1638; 538 F.3d, at 476. We do not dispute that some entities may maintain procedures to avoid legal errors. But legal reasoning is not a mechanical or strictly linear process. For this reason, we find force in the suggestion by the Government (as amicus curiae supporting Jerman) that the broad statutory requirement of procedures reasonably designed to avoid "any" bona fide error indicates that the relevant procedures are ones that help to avoid errors like clerical or factual mistakes. 1615*1615 Such procedures are more likely to avoid error than those applicable to legal reasoning, particularly in the context of a comprehensive and complex federal statute such as the FDCPA that imposes openended prohibitions on, inter alia, "false, deceptive," § 1692e, or "unfair" practices, § 1692f. See Brief for United States as Amicus Curiae 16-18.

Even if the text of § 1692k(c), read in isolation, leaves room for doubt, the context and history of the FDCPA provide further reinforcement for construing that provision not to shield violations resulting from misinterpretations of the requirements of the Act. See Dada

v. Mukasey, 554 U.S. 1, ___, 128 S.Ct. 2307, 2317, 171 L.Ed.2d 178 (2008) ("In reading a statute we must not look merely to a particular clause, but consider in connection with it the whole statute" (internal quotation marks omitted)). As described above, Congress included in the FDCPA not only the bona fide error defense but also a separate protection from liability for "any act done or omitted in good faith in conformity with any advisory opinion of the [FTC]." § 1692k(e). In our view, the Court of Appeals' reading is at odds with the role Congress evidently contemplated for the FTC in resolving ambiguities in the Act. Debt collectors would rarely need to consult the FTC if § 1692k(c) were read to offer immunity for good-faith reliance on advice from private counsel. Indeed, debt collectors might have an affirmative incentive not to seek an advisory opinion to resolve ambiguity in the law, as receipt of such advice would prevent them from claiming good-faith immunity for violations and would potentially trigger civil penalties for knowing violations under the FTC Act.[8] More importantly, the existence of a separate provision that, by its plain terms, is more obviously tailored to the concern at issue (excusing civil liability when the Act's prohibitions are uncertain) weighs against stretching the language of the bona fide error defense to accommodate Carlisle's expansive reading.[9]

Any remaining doubt about the proper interpretation of § 1692k(c) is dispelled by evidence of the meaning attached to the language Congress copied into the FDCPA's bona fide error defense from a parallel provision in an existing statute. TILA, 82 Stat. 146, was the first of several statutes collectively known as the Consumer Credit Protection Act (CCPA) that now include the FDCPA. As enacted in 1968, § 130(c) of TILA provided an affirmative defense that was in pertinent part identical to the provision Congress later enacted into the FDCPA: "A creditor may not be held liable in any action brought under [TILA] if the creditor shows by a preponderance of evidence that the violation was not intentional and resulted from a bona fide error notwithstanding the maintenance of procedures reasonably adapted to 1616*1616 avoid any such error." 82 Stat. 157 (codified at 15 U.S.C. § 1640(c)).

During the 9-year period between the enactment of TILA and passage of the FDCPA, the three Federal Courts of Appeals to consider the question interpreted TILA's bona fide error defense as referring to clerical errors; no such court interpreted TILA to extend to violations resulting from a mistaken legal interpretation of that Act.[10] We have often observed that when "judicial interpretations have settled the meaning of an existing statutory provision, repetition of the same language in a new statute indicates, as a general matter, the intent to incorporate its . . . judicial interpretations as well." Bragdon v. Abbott, 524 U.S. 624, 645, 118 S.Ct. 2196, 141 L.Ed.2d 540 (1998); see also Rowe v. New Hampshire Motor Transp. Assn., 552 U.S. 364, 370, 128 S.Ct. 989, 169 L.Ed.2d 933 (2008). While the interpretations of three Federal Courts of Appeals may not have "settled" the meaning of TILA's bona fide error defense, there is no reason to suppose that Congress disagreed with those interpretations when it enacted the FDCPA. Congress copied verbatim the pertinent portions of TILA's bona fide error defense into the FDCPA. Compare 15 U.S.C. § 1640(c)

(1976 ed.) with § 813(c), 91 Stat. 881. This close textual correspondence supports an inference that Congress understood the statutory formula it chose for the FDCPA consistent with Federal Court of Appeals interpretations of TILA.[11]

1617*1617 Carlisle and the dissent urge reliance, consistent with the approach taken by the Court of Appeals, on a 1980 amendment to TILA that added the following sentence to that statute's bona fide error defense: "Examples of a bona fide error include, but are not limited to, clerical, calculation, computer malfunction and program[m]ing, and printing errors, except that an error of legal judgment with respect to a person's obligations under [TILA] is not a bona fide error." See Truth in Lending Simplification and Reform Act, § 615, 94 Stat. 181. The absence of a corresponding amendment to the FDCPA, Carlisle reasons, is evidence of Congress' intent to give a more expansive scope to the FDCPA defense. For several reasons, we decline to give the 1980 TILA amendment such interpretative weight. For one, it is not obvious that the amendment changed the scope of TILA's bona fide error defense in a way material to our analysis, given the uniform interpretations of three Courts of Appeals holding that the TILA defense does not extend to mistakes of law.[12] (Contrary to the dissent's suggestion, post, at 1639, this reading does not render the 1980 amendment surplusage. Congress may simply have intended to codify existing judicial interpretations 1618*1618 to remove any potential for doubt in jurisdictions where courts had not yet addressed the issue.) It is also unclear why Congress would have intended the FDCPA's defense to be broader than the one in TILA, which presents at least as significant a set of concerns about imposing liability for uncertain legal obligations. See, e.g., Ford Motor Credit Co. v. Milhollin, 444 U.S. 555, 566, 100 S.Ct. 790, 63 L.Ed.2d 22 (1980) (TILA is "`highly technical'"). Our reluctance to give controlling weight to the TILA amendment in construing the FDCPA is reinforced by the fact that Congress has not expressly included mistakes of law in any of the numerous bona fide error defenses, worded in pertinent part identically to § 1692k(c), elsewhere in the U.S.Code. Compare, e.g., 12 U.S.C. § 4010(c)(2) (bona fide error defense in Expedited Funds Availability Act expressly excluding "an error of legal judgment with respect to [obligations under that Act]") with 15 U.S.C. §§ 1693m(c), 1693h(c) (bona fide error provisions in the Electronic Fund Transfer Act that are silent as to errors of legal judgment).[13] Although Carlisle points out that Congress has amended the FDCPA on several occasions without expressly restricting the scope of § 1692k(c), that does not suggest Congress viewed the statute as having the expansive reading Carlisle advances, particularly as not until recently had a Court of Appeals interpreted the bona fide error defense to include a violation of the FDCPA resulting from a mistake of law. See Johnson v. Riddle, 305 F.3d 1107, 1121-1124, and nn. 14-15 (CA10 2002).

Carlisle's reliance on Heintz, 514 U.S. 291, 115 S.Ct. 1489, 131 L.Ed.2d 395, is also unavailing. We held in that case that the FDCPA's definition of "debt collector" includes lawyers who regularly, through litigation, attempt to collect consumer debts. Id., at 292,

115 S.Ct. 1489. We addressed a concern raised by the petitioner (as here, a lawyer collecting a debt on behalf of a client) that our reading would automatically render liable "any litigating lawyer who brought, and then lost, a claim against a debtor," on the ground that § 1692e(5) prohibits a debt collector from making any "`threat to take action that cannot legally be taken.'" Id., at 295, 115 S.Ct. 1489. We expressed skepticism that § 1692e(5) itself demanded such a result. But even assuming the correctness of petitioner's reading of § 1692e(5), we suggested that the availability of the bona fide error defense meant that the prospect of liability for litigating lawyers was not "so absurd" as to warrant implying a categorical exemption unsupported by the statutory text. Ibid. We had no occasion in Heintz to address the overall scope of the bona fide error defense. Our discussion of § 1692e(5) did not depend on the premise that a misinterpretation of the requirements of the Act would fall under the bona fide error defense. In the mine-run lawsuit, 1619*1619 a lawyer is at least as likely to be unsuccessful because of factual deficiencies as opposed to legal error. Lawyers can, of course, invoke § 1692k(c) for violations resulting from qualifying factual errors.

Carlisle's remaining arguments do not change our view of § 1692k(c). Carlisle perceives an inconsistency between our reading of the term "intentional" in that provision and the instruction in § 1692k(b) that a court look to whether "noncompliance was intentional" in assessing statutory additional damages. But assuming § 1692k(b) encompasses errors of law, we see no conflict, only congruence, in reading the Act to permit a court to adjust statutory damages for a good-faith misinterpretation of law, even where a debt collector is not entitled to the categorical protection of the bona fide error defense. Carlisle is also concerned that under our reading, § 1692k(c) would be unavailable to a debt collector who violates a provision of the FDCPA applying to acts taken with particular intent because in such instances the relevant act would not be unintentional. See, e.g., § 1692d(5) (prohibiting a debt collector from "[c]ausing a telephone to ring . . . continuously with intent to annoy, abuse, or harass"). Including mistakes as to the scope of such a prohibition, Carlisle urges, would ensure that § 1692k(c) applied throughout the FDCPA. We see no reason, however, why the bona fide error defense must cover every provision of the Act.

The parties and amici make arguments concerning the legislative history that we address for the sake of completeness. Carlisle points to a sentence in a Senate Committee Report stating that "[a] debt collector has no liability . . . if he violates the act in any manner, including with regard to the act's coverage, when such violation is unintentional and occurred despite procedures designed to avoid such violations." S.Rep. No. 95-382, p. 5 (1977), U.S.Code Cong. & Admin.News 1977, pp. 1695, 1699; see also post, at 1627-1628 (opinion of SCALIA, J.) (discussing report). But by its own terms, the quoted sentence does not unambiguously support Carlisle's reading. Even if a bona fide mistake "with regard to the act's coverage" could be read in isolation to contemplate a mistake of law, that reading does not exclude mistakes of fact. A mistake "with regard to the act's coverage" may derive wholly from a debt collector's factually mistaken belief, for example, that a particular debt arose out of a nonconsumer transaction and was therefore not "covered" by the Act. There is no reason to read this passing statement in the Senate Report as contemplating an exemption for legal error that is the product of an attorney's erroneous interpretation of the FDCPA—particularly when attorneys were excluded from the Act's definition of "debt collector" until 1986. 100 Stat. 768. Moreover, the reference to "any manner" of violation is expressly qualified by the requirements that the violation be "unintentional" and occur despite maintenance of appropriate procedures. In any event, we need not choose between these possible readings of the Senate Report, as the legislative record taken as a whole does not lend strong support to Carlisle's view.[14] 1620*1620 We therefore decline to give controlling weight to this isolated passage.

B

Carlisle, its amici, and the dissent raise the additional concern that our reading will have unworkable practical consequences for debt collecting lawyers. See, e.g., Brief for Respondents 40-41, 45-48; NARCA Brief 4-16; post, at 1630-1636. Carlisle claims the FDCPA's private enforcement provisions have fostered a "cottage industry" of professional plaintiffs who sue debt collectors for trivial violations of the Act. See Brief for Respondents 40-41. If debt collecting attorneys can be held personally liable for their reasonable misinterpretations of the requirements of the Act, Carlisle and its amici foresee a flood of lawsuits against creditors' lawyers by plaintiffs (and their attorneys) seeking damages and attorney's fees. The threat of such liability, in the dissent's view, creates an irreconcilable conflict between an attorney's personal financial interest and her ethical obligation of zealous advocacy on behalf of a client: An attorney uncertain about what the FDCPA requires must choose between, on the one hand, exposing herself to liability and, on the other, resolving the legal ambiguity against her client's interest or advising the client to settle—even where there is substantial legal authority for a position favoring the client. Post, at 1633-1636.[15]

We do not believe our holding today portends such grave consequences. For one, the FDCPA contains several provisions that expressly guard against abusive lawsuits, thereby mitigating the financial risk to creditors' attorneys. When an alleged 1621*1621 violation is trivial, the "actual damage[s]" sustained, § 1692k(a)(1), will likely be de minimis or even zero. The Act sets a cap on "additional" damages, § 1692k(a)(2), and vests courts with discretion to adjust such damages where a violation is based on a good-faith error, § 1692k(b). One amicus suggests that attorney's fees may shape financial incentives even where actual and statutory damages are modest. NARCA Brief 11. The statute does contemplate an award of costs and "a reasonable attorney's fee as determined by the court" in the case of "any successful action to enforce the foregoing liability." § 1692k(a)(3). But courts have discretion in calculating reasonable attorney's fees under this statute,[16] and § 1692k(a)(3) authorizes courts to award attorney's fees to the defendant if a plaintiff's suit "was brought in bad faith and for the purpose of harassment."

Lawyers also have recourse to the affirmative defense in § 1692k(c). Not every uncertainty presented in litigation stems from interpretation of the requirements of the Act itself; lawyers may invoke the bona fide error defense, for instance, where a violation results from a qualifying factual error. Jerman and the Government suggest that lawyers can entirely avoid the risk of misinterpreting the Act by obtaining an advisory opinion from the FTC under § 1692k(e). Carlisle fairly observes that the FTC has not frequently issued such opinions, and that the average processing time may present practical difficulties. Indeed, the Government informed us at oral argument that the FTC has issued only four opinions in the past decade (in response to seven requests), and the FTC's response time has typically been three or four months. Tr. of Oral Arg. 27-28, 30. Without disregarding the possibility that the FTC advisory opinion process might be useful in some cases, evidence of present administrative practice makes us reluctant to place significant weight on § 1692k(e) as a practical remedy for the concerns Carlisle has identified.

We are unpersuaded by what seems an implicit premise of Carlisle's arguments: 1622*1622 that the bona fide error defense is a debt collector's sole recourse to avoid potential liability. We addressed a similar argument in Heintz, in which the petitioner urged that certain of the Act's substantive provisions would generate "`anomalies'" if the term "debt collector" was read to include litigating lawyers. 514 U.S., at 295, 115 S.Ct. 1489. Among other things, the petitioner in Heintz contended that § 1692c(c)'s bar on further communication with a consumer who notifies a debt collector that she is refusing to pay the debt would prohibit a lawyer from filing a lawsuit to collect the debt. Id., at 296-297, 115 S.Ct. 1489. We agreed it would be "odd" if the Act interfered in this way with "an ordinary debt-collecting lawsuit" but suggested § 1692c(c) did not demand such a reading in light of several exceptions in the text of that provision itself. Ibid. As in Heintz, we need not authoritatively interpret the Act's conduct-regulating provisions to observe that those provisions should not be assumed to compel absurd results when applied to debt collecting attorneys.

To the extent the FDCPA imposes some constraints on a lawyer's advocacy on behalf of a client, it is hardly unique in our law. "[A]n attorney's ethical duty to advance the interests of his client is limited by an equally solemn duty to comply with the law and standards of professional conduct." Nix v. Whiteside, 475 U.S. 157, 168, 106 S.Ct. 988, 89 L.Ed.2d 123 (1986). Lawyers face sanctions, among other things, for suits presented "for any improper purpose, such as to harass, cause unnecessary delay, or needlessly increase the cost of litigation." Fed. Rules Civ. Proc. 11(b), (c). Model rules of professional conduct adopted by many States impose outer bounds on an attorney's pursuit of a client's interests. See, e.g., ABA Model Rules of Professional Conduct 3.1 (2009) (requiring nonfrivolous basis in law and fact for claims asserted); 4.1 (truthfulness to third parties). In some circumstances, lawyers may face personal liability for conduct undertaken during representation of a client. See, e.g., Central Bank of Denver, N.A. v. First Interstate Bank of Denver, N. A., 511 U.S. 164, 191, 114 S.Ct. 1439, 128 L.Ed.2d 119 (1994) ("Any person or entity, including a lawyer, . . . who employs a manipulative device or makes a material misstatement (or omission) on which a purchaser or seller of securities relies may be liable as a primary violator under [Securities and Exchange Commission Rule] 10b-5").

Moreover, a lawyer's interest in avoiding FDCPA liability may not always be adverse to her client. Some courts have held clients vicariously liable for their lawyers' violations of the FDCPA. See, e.g., Fox v. Citicorp Credit Servs., Inc., 15 F.3d 1507, 1516 (C.A.9 1994); see also First Interstate Bank of Fort Collins, N.A. v. Soucie, 924 P.2d 1200, 1202 (Colo.App.1996).

The suggestion that our reading of § 1692k(c) will create unworkable consequences is also undermined by the existence of numerous state consumer protection and debt collection statutes that contain bona fide error defenses that are either silent as to, or expressly exclude, legal errors.[17] Several States have enacted debt collection statutes that contain neither an exemption for attorney debt collectors nor any bona fide error defense at all. See, e.g., Mass. Gen. Laws, ch. 93, § 49 (West 2008); Md. Com. Law Code Ann. § 14-203 (Lexis 2005); Ore. Rev.Stat. § 646.641 (2007); Wis. Stat. 1623*1623 § 427.105 (2007-2008). More generally, a group of 21 States as amici supporting Jerman inform us they are aware of "no [judicial] decisions interpreting a parallel state bona fide error provision [in a civil regulatory statute] to immunize a defendant's mistake of law," except in a minority of statutes that expressly provide to the contrary.[18] See Brief for State of New York et al. as Amici Curiae 11, and n. 6. Neither Carlisle and its amici nor the dissent demonstrate that lawyers have suffered drastic consequences under these state regimes.

In the dissent's view, these policy concerns are evidence that "Congress could not have intended" the reading we adopt today. Post, at 1630. But the dissent's reading raises concerns of its own. The dissent focuses on the facts of this case, in which an attorney debt collector, in the dissent's view, "acted reasonably at every step" and committed a "technical violation" resulting in no "actual harm" to the debtor. Post, at 1634, 1631, 1632. But the dissent's legal theory does not limit the defense to attorney debt collectors or "technical" violations.[19] Under that approach, it appears, nonlawyer debt collectors could obtain blanket immunity for mistaken interpretations of the FDCPA simply by seeking the advice of legal counsel. Moreover, many debt collectors are compensated with a percentage of money recovered, and so will have a financial incentive to press the boundaries of the Act's prohibitions on collection techniques. It is far from obvious why immunizing debt collectors who adopt aggressive but mistaken interpretations of the law would be consistent with the statute's broadly worded prohibitions on debt collector misconduct. Jerman and her amici express further concern that the dissent's reading would give a competitive advantage to debt collectors who press the boundaries of lawful conduct. They foresee a "race to the bottom" driving ethical collectors out of business. Brief for Petitioner 32; Brief for Public Citizen et al. as Amici Curiae 16-18. It is difficult to square such a result with Congress' express purpose "to eliminate abusive debt collection practices by debt collectors, [and] to insure that those debt collectors who refrain from using abusive debt collection practices are not competitively disadvantaged," § 1692(e).

The dissent's reading also invites litigation about a debt collector's subjective intent to violate the FDCPA and the adequacy of procedures maintained to avoid legal error. Cf. Barlow, 7 Pet., at 411, 8 L.Ed. 728 (maxim that ignorance of the law will not excuse civil or criminal liability "results from the extreme difficulty of ascertaining what is, bona fide, the interpretation of the party"). Courts that read § 1692k(c) to permit a mistake-of-law defense have adopted varying formulations of what legal procedures are "reasonably adapted to avoid any [legal] error."[20] 1624*1624 Among other uncertainties, the dissent does not explain whether it would read § 1692k(c) to impose a heightened standard for the procedures attorney debt collectors must maintain, as compared to nonattorney debt collectors. The increased cost to prospective plaintiffs in time, fees, and uncertainty of outcome may chill private suits under the statutory right of action, undermining the FDCPA's calibrated scheme of statutory incentives to encourage self-enforcement. Cf. FTC, Collecting Consumer Debts: The Challenge of Change 67 (2009) ("Because the Commission receives more than 70,000 third-party debt collection complaints per year, it is not feasible for federal government law enforcement to be the exclusive or primary means of deterring all possible law violations"). The state amici predict that, on the dissent's reading, consumers will have little incentive to bring enforcement actions "where the law [i]s at all unsettled, because in such circumstances a debt collector could easily claim bona fide error of law"; in the States' view, the resulting "enforcement gap" would be "extensive" at both the federal and State levels. See Brief for State of New York et al. as Amici Curiae 7-10. In short, the policy concerns identified by the dissent tell only half the story.[21]

In sum, we do not foresee that our decision today will place unmanageable burdens on lawyers practicing in the debt collection industry. To the extent debt collecting lawyers face liability for mistaken interpretations of the requirements of the FDCPA, Carlisle, its amici, and the dissent have not shown that "the result [will be] so absurd as to warrant" disregarding the weight of textual authority discussed above. Heintz, 514 U.S., at 295, 115 S.Ct. 1489. Absent such a showing, arguments that the Act strikes an undesirable balance in assigning the risks of legal misinterpretation are properly addressed to Congress. To the extent Congress is persuaded that the policy concerns identified by the dissent require a recalibration of the FDCPA's liability scheme, it is, of course, free to amend the statute accordingly.[22] Congress has wide latitude, for instance, to revise § 1692k to excuse some or all mistakes of law or grant broader discretion to district courts to adjust a plaintiff's recovery. This Court may not, however, read more into § 1692k(c) than the statutory language naturally supports. We therefore hold that the bona fide error defense in § 1692k(c) does not apply to a violation of the FDCPA resulting from a debt collector's incorrect interpretation of the requirements of that statute.

1625*1625 * * *

For the reasons discussed above, the judgment of the United States Court of Appeals for the Sixth Circuit is reversed, and the case is remanded for further proceedings consistent with this opinion.

It is so ordered.

Justice BREYER, concurring.

As respondents point out, the Court's interpretation of the Fair Debt Collection Practices Act may create a dilemma for lawyers who regularly engage in debt collection, including through litigation. See Brief for Respondents 44-48; Heintz v. Jenkins, 514 U.S. 291, 115 S.Ct. 1489, 131 L.Ed.2d 395 (1995). Can those lawyers act in the best interests of their clients if they face personal liability when they rely on good-faith interpretations of the Act that are later rejected by a court? Or will that threat of personal liability lead them to do less than their best for those clients?

As the majority points out, however, the statute offers a way out of—though not a panacea for—this dilemma. Ante, at 1615-1616, 1621-1622. Faced with legal uncertainty, a lawyer can turn to the Federal Trade Commission (FTC or Commission) for an advisory opinion. 16 CFR §§ 1.1 to 1.4 (2009). And once he receives that opinion and acts upon it the dilemma disappears: If he fails to follow the opinion, he has not acted in good faith and can fairly be held liable. If he follows the opinion, the statute frees him from any such liability. 15 U.S.C. § 1692k(e) (debt collectors immune from liability for "any act done or omitted in . . . conformity with any advisory opinion of the [Federal Trade] Commission"). See also R. Hobbs et al., National Consumer Law Center, Fair Debt Collection §§ 6.12.2, 7.3 (6th ed.2008).

The FTC, of course, may refuse to issue such an opinion. See, e.g., 16 CFR § 1.1 (providing that the Commission will issue advisory opinions "where practicable" and only when "[t]he matter involves a substantial or novel question of fact or law and there is no clear Commission or court precedent" or "is of significant public interest"). Apparently, within the past decade, the FTC has received only seven requests and issued four opinions. See Tr. of Oral Arg. 27-28; see also Federal Trade Commission, Commission FDCPA Advisory Opinions, online at http://www.ftc.gov/ os/statutes/fdcpajump.shtm (as visited Apr.

19, 2010, and available in Clerk of Court's case file). Yet, should the dilemma I have described above prove serious, I would expect the FTC to receive more requests and to respond to them, thereby reducing the scope of the problem to the point where other available tools, e.g., damages caps and vicarious liability, will prove adequate. See ante, at 1620-1623. On this understanding, I agree with the Court and join its opinion.

Justice SCALIA, concurring in part and concurring in the judgment.

I join the Court's opinion except for its reliance upon two legal fictions. A portion of the Court's reasoning consists of this: The language in the Fair Debt Collection Practices Act (FDCPA or Act) tracks language in the Truth in Lending Act (TILA); and in the nine years between the enactment of TILA and the enactment of the FDCPA, three Courts of Appeals had "interpreted TILA's bona fide error defense as referring to clerical errors." Ante, at 1616. Relying on our statement in Bragdon v. Abbott, 524 U.S. 624, 645, 118 S.Ct. 2196, 141 L.Ed.2d 540 (1998), that Congress's repetition, in a new statute, of statutory language with a "`settled'" judicial interpretation indicates "`the intent to incorporate its . . . judicial interpretations as well,'" the Court concludes that these 1626*1626 three Court of Appeals cases "suppor[t] an inference that Congress understood the statutory formula it chose for the FDCPA consistent with Federal Court of Appeals interpretations of TILA." Ante, at 1615-1617.

Let me assume (though I do not believe it) that what counts is what Congress "intended," even if that intent finds no expression in the enacted text. When a large majority of the Circuits, over a lengthy period of time, have uniformly reached a certain conclusion as to the meaning of a particular statutory text, it may be reasonable to assume that Congress was aware of those holdings, took them to be correct, and intended the same meaning in adopting that text.[1] It seems to me unreasonable, however, to assume that, when Congress has a bill before it that contains language used in an earlier statute, it is aware of, and approves as correct, a mere three Court of Appeals decisions interpreting that earlier statute over the previous nine years. Can one really believe that a majority in both Houses of Congress knew of those three cases, and accepted them as correct (even when, as was the case here, some District Court opinions and a State Supreme Court opinion had concluded, to the contrary, that the defense covered legal errors, see ante, at 1615-1616, n. 10)? This is a legal fiction, which has nothing to be said for it except that it can sometimes make our job easier. The Court acknowledges that "the interpretations of three Federal Courts of Appeals may not have `settled' the meaning of TILA's bona fide error defense," but says "there is no reason to suppose that Congress disagreed with those interpretations." Ante, at 1616-1617. Perhaps not; but no reason to suppose that it knew of and agreed with them either—which is presumably the proposition for which the Court cites them.

Even assuming, moreover, that Congress knew and approved of those cases, they would not support the Court's conclusion today. All three of them said that TILA's bona fide error defense covered only clerical errors. See Ives v. W.T. Grant Co., 522 F.2d 749, 758 (C.A.2 1975) ("only available for clerical errors"); Haynes v. Logan Furniture Mart, Inc., 503 F.2d 1161, 1167 (C.A.7 1974) ("basically only clerical errors"); Palmer v. Wilson, 502 F.2d 860, 861 (C.A.9 1974) ("[C]lerical errors . . . are the only violations this section was designed to excuse"). Yet the Court specifically interprets the identical language in the FDCPA as providing a defense not only for clerical errors, but also for factual errors. See ante, at 1618, 1621; see also ante, at 1619 (suggesting the same). If the Court really finds the three Courts of Appeals' interpretations of TILA indicative of congressional intent in the FDCPA, it should restrict its decision accordingly. As for me, I support the Court's inclusion of factual errors, because there is nothing in the text of the FDCPA limiting the excusable "not intentional" violations to those based on clerical errors, and since there is a long tradition in the common law and in our construction of federal statutes distinguishing errors of fact from errors of law.

The Court's opinion also makes fulsome use of that other legal fiction, legislative history, ranging from a single Representative's 1627*1627 floor remarks on the House bill that became the FDCPA, ante, at 1616-1617, n. 11, to a single Representative's remarks in a Senate Subcommittee hearing on the House bill and three Senate bills, ibid., to two 1979 Senate Committee Reports dealing not with the FDCPA but with the 1980 amendments to TILA, ante, at 1617, n. 12, to remarks in a Committee markup of the Senate bill on the FDCPA, ante, at 1619-1620, n. 14, to a House Report dealing with an earlier version of the FDCPA, ibid. Is the conscientious attorney really expected to dig out such mini-nuggets of "congressional intent" from floor remarks, committee hearings, committee markups, and committee reports covering many different bills over many years? When the Court addresses such far-afield legislative history merely "for the sake of completeness," ante, at 1619, it encourages and indeed prescribes such wasteful over-lawyering.

As it happens, moreover, one of the supposedly most "authoritative" snippets of legislative history, a Senate Committee Report dealing with the meaning of TILA, states very clearly that the 1980 amendment to TILA's bona fide error defense "clarified" the defense "to make clear that it applies to mechanical and computer errors," S.Rep. No. 96-73, pp. 7-8 (1979). Likewise, the 1999 American Law Report the Court cites, ante, at 1617, n. 12, which relies on another Senate Committee Report, describes the amendment as clarifying the "prevailing view" that the defense "applies to clerical errors," Lockhart, 153 A.L.R. Fed. 211-212, § 2[a] (1999).[2] Once again, the legal fiction contradicts the Court's conclusion that the language in the FDCPA, identical to the original TILA defense, applies to mistakes of fact.

But if legislative history is to be used, it should be used impartially. (Legislative history, after all, almost always has something for everyone!) The Court dismisses with a wave of the hand what seems to me the most persuasive legislative history (if legislative history could ever be persuasive) in the case. The respondents point to the Senate Committee Report on the FDCPA, which says that "[a] debt collector has no liability . . . if he violates the act in any manner, including with regard to the act's coverage, when such violation is unintentional and occurred despite procedures designed to avoid such violations." S.Rep. No. 95-382, p. 5 (1977), U.S.Code Cong. & Admin.News 1977, pp. 1695, 1699 (emphasis added). The Court claims that a mistake about "the act's coverage" in this passage might refer to factual mistakes, such as a debt collector's mistaken belief "that a particular debt arose out of a nonconsumer transaction and was therefore not `covered' by the Act," ante, at 1619. The Court's explanation seems to me inadequate. No lawyer—indeed, no one speaking accurately—would equate a mistake regarding the Act's coverage with a mistake regarding whether a particular fact situation falls within the Act's coverage. What the Act covers ("the act's coverage") is one thing; whether a particular case falls within the Act's coverage is something else.

Even if (contrary to my perception) the phrase could be used to refer to both these things, by what principle does the Court reject the more plausible meaning? The fact that "attorneys were excluded from the Act's definition of `debt collector' until 1986," ibid., does not, as the Court 1628*1628 contends, support its conclusion that errors of law are not covered. Attorneys are not the only ones who would have been able to claim a legal-error defense; non-attorneys make legal mistakes too. They also sometimes receive and rely upon erroneous legal advice from attorneys. Indeed, if anyone could satisfy the defense's requirement of maintaining "procedures reasonably adapted to avoid" a legal error, it would be a non-attorney debt collector who follows the procedure of directing all legal questions to his attorney.

The Court also points to "equivocal" evidence from the Senate Committee's final markup session, ante, at 1619-1620, n. 14, but it minimizes a decidedly unhelpful discussion of the scope of the defense during the session. In response to concern that the defense would be construed, like the TILA defense, as "only protecting against a mathematical error," a staff member explained that, because of differences in the nature of the statutes, the FDCPA defense was broader than the TILA defense and "would apply to any violation of the act which was unintentional." See Senate Committee on Banking, Housing and Urban Affairs, Markup Session: S. 1130— Debt Collection Legislation 20-21 (July 26, 1977) (emphasis added). The Chairman then asked: "So it's not simply a mathematical error but any bona fide error without intent?" Id., at 21 (emphasis added). To which the staff member responded: "That's correct." Ibid. The repeated use of "any"—"any violation" and "any bona fide error"—supports the natural reading of the Committee Report's statement regarding "the act's coverage" as including legal errors about the scope of the Act, rather than just factual errors.

The Court ultimately dismisses the Senate Committee Report on the ground that "the legislative record taken as a whole does not lend strong support to Carlisle's view." Ante, at 1619. I think it more reasonable to give zero weight to the other snippets of legislative history that the Court relies upon, for the reason that the Senate Committee Report on the very bill that became the FDCPA flatly contradicts them. It is almost invariably the case that our opinions benefit not at all from the make-weight use of legislative history. But today's opinion probably suffers from it. Better to spare us the results of legislative-history research, however painfully and exhaustively conducted it might have been.

The Court's textual analysis stands on its own, without need of (or indeed any assistance from) the two fictions I have discussed. Accordingly, I concur in the judgment of the Court.

Justice KENNEDY, with whom Justice ALITO joins, dissenting.

The statute under consideration is the Fair Debt Collection Practices Act (FDCPA), 15 U.S.C. § 1692 et seq. The statute excepts from liability a debt collector's "bona fide error[s]," provided that they were "not intentional" and reasonable procedures have been maintained to avoid them. § 1692k(c). The Court today interprets this exception to exclude legal errors. In doing so, it adopts a questionable interpretation and rejects a straightforward, quite reasonable interpretation of the statute's plain terms. Its decision aligns the judicial system with those who would use litigation to enrich themselves at the expense of attorneys who strictly follow and adhere to professional and ethical standards.

When the law is used to punish good-faith mistakes; when adopting reasonable safeguards is not enough to avoid liability; when the costs of discovery and litigation are used to force settlement even absent 1629*1629 fault or injury; when class-action suits transform technical legal violations into windfalls for plaintiffs or their attorneys, the Court, by failing to adopt a reasonable interpretation to counter these excesses, risks compromising its own institutional responsibility to ensure a workable and just litigation system. The interpretation of the FDCPA the Court today endorses will entrench, not eliminate, some of the most troubling aspects of our legal system. Convinced that Congress did not intend this result, I submit this respectful dissent.

I

A

The FDCPA addresses "abusive debt collection practices," § 1692(e), by regulating interactions between commercial debt collectors and consumers. See ante, at 1608-1609. The statute permits private suits against debt collectors who violate its provisions. § 1692k(a). An exception to liability is provided by the so-called bona fide error defense:

"A debt collector may not be held liable in any action . . . if the debt collector shows by a preponderance of evidence that the violation was not intentional and resulted from a bona fide error notwithstanding the maintenance of procedures reasonably adapted to avoid any such error." § 1692k(c).

This language does not exclude mistakes of law and is most naturally read to include them. Certainly a mistaken belief about the law is, if held in good faith, a "bona fide error" as that phrase is normally understood. See Black's Law Dictionary 582 (8th ed.2004) (defining "error" as "a belief that what is false is true or that what is true is false," def. 1); ibid. ("[a] mistake of law or of fact in a tribunal's judgment, opinion, or order," def. 2); ibid. (listing categories of legal errors).

The choice of words provides further reinforcement for this view. The bona fide error exception in § 1692k(c) applies if "the violation was not intentional and resulted from a bona fide error." The term "violation" specifically denotes a legal infraction. See id., at 1600 ("An infraction or breach of the law; a transgression," def. 1). The statutory term "violation" thus stands in direct contrast to other provisions of the FDCPA that describe conduct itself. This applies both to specific terms, e.g., § 1692e ("A debt collector may not use any false, deceptive, or misleading representation or means in connection with the collection of any debt"), and to more general ones, e.g., § 1692k(e) (referring to "any act done or omitted in good faith"). By linking the mens rea requirement ("not intentional") with the word "violation"— rather than with the conduct giving rise to the violation—the Act by its terms indicates that the bona fide error exception applies to legal errors as well as to factual ones.

The Court's precedents accord with this interpretation. Federal statutes that link the term "violation" with a mens rea requirement have been interpreted to excuse good-faith legal mistakes. See, e.g., McLaughlin v. Richland Shoe Co., 486 U.S. 128, 129, 133, 108 S.Ct. 1677, 100 L.Ed.2d 115 (1988) (the phrase "arising out of a willful violation" in the Fair Labor Standards Act applies where an employer "either knew or showed reckless disregard for the matter of whether its conduct was prohibited by the statute"); Trans World Airlines, Inc. v. Thurston, 469 U.S. 111, 125, 126, 105 S.Ct. 613, 83 L.Ed.2d 523 (1985) (damages provision under the Age Discrimination in Employment Act, which applies "only in cases of willful violations," creates liability where an employer "knew or showed reckless disregard for the matter of whether its conduct was prohibited by the ADEA" (internal quotation marks 1630*1630 omitted)); cf. Liparota v. United States, 471 U.S. 419, 428, 105 S.Ct. 2084, 85 L.Ed.2d 434 (1985) (prohibition on use of food stamps "'knowing [them] to have been received . . . in violation of'" federal law "undeniably requires a knowledge of illegality" (emphasis deleted)). The FDCPA's use of "violation" thus distinguishes it from most of the authorities relied upon by the Court to demonstrate that mistake-of-law defenses are disfavored. See, e.g., ante, at 1612 (citing Kolstad v. American Dental Assn., 527 U.S. 526, 119 S.Ct. 2118, 144 L.Ed.2d 494 (1999)).

The Court's response is that there is something distinctive about the word "willful" that suggests an excuse for mistakes of law. This may well be true for criminal statutes, in which the terms "`knowing,' `intentional' [and] `willful'" have been distinguished in this regard. Ante, at 1613 (citing Safeco Ins. Co. of America v. Burr, 551 U.S. 47, 57, 127 S.Ct. 2201, 167 L.Ed.2d 1045 (2007)). But this distinction is specific to the criminal context:

"It is different in the criminal law. When the term `willful' or `willfully' has been used in a criminal statute, we have regularly read the modifier as limiting liability to knowing violations. This reading of the term, however, is tailored to the criminal law, where it is characteristically used to require a criminal intent beyond the purpose otherwise required for guilt, or an additional `bad purpose,' or specific intent to violate a known legal duty created by highly technical statutes." Id., at 57-58, n. 9, 127 S.Ct. 2201 (citations omitted).

For this reason, the Court's citation to criminal cases, which are themselves inconsistent, see Ratzlaf v. United States, 510 U.S. 135, 114 S.Ct. 655, 126 L.Ed.2d 615 (1994), is unavailing. See ante, at 1613-1614, and n. 7.

In the civil context, by contrast, the word "willful" has been used to impose a mens rea threshold for liability that is lower, not higher, than an intentionality requirement. See Safeco, supra, at 57, 127 S.Ct. 2201 ("[W]here willfulness is a statutory condition of civil liability, we have generally taken it to cover not only knowing violations of a standard, but reckless ones as well"). Avoiding liability under a statute aimed at intentional violations should therefore be easier, not harder, than avoiding liability under a statute aimed at willful violations. And certainly there is nothing in Thurston or McLaughlin —both civil cases— suggesting that they would have come out differently had the relevant statutes used "intentional violation" rather than "willful violation."

B

These considerations suffice to show that § 1692k(c) is most reasonably read to include mistakes of law. Even if this were merely a permissible reading, however, it should be adopted to avoid the adverse consequences that must flow from the Court's contrary decision. The Court's reading leads to results Congress could not have intended.

1

The FDCPA is but one of many federal laws that Congress has enacted to protect consumers. A number of these statutes authorize the filing of private suits against those who use unfair or improper practices. See, e.g., 15 U.S.C. § 1692k (FDCPA); § 1640 (Truth in Lending Act); § 1681n (Fair Credit Reporting Act); 49 U.S.C. § 32710 (Federal Odometer Disclosure Act); 11 U.S.C. § 526(c)(2) (Bankruptcy Abuse Prevention and Consumer Protection Act of 2005). Several of these provisions permit a successful plaintiff to recover—in addition to actual damages— 1631*1631 statutory damages, attorney's fees and costs, and in some cases punitive damages. E.g., 15 U.S.C. § 1640(a)(2) (statutory damages); § 1640(a)(3) (attorney's fees and costs); § 1681n(a)(1)(B) (statutory and punitive damages); § 1681n(a)(1)(B)(3) (costs and attorney's fees); 49 U.S.C. § 32710(a) ("3 times the actual damages or $1,500, whichever is greater"); § 32710(b) (costs and attorney's fees); 11 U.S.C. § 526(c)(3)(A) (costs and attorney's fees). Some also explicitly permit class-action suits. E.g., 15 U.S.C. § 1640(a)(2)(B); § 1692k(a)(2)(B).

A collateral effect of these statutes may be to create incentives to file lawsuits even where no actual harm has occurred. This happens when the plaintiff can recover statutory damages for the violation and his or her attorney will receive fees if the suit is successful, no matter how slight the injury. A favorable verdict after trial is not necessarily the goal; often the plaintiff will be just as happy with a settlement, as will his or her attorney (who will receive fees regardless). The defendant, meanwhile, may conclude a quick settlement is preferable to the costs of discovery and a protracted trial. And if the suit attains class-action status, the financial stakes rise in magnitude. See, e.g., § 1640(a)(2)(B) (class-action recovery of up to "the lesser of $500,000 or 1 per centum of the net worth of the [defendant]"); § 1692k(a)(2)(B) (same).

The present case offers an object lesson. Respondents filed a complaint in state court on behalf of a client that mistakenly believed Jerman owed money to it. Jerman's attorney then informed respondents that the debt had been paid in full. Respondents confirmed this fact with the client and withdrew the lawsuit.

This might have been the end of the story. But because respondents had informed Jerman that she was required to dispute the debt in writing, she filed a class-action complaint. It did not matter that Jerman had claimed no harm as a result of respondents' actions. Jerman sued for damages, attorney's fees, and costs—including class damages of "$500,000 or 1% of defendants' net worth whichever is less." Amended Complaint in No. 1:06-CV-01397 (ND Ohio), p. 4. In addition to merits-related discovery, Jerman sought information from respondents concerning the income and net worth of each partner in the firm. At some point, Jerman proposed to settle with respondents for $15,000 in damages and $7,500 in attorney's fees. Amended Joint App. in No. 07-3964(CA6), pp. 256-262. The case illustrates how a technical violation of a complex federal statute can give rise to costly litigation with incentives to settle simply to avoid attorney's fees.

Today's holding gives new impetus to this already troubling dynamic of allowing certain actors in the system to spin even good-faith, technical violations of federal law into lucrative litigation, if not for themselves then for the attorneys who conceive of the suit. See Federal Home Loan Mortgage Corp. v. Lamar, 503 F.3d 504, 513 (C.A.6 2007) (referring to the "cottage industry" of litigation that has arisen out of the FDCPA (internal quotation marks omitted)). It is clear that Congress, too, was troubled by this dynamic. That is precisely why it enacted a bona fide error defense. The Court's ruling, however, endorses and drives forward this dynamic, for today's holding leaves attorneys and their clients vulnerable to civil liability for adopting good-faith legal positions later determined to be mistaken, even if reasonable efforts were made to avoid mistakes.

The Court seeks to brush aside these concerns by noting that trivial violations will give rise to little in the way of actual damages and that trial courts "have discretion 1632*1632 in calculating reasonable attorney's fees under [the] statute." Ante, at 1620. It is not clear, however, that a court is permitted to adjust a fee award based on its assessment of the suit's utility. Cf. Perdue v. Kenny A., post, at 1633 (noting a "`strong presumption'" of reasonableness that attaches to a lodestar calculation of attorney's fees). Though the Court, properly, does not address the question here, it acknowledges that some courts have deemed fee awards to victorious plaintiffs to be "`mandatory,'" even if the plaintiff suffered no damage. Ante, at 1621, n. 16.

The Court's second response is that the FDCPA guards against abusive suits and that suits brought "`in bad faith and for the purpose of harassment'" can lead to a fee award for the defendant. Ante, at 1621 (quoting § 1692k(a)(3)). Yet these safeguards cannot deter suits based on technical—but harmless—violations of the statute. If the plaintiff obtains a favorable judgment or a settlement, then by definition the suit will not have been brought in bad faith. See Emanuel v. American Credit Exch., 870 F.2d 805, 809 (C.A.2 1989) (FDCPA defendant's "claim for malicious prosecution cannot succeed unless the action subject of the claim is unsuccessful").

Again the present case is instructive. Jerman brought suit without pointing to any actual harm that resulted from respondents' actions. At the time her complaint was filed, it was an open question in the Sixth Circuit whether a debt collector could demand that a debt be disputed in writing, and the district courts in the Circuit had reached different answers. Ante, at 1610, n. 2. The trial court in this case happened to side with Jerman on the issue, 464 F.Supp.2d 720, 722-725 (N.D.Ohio 2006), but it seems unlikely that the court would have labeled her suit "abusive" or "in bad faith" even if it had gone the other way.

There is no good basis for optimism, then, when one contemplates the practical consequences of today's decision. Given the complexity of the FDCPA regime, see 16 CFR pt. 901 (2009) (FDCPA regulations), technical violations are likely to be common. Indeed, the

Court acknowledges that they are inevitable. See ante, at 1614-1615. As long as legal mistakes occur, plaintiffs and their attorneys will have an incentive to bring suits for these infractions. It seems unlikely that Congress sought to create a system that encourages costly and time-consuming litigation over harmless violations committed in good faith despite reasonable safeguards.

When construing a federal statute, courts should be mindful of the effect of the interpretation on congressional purposes explicit in the statutory text. The FDCPA states an objective that today's decision frustrates. The statutory purpose was to "eliminate abusive debt collection practices" and to ensure that debt collectors who refrain from using those practices "are not competitively disadvantaged." 15 U.S.C. § 1692(e) ("Purposes"). The practices Congress addressed involved misconduct that is deliberate, see § 1692(a) ("abusive, deceptive, and unfair debt collection practices"); § 1692(c) ("misrepresentation or other abusive debt collection practices"), or unreasonable, see § 1692c(a)(1) (prohibiting debt collectors from communicating with debtors at times "which should be known" to be inconvenient); § 1692e(8) (prohibiting the communication of credit card information "which should be known to be false"). That explains the statutory objective not to disadvantage debt collectors who "refrain" from abusive practices—that is to say, debt collectors who do not intentionally or unreasonably adopt them. It further explains 1633*1633 why Congress included a good-faith error exception, which exempts violations that are not intentional or unreasonable.

In referring to "abusive debt collection practices," however, surely Congress did not contemplate attorneys who act based on reasonable, albeit ultimately mistaken, legal interpretations. A debt collector does not gain a competitive advantage by making good-faith legal errors any more than by making good-faith factual errors. This is expressly so if the debt collector has implemented "procedures reasonably adapted to avoid" them. By reading § 1692k(c) to exclude good-faith mistakes of law, the Court fails to align its interpretation with the statutory objectives.

The Court urges, nevertheless, that there are policy concerns on the other side. The Court frets about debt collectors who "press the boundaries of the Act's prohibitions" and about a potential "`race to the bottom.'" Ante, at 1623 (quoting Brief for Petitioner 32). For instance, in its view, interpreting § 1692k(c) to encompass legal mistakes might mean that "nonlawyer debt collectors could obtain blanket immunity for mistaken interpretations of the FDCPA simply by seeking the advice of legal counsel." Ante, at 1623. It must be remembered, however, that § 1692k(c) may only be invoked where the debt collector's error is "bona fide" and where "reasonable procedures" have been adopted to avoid errors. There is no valid or persuasive reason to assume that Congress would want to impose liability on a debt collector who relies in good faith on the reasonable advice of counsel. If anything, we should expect Congress to think that such behavior should be encouraged, not discouraged.

The Court also suggests that reading § 1692k(c) to include legal errors would encourage litigation over a number of issues: what subjective intent is necessary for liability; what procedures are necessary to avoid legal mistakes; what standard applies to procedures adopted by attorney debt collectors as compared to non-attorney debt collectors. Yet these questions are no different from ones already raised by the statute. Whether the debt collector is an attorney or not, his or her subjective intent must be assessed before liability can be determined. Procedures to avoid mistakes—whether legal or otherwise—must be "reasonable," which is always a context-specific inquiry. The Court provides no reason to think that legal errors raise concerns that differ in these respects from those raised by non-legal errors.

2

There is a further and most serious reason to interpret § 1692k(c) to include good-faith legal mistakes. In Heintz v. Jenkins, 514 U.S. 291, 115 S.Ct. 1489, 131 L.Ed.2d 395 (1995), the Court held that attorneys engaged in debt-collection litigation may be "debt collectors" for purposes of the FDCPA. In reaching this conclusion the Court confronted the allegation that its interpretation would produce the anomalous result that attorneys could be liable for bringing legal claims against debtors if those claims ultimately proved unsuccessful. Id., at 295, 115 S.Ct. 1489. The Court rejected this argument. In doing so it said that § 1692k(c) provides debt collectors with a defense for their bona fide errors. Id., at 295, 115 S.Ct. 1489.

Today the Court relies on Heintz to allay concerns about the practical implications of its decision. Ante, at 1622. Yet the Court reads § 1692k(c) to exclude mistakes of law, thereby producing the very result that Heintz said would not come about. Attorneys may now be held liable for taking reasonable legal positions in good faith if those positions are ultimately rejected.

1634*1634 Attorneys are duty-bound to represent their clients with diligence, creativity, and painstaking care, all within the confines of the law. When statutory provisions have not yet been interpreted in a definitive way, principled advocacy is to be prized, not punished. Surely this includes offering interpretations of a statute that are permissible, even if not yet settled. The FDCPA is a complex statute, and its provisions are subject to different interpretations. See, e.g., ante, at 1610-1611, n. 4 (identifying splits of authority on two different FDCPA issues); Brief for National Association of Retail Collection Attorneys as Amicus Curiae 5-6 (identifying another split); see also ante, at 1614-1615. Attorneys will often find themselves confronted with a statutory provision that is susceptible to different but still reasonable interpretations.

An attorney's obligation in the face of uncertainty is to give the client his or her best professional assessment of the law's mandate. Under the Court's interpretation of the FDCPA, however, even that might leave the attorney vulnerable to suit. For if the attorney proceeds based on an interpretation later rejected by the courts, today's decision deems that to be actionable as an intentional "violation," with personal financial liability soon to follow. Indeed, even where a particular practice is compelled by existing precedent, the attorney may be sued if that precedent is later overturned.

These adverse consequences are evident in the instant case. When respondents filed a foreclosure complaint against Jerman on behalf of their client, they had no reason to doubt that the debt was valid. They had every reason, furthermore, to believe that they were on solid legal ground in asking her to dispute the amount owed in writing. See, e.g., Graziano v. Harrison, 950 F.2d 107, 112 (C.A.3 1991) (written objection is necessary for coherent statutory scheme and protects the debtor by "creat[ing] a lasting record of the fact that the debt has been disputed"). When Jerman disputed the debt, respondents verified that the debt had been satisfied and withdrew the lawsuit. Respondents acted reasonably at every step, and yet may still find themselves liable for a harmless violation.

After today's ruling, attorneys can be punished for advocacy reasonably deemed to be in compliance with the law or even required by it. This distorts the legal process. Henceforth, creditors' attorneys of the highest ethical standing are encouraged to adopt a debtor-friendly interpretation of every question, lest the attorneys themselves incur personal financial risk. It is most disturbing that this Court now adopts a statutory interpretation that will interject an attorney's personal financial interests into the professional and ethical dynamics of the attorney-client relationship. These consequences demonstrate how untenable the Court's statutory interpretation is and counsel in favor of a different reading. See Milavetz, Gallop & Milavetz, P.A. v. United States, 559 U.S. ___, ___, n. 5, 130 S.Ct. 1324, 1338 n. 5, ___ L.Ed.2d ___ (2010) (rejecting a reading of federal law that "would seriously undermine the attorney-client relationship").

The Court's response is that this possibility is nothing new, because attorneys are already duty-bound to comply with the law and with standards of professional conduct. Attorneys face sanctions for harassing behavior and frivolous litigation, and in some cases misconduct may give rise to personal liability. Ante, at 1621-1622.

This response only underscores the problem with the Court's approach. By reading § 1692k(c) to exclude mistakes of law, the Court ensures that attorneys will 1635*1635 face liability even when they have done nothing wrong—indeed, even when they have acted in accordance with their professional responsibilities. Here respondents' law firm did not harass Jerman; it did not file a frivolous suit against her; it did not intentionally mislead her; it caused her no damages or injury. The firm acted upon a reasonable legal interpretation that the District Court later thought to be mistaken. The District Court's position, as all concede, was in conflict with other published, reasoned opinions. Ante, at 1610, n. 2. (And in the instant case, neither the Court of Appeals nor this Court has decided the issue. See ante, at 1610, n. 3.) If the law firm can be punished for making a good-faith legal error, then to be safe an attorney must always stick to the most debtor-friendly interpretation of the statute, lest automatic liability follow if some later decision adopts a different rule. This dynamic creates serious concerns, not only for the attorney-client relationship but also for First Amendment rights. Cf. Legal Services Corporation v. Velazquez, 531 U.S. 533, 545, 121 S.Ct. 1043, 149 L.Ed.2d 63 (2001) (law restricting arguments available to attorneys "prohibits speech and expression upon which courts must depend for the proper exercise of the judicial power"). We need not decide that these concerns rise to the level of an independent constitutional violation, see ante, at 1624, n. 21, to recognize that they counsel against a problematic interpretation of the statute. See Edward J. DeBartolo Corp. v. Florida Gulf Coast Building & Constr. Trades Council, 485 U.S. 568, 575, 108 S.Ct. 1392, 99 L.Ed.2d 645 (1988) ("[W]here an otherwise acceptable construction of a statute would raise serious constitutional problems, the Court will construe the statute to avoid such problems unless such construction is plainly contrary to the intent of Congress").

Justice BREYER—although not the Court—argues that an attorney faced with legal uncertainty only needs to turn to the Federal Trade Commission (FTC) for an advisory opinion. An attorney's actions in conformity with the opinion will be shielded from liability. Ante, at 1625 (concurring opinion) (citing 15 U.S.C. § 1692k(e)). This argument misconceives the practical realities of litigation. Filings and motions are made under pressing time constraints; arguments must be offered quickly in reply; and strategic decisions must be taken in the face of incomplete information. Lawyers in practice would not consider this alternative at all realistic, particularly where the defense is needed most.

And even were there time to generate a formal request to the FTC and wait an average of three or four months for a response (assuming the FTC responds at all), the argument assumes that an ambiguity in the statute is obvious, not latent, that the problem is at once apparent, and that a conscious decision to invoke FTC procedures can be made. But the problem in many instances is that interpretive alternatives are not at once apparent. All this may explain why, in the past decade, the FTC has issued only four opinions in response to just seven requests. See Tr. of Oral Arg. 27-28, 30. The FTC advisory process does not remedy the difficulties that the Court's opinion will cause.

Even if an FTC opinion is obtained, moreover, the ethical dilemma of counsel is not resolved. If the FTC adopts a position unfavorable to the client, the attorney may still believe the FTC is mistaken. Yet under today's decision, the attorney who in good faith continues to assert a reasonable position to the contrary does so at risk of personal liability. This alters the ethical balance central to the adversary system; and it is, again, a reason for the Court to 1636*1636 adopt a different, but still reasonable, interpretation to avoid systemic disruption.

II

The Court does not assert that its interpretation is clearly commanded by the text. Instead, its decision relies on an amalgam of arguments that, taken together, are said to establish the superiority of its preferred reading. This does not withstand scrutiny.

First, the Court relies on the maxim that "`ignorance of the law will not excuse any person, either civilly or criminally.'" Ante, at 1611 (quoting Barlow v. United States, 7 Pet. 404, 411, 8 L.Ed. 728 (1833)). There is no doubt that this principle "is deeply rooted in the American legal system." Cheek v. United States, 498 U.S. 192, 199, 111 S.Ct. 604, 112 L.Ed.2d 617 (1991). Yet it is unhelpful to the Court's position. The maxim the Court cites is based on the premise "that the law is definite and knowable," so that all must be deemed to know its mandate. Ibid. See also O. Holmes, The Common Law 48 (1881) ("[T]o admit the excuse [of ignorance] at all would be to encourage ignorance where the law-maker has determined to make men know and obey"). In other words, citizens cannot avoid compliance with the law simply by demonstrating a failure to learn it.

The most straightforward application of this principle is to statutory provisions that delineate a category of prohibited conduct. These statutes will not be read to excuse legal mistakes absent some indication that the legislature meant to do so. See, e.g., Armour Packing Co. v. United States, 209 U.S. 56, 70, 85-86, 28 S.Ct. 428, 52 L.Ed. 681 (1908) (rejecting the defendant's attempt to read a mistake-of-law defense into a criminal statute forbidding shippers to "obtain or dispose of property at less than the regular rate established"); ante, at 1612 (discussing a federal statute imposing liability for "intentional discrimination").

In the present case, however, the Court is not asked whether a mistake of law should excuse respondents from a general prohibition that would otherwise cover their conduct. Rather, the issue is the scope of an express exception to a general prohibition. There is good reason to think the distinction matters. It is one thing to presume that Congress does not intend to create an exception to a general rule through silence; it is quite another to presume that an explicit statutory exception should be confined despite the existence of other sensible interpretations. Cf. Kosak v. United States, 465 U.S. 848, 853, n. 9, 104 S.Ct. 1519, 79 L.Ed.2d 860 (1984) (although the Federal Tort Claims Act waives sovereign immunity, "the proper objective of a court attempting to construe [an exception to the Act] is to identify those circumstances which are within the words and reason of the exception—no less and no more" (internal quotation marks omitted)). This is all the more true where the other possible interpretations are more consistent with the purposes of the regulatory scheme. By its terms, § 1692k(c) encompasses—without limitation—all violations that are "not intentional and resul[t] from a bona fide error." The Court provides no reason to read this language narrowly.

The Court responds that "our precedents have made clear for more than 175 years" that the presumption against mistake-of-law defenses applies even to explicit statutory exceptions. Ante, 1611-1612, n. 5. By this the Court means that one case applied the presumption to an exception more than 175 years ago. In Barlow, the Court declined to excuse an alleged mistake of law despite a statutory provision that excepted "false denomination[s] 1637*1637. . . [that] happened by mistake or accident, and not from any intention to defraud the revenue." 7 Pet., at 406, 8 L.Ed. 728. In construing this language, the Barlow Court noted that it demonstrated congressional intent to exclude mistakes of law:

"The very association of mistake and accident, in this [connection], furnishes a strong ground to presume that the legislature had the same classes of cases in view . . . . Mistakes in the construction of the law, seem as little intended to be excepted by the proviso, as accidents in the construction of the law." Id., at 411-412.

Unlike the provision at issue in Barlow, § 1692k(c) gives no indication that its broad reference to "bona fide error[s]" was meant to exclude legal mistakes.

Even if statutory exceptions should normally be construed to exclude mistakes of law, moreover, that guideline would only apply absent intent to depart from the general rule. There is no doubt that Congress may create a mistake-of-law defense; the question is whether it has done so here. See Ratzlaf, 510 U. S, at 149, 114 S.Ct. 655. As explained above, see Part I-A, supra, Congress has made its choice plain by using the word "violation" in § 1692k(c) to indicate that mistakes of law are to be included.

Second, the Court attempts to draw a contrast between § 1692k(c) and the administrative penalties in the Federal Trade Commission Act (FTC Act), 38 Stat. 717, 15 U.S.C. § 41 et seq. Under the FTC Act, a debt collector may face civil penalties of up to $16,000 per day for acting with "actual knowledge or knowledge fairly implied on the basis of objective circumstances that [an] act is" prohibited under the FDCPA. §§ 45(m)(1)(A), (C); 74 Fed. Reg. 858 (2009) (amending 16 CFR § 1.98(d) (2009)). The Court reasons that the FTC provision is meant to provide relatively harsh penalties for intentional violations. By contrast, the argument continues, the penalties in the FDCPA itself must cover—and hence § 1692k(c) must not excuse—unintentional violations. Ante, at 1612-1613.

The argument rests on a mistaken premise—namely, that § 1692k(c) must immunize all legal errors or none. This misreads the statute. As the text states, it applies only to "bona fide" errors committed despite "the maintenance of procedures reasonably adapted to avoid" these mistakes. So under a sensible reading of the statute, (1) intentional violations are punishable under the heightened penalties of the FTC Act; (2) unintentional violations are generally subject to punishment under the FDCPA; and (3) a defendant may escape liability altogether by proving that a violation was based on a bona fide error and that reasonable error-prevention procedures were in place. There is nothing incongruous in this scheme. Indeed, for the reasons described in Part I, supra, it is far less peculiar than the Court's reading, which would subject attorneys to liability for good-faith legal advocacy, even advocacy based on an accurate assessment of then-existing case law.

Third, in construing § 1692k(c) to exclude legal errors, the Court points to the requirement that a debt collector maintain "procedures reasonably adapted to avoid any such error." The Court asserts that this phrase most naturally evokes procedures to avoid clerical or factual mistakes. There is nothing natural in reading this phrase contrary to its plain terms, which do not distinguish between different categories of mistakes. Nor is there anything unusual about procedures adopted to avoid legal mistakes. The present case is again instructive. According to the District Court, respondents designated a lead 1638*1638 FDCPA compliance attorney, who regularly attended conferences and seminars; subscribed to relevant periodicals; distributed leading FDCPA cases to all attorneys; trained new attorneys on their statutory obligations; and held regular firm-wide meetings on FDCPA issues. See 538 F.3d 469, 477 (C.A.6 2008). These procedures are not only "reasonably adapted to avoid [legal] error[s]," but also accord with the FDCPA's purposes.

The Court argues, nonetheless, that the statute contemplates only clerical or factual errors, for these are the type of errors that can mostly naturally be addressed through "`a series of steps followed in a regular orderly definite way.'" Ante, at 1614 (quoting Webster's Third New International Dictionary 1807 (1976)). As made clear by the steps that respondents have taken to ensure FDCPA compliance, this is simply not true. The Court also speculates that procedures to avoid clerical or factual errors will be easier to implement than procedures to avoid legal errors. Even if this were not pure conjecture, it has nothing to do with what the statute requires. The statute does not talk about procedures that eliminate all—or even most—errors. It merely requires procedures "reasonably adapted to avoid any such error." The statute adopts the sensible approach of requiring reasonable safeguards if liability is to be avoided. This approach, not the Court's interpretation, reflects the reality of debt-collection practices.

Fourth, the Court argues that construing § 1692k(c) to encompass a mistake-of-law defense "is at odds with" the role contemplated for the FTC. Ante, at 1615. This is so, it contends, because the FTC is authorized to issue advisory opinions, and the statute shields from liability "any act done or omitted in good faith in conformity" with such opinions. § 1692k(e). But why, asks the Court, would a debt collector seek an opinion from the FTC if immunity under § 1692k(c) could be obtained simply by relying in good faith on advice from private counsel? Going further, the Court suggests that debt collectors might "have an affirmative incentive not to seek an advisory opinion to resolve ambiguity in the law, which would then prevent them from claiming good-faith immunity for violations." Ante, at 1615.

There is little substance to this line of reasoning. As the Court itself acknowledges, debt collectors would have an incentive to invoke the FTC safe harbor even if § 1692k(c) is construed to include a mistake-of-law defense, because the safe harbor provides a "more categorical immunity." Ante, at 1615, n. 8. Additionally, if a debt collector avoids seeking an advisory opinion from the FTC out of concern that the answer will be unfavorable, that seems quite at odds with saying that his or her ignorance is "bona fide."

It should be noted further that the Court's concern about encouraging ignorance could apply just as well to § 45(m)(1)(A). That provision subjects a debt collector to harsh penalties for violating an FTC rule "with actual knowledge or knowledge fairly implied on the basis of objective circumstances that such act is unfair or deceptive and is prohibited by such rule." No one contends that this will encourage debt collectors to avoid learning the FTC's rules. Yet there is no doubt that § 45(m)(1)(A) permits a mistake-of-law defense.

All this assumes, of course, that obtaining an FTC advisory opinion will be a reasonably practical possibility. For the reasons stated above, see Part I-B-2, supra, this is to be doubted. Even the Court recognizes the limited role that the FTC has played. Ante, at 1621 ("[E]vidence of present administrative practice makes us 1639*1639 reluctant to place significant weight on § 1692k(e) as a practical remedy").

Fifth, the Court asserts that "[a]ny remaining doubt" about its preferred interpretation is dispelled by the FDCPA's statutory history. The Court points to the fact that § 1692k(c) mirrors a bona fide error defense provision in the earlier enacted Truth in Lending Act (TILA), arguing that Congress sought to incorporate into the FDCPA the view of the Courts of Appeals that the TILA defense applied only to clerical errors. Ante, at 1615-1616. As Justice SCALIA points out, the Court's claims of judicial uniformity are overstated. See ante, at 1626-1627 (opinion concurring in part and concurring in judgment). They rest on three Court of Appeals decisions, which are contradicted by several District Court opinions and a State Supreme Court opinion—hardly a consistent legal backdrop against which to divine legislative intent. The Court also ignores the fact that those three Courts of Appeals had construed the TILA provision to apply only to clerical errors. See Ives v. W.T. Grant Co., 522 F.2d 749, 758 (C.A.2 1975); Haynes v. Logan Furniture Mart, Inc., 503 F.2d 1161, 1167 (C.A.7 1974); Palmer v. Wilson, 502 F.2d 860, 861 (C.A.9 1974). The Court therefore cannot explain why it reads § 1692k(c) more broadly to encompass factual mistakes as well.

It is of even greater significance that in 1980 Congress amended the TILA's bona fide error exception explicitly to exclude "an error of legal judgment with respect to a person's obligations under [the TILA]." See Truth in Lending Simplification and Reform Act, § 615(c), 94 Stat. 181. This amendment would have been unnecessary if Congress had understood the pre-1980 language to exclude legal errors. The natural inference is that the pre-amendment TILA language—the same language later incorporated nearly verbatim into § 1692k(c)—was understood to cover those errors.

The Court's responses to this point are perplexing. The Court first says that the 1980 amendment did not "obvious[ly]" change the scope of the TILA's bona fide error defense, given the "uniform interpretation" that the defense had been given in the Courts of Appeals. Ante, at 1617. The Court thus prefers to make an entire statutory amendment surplusage rather than abandon its dubious assumption that Congress meant to ratify a nascent Court of Appeals consensus. Cf. Corley v. United States, 556 U.S. ___, ___, 129 S.Ct. 1558, 1560, 173 L.Ed.2d 443 (2009) ("[O]ne of the most basic interpretive canons [is] that [a] statute should be construed so that effect is given to all its provisions, so that no part will be inoperative or superfluous, void or insignificant" (internal quotation marks omitted; second alteration in original)). (Without any evidence, the Court speculates that perhaps the amendment was intended to codify existing judicial interpretations that excluded legal errors. Ante, at 1617-1618. If those judicial interpretation were truly as uniform as the Court suggests—and the presumption against mistake-of-law defenses as ironclad—there would have been no need for such a recodification.)

The Court is hesitant as well to give the 1980 amendment weight because Congress "has not expressly included mistakes of law in any of the numerous bona fide error defenses, worded in pertinent part identically to § 1692k(c), elsewhere in the U.S.Code." Ante, at 1618 (emphasis in original). In other words, the Court refuses to read § 1692k(c) to cover mistakes of law because other bona fide error statutes do not expressly refer to such mistakes. But the reverse should be true: If other bona fide error provisions included mistake-of-law language but § 1692k(c) did 1640*1640 not, we might think that the omission in § 1692k(c) signaled Congress's intent to exclude mistakes of law. The absence of mistake-of-law language in § 1692k(c) is consequently less noteworthy because other statutes also omit such language.

The Court emphasizes that some bona fide error defenses, like the one in the current version of the TILA, expressly exclude legal errors from their scope. Ante, at 1617-1618 (citing 12 U.S.C. § 4010(c)(2)). Yet this also can prove the opposite of what the Court says it does: If a bona fide error defense were generally assumed not to include legal mistakes (as the Court argues), there would be no need to expressly exclude them. It is only if the defense would otherwise include such errors that exclusionary language becomes necessary. By writing explicit exclusionary language into the TILA (and some other federal provisions), Congress has indicated that those provisions would otherwise cover good-faith legal errors.

* * *

For these reasons, § 1692k(c) is best read to encompass mistakes of law. I would affirm the judgment of the Court of Appeals.

[1] Section 1692g(a)(3) requires a debt collector, within five days of an "initial communication" about the collection of a debt, to send the consumer a written notice containing, inter alia, "a statement that unless the consumer, within thirty days after receipt of the notice, disputes the validity of the debt, or any portion thereof, the debt will be assumed to be valid by the debt collector."

[2] The District Court distinguished, for instance, Graziano v. Harrison, 950 F.2d 107, 112 (C.A.3 1991), which held a consumer's dispute of a debt under § 1692g must be in writing to be effective. Noting that district courts within the Sixth Circuit had reached different results, and distinguishing one unpublished Sixth Circuit decision which Carlisle suggested approved a form with an in-writing requirement, the court adopted the reasoning from Camacho v. Bridgeport Financial, Inc., 430 F.3d 1078, 1080-1082 (C.A.9 2005), and held that the plain language of § 1692g does not impose an "in writing" requirement on consumers. See 464 F.Supp.2d, at 725.

[3] Because the question was not raised on appeal, the Court of Appeals did not address whether Carlisle's inclusion of the "in writing" requirement violated § 1692g. 538 F.3d, at 472, n. 2. We likewise express no view about whether inclusion of an "in writing" requirement in a notice to a consumer violates § 1692g, as that question was not presented in the petition for certiorari. Compare Graziano, supra, at 112 (reading § 1692g(a)(3) to require that "any dispute, to be effective, must be in writing"), with Camacho, supra, at 1082 (under § 1692g(a)(3), "disputes need not be made in writing").

[4] Compare, e.g., 538 F.3d, at 476 (case below), with Baker v. G.C. Servs. Corp., 677 F.2d 775, 779 (C.A.9 1982), and Hulshizer v. Global Credit Servs., Inc., 728 F.2d 1037, 1038 (C.A.8 1984) (per curiam).

The Courts of Appeals have also expressed different views about whether 15 U.S.C. § 1692k(c) applies to violations of the FDCPA resulting from a misinterpretation of the requirements of state law. Compare Johnson v. Riddle, 305 F.3d 1107, 1121 (C.A.10 2002) (concluding that § 1692k(c) applies where a debt collector's misinterpretation of a Utah dishonored check statute resulted in a violation of § 1692f(1), which prohibits collection of any amount not "permitted by law"), with Picht v. Jon R. Hawks, Ltd., 236 F.3d 446, 451-452 (C.A.8 2001) (stating that § 1692k(c) does not preclude FDCPA liability resulting from a creditor's mistaken legal interpretation of a Minnesota garnishment statute). The parties disagree about whether § 1692k(c) applies when a violation results from a debt collector's misinterpretation of the legal requirements of state law or federal law other than the FDCPA. Compare Brief for Petitioner 47-49, with Brief for Respondents 60-62. Because this case involves only an alleged misinterpretation of the requirements of the FDCPA, we need not, and do not, reach those other questions.

[5] The dissent discounts the relevance of the principle here, on grounds that this case involves the scope of a statutory exception to liability, rather than a provision "delineat[ing] a category of prohibited conduct." Post, at 1636 (opinion of KENNEDY, J.). That is a distinction without a difference, as our precedents have made clear for more than 175 years. Barlow involved a statute providing for forfeiture of any goods entered "by a false denomination" in the office of a customs collector "for the benefit of drawback or bounty upon the exportation"; the statute included, however, an exception under which "said forfeiture shall not be incurred, if it shall be made appear . . . that such false denomination. . . happened by mistake or accident, and not from any intention to defraud the revenue." 7 Pet., at 406, 8 L.Ed. 728; see also Act of Mar. 2, 1799, § 84, 1 Stat. 694. The Court concluded that the shipment at issue, entered as "refined sugars," was mislabeled under the prevailing meaning of that term and thus was subject to forfeiture "unless the [petitioner] c[ould] bring himself within the exceptio[n]." 7 Pet., at 409-410, 8 L.Ed. 728. As there had been no "accident" or "mistake" of fact, the "only mistake, if there ha[d] been any, [wa]s a mistake of law." Id., at 410-411. The Court observed that the shipper's conduct, even if "entirely compatible with good faith, [wa]s not wholly free from the suspicion of an intention to overreach. . . by passing off, as refined sugars, what he well knew were not admitted to be such." Id., at 411. But the Court declined to resolve the case on the ground of the shipper's intent, instead invoking the "common maxim, familiar to all minds, that ignorance of the law will not excuse any person, either civilly or criminally." Ibid. Notwithstanding the existence of a statutory exception—which did not expressly exclude legal errors from the category of "mistake[s]" made without "intention to defraud"—the Court saw "not the least reason to suppose that the legislature, in this enactment, had any intention to supersede the common principle." Ibid.

The dissent implies Barlow is too old to be relevant. Post, at 1636-1637. But at least in the context of stare decisis, this Court has suggested precedents tend to gain, not lose, respect with age. See Montejo v. Louisiana, 556 U.S. ___, ___, 129 S.Ct. 2079, 2088, 173 L.Ed.2d 955 (2009). In any event, Justice Story's opinion for a unanimous Court in Barlow is hardly a relic. As recently as 1994 this Court cited it for the "venerable principle" that ignorance of the law generally is no defense. Ratzlaf v. United States, 510 U.S. 135, 149,

114 S.Ct. 655, 126 L.Ed.2d 615; see also Cheek v. United States, 498 U.S. 192, 199, 111 S.Ct. 604, 112 L.Ed.2d 617 (1991) (citing Barlow for a similar proposition).

[6] Different considerations apply, of course, in interpreting criminal statutes. Safeco Ins. Co. of America v. Burr, 551 U.S. 47, 57-58, n. 9, 127 S.Ct. 2201, 167 L.Ed.2d 1045 (2007). But even in that context, we have not consistently required knowledge that the offending conduct is unlawful. See, e.g., Ellis v. United States, 206 U.S. 246, 255, 257, 27 S.Ct. 600, 51 L.Ed. 1047 (1907) (observing, in the context of a statute imposing liability for "intentiona[l] violat[ions]," that "[i]f a man intentionally adopts certain conduct in certain circumstances known to him, and that conduct is forbidden by the law under those circumstances, he intentionally breaks the law in the only sense in which the law ever considers intent").

[7] Indeed, in International Minerals, the Court faced, and evidently rejected, the distinction the dissent would draw today between the term "`violation'" and a reference to "the conduct giving rise to the violation." Post, at 1629. As noted, in International Minerals, the Court rejected a mistake-of-law defense for a statute that applied to those who "knowingly violat[e]" certain regulations. 402 U.S., at 559, 563, 91 S.Ct. 1697. In so doing, however, we expressly acknowledged the contrary view adopted by one lower court opinion that knowledge of the regulations was necessary. Id., at 562, 91 S.Ct. 1697 (citing St. Johnsbury Trucking Co. v. United States, 220 F.2d 393, 397 (C.A.1 1955) (Magruder, C.J., concurring)). The dissenting opinion in International Minerals quoted extensively portions of the St. Johnsbury concurrence that reached its result by contrasting a statute making it an offense "`"knowingly" to sell adulterated milk'" with one that makes it an offense "`knowingly [to] violat[e] a regulation.'" 402 U.S., at 566, 91 S.Ct. 1697 (Stewart, J., dissenting) (quoting St. Johnsbury, supra, at 398).

Liparota v. United States, 471 U.S. 419, 105 S.Ct. 2084, 85 L.Ed.2d 434 (1985), is also inapposite. Cf. post, at 1630 (KENNEDY, J., dissenting). Concluding that a mistake-of-law defense is available under a provision that specifies particular conduct undertaken while "`knowing'" that food stamp coupons had been "`used in any manner in violation of [law],'" 471 U.S., at 428, n. 12 [105 S.Ct. 2084], says little about the meaning of a "not intentional" "violation" in 15 U.S.C. § 1692k(c). Indeed, the statute in Liparota bears a closer resemblance to the administrative penalty provision in § 45(m)(1)(A). See supra, at 1612-1613.

[8] One of Carlisle's amici suggests the FTC safe harbor would provide a more categorical immunity than § 1692k(c), obviating the need, e.g., to maintain "procedures reasonably adapted to avoid any such error." Brief for National Association of Retail Collection Attorneys as Amicus Curiae 18-19 (NARCA Brief). Even if that is true, we need not conclude

that the FTC safe harbor would be rendered entirely superfluous to reason that the existence of that provision counsels against extending the bona fide error defense to serve an overlapping function.

[9] Carlisle raises concerns about whether, in light of contemporary administrative practice, the FTC safe harbor is a realistic way for debt collectors and their lawyers to seek guidance on the numerous time-sensitive legal issues that arise in litigation. These practical concerns, to which we return below, do not change our understanding of the statutory text itself or the likely intent of the enacting Congress.

[10] See Ives v. W.T. Grant Co., 522 F.2d 749, 757-758 (C.A.2 1975) (concluding that the bona fide error defense in § 1640(c) was unavailable despite creditor's reliance, in selecting language for credit contract forms, on a pamphlet issued by the Federal Reserve Board); Haynes v. Logan Furniture Mart, Inc., 503 F.2d 1161, 1167 (C.A.7 1974) ("[Section] 1640(c) offers no shelter from liability for the defendant, whose error . . . was judgmental with respect to legal requirements of the Act and not clerical in nature"); Palmer v. Wilson, 502 F.2d 860, 861 (C.A.9 1974) (similar). Carlisle contends the meaning of TILA's defense was unsettled at the time of the FDCPA's enactment, relying first on several District Court opinions extending the defense to good-faith legal errors. See, e.g., Welmaker v. W.T. Grant Co., 365 F.Supp. 531, 544 (N.D.Ga.1972). But even assuming Congress would have looked to district court, rather than court of appeals, opinions in discerning the meaning of the statutory language, applicable Circuit precedent had cast some doubt on those decisions by the time the FDCPA was enacted. See, e.g., Turner v. Firestone Tire & Rubber Co., 537 F.2d 1296, 1298 (C.A.5 1976) (per curiam) (referring to § 1640(c) as the "so-called clerical error defense"). Carlisle also relies on the holding in Thrift Funds of Baton Rouge, Inc. v. Jones, 274 So.2d 150 (La. 1973). But in that case, the Louisiana Supreme Court concluded only that a lender's mistaken interpretation of state usury law did not "amoun[t] to an intentional violation of [TILA's] disclosure requirements." Id., at 161. The Louisiana court had no occasion to address the question analogous to the one we consider today: whether TILA's bona fide error defense extended to violations resulting from mistaken interpretation of TILA itself. See n. 4, supra; see also Starks v. Orleans Motors, Inc., 372 F.Supp. 928, 931 (E.D.La.) (distinguishing Thrift Funds on this basis), aff'd, 500 F.2d 1182 (C.A.5 1974). These precedents therefore do not convince us that Congress would have ascribed a different meaning to the statutory language it chose for the FDCPA. Compare post, at 1626 (SCALIA, J., concurring in part and concurring in judgment), with Herman & MacLean v. Huddleston, 459 U.S. 375, 384-386, and n. 21, 103 S.Ct. 683, 74 L.Ed.2d 548 (1983) (concluding that Congress had "ratified" the "well-established judicial interpretation" of a statute by leaving it intact during a comprehensive revision, notwithstanding "[t]wo early district court decisions," not subsequently followed, that had adopted a contrary view).

[11] That only three Courts of Appeals had occasion to address the question by the time the FDCPA was enacted does not render such an inference unreasonable. Contra, post, at 1625-1626 (opinion of SCALIA, J.). Whether or not we would take that view when such an inference serves as a court's sole interpretative guide, here our conclusion also relies on common principles of statutory interpretation, as well as the statute's text and structure. Moreover, the inference is supported by the fact that TILA and the FDCPA were enacted as complementary titles of the CCPA, a comprehensive consumer-protection statute. While not necessary to our conclusion, evidence from the legislative record demonstrates that some Members of Congress understood the relationship between the FDCPA and existing provisions of the CCPA. See, e.g., 123 Cong. Rec. 10242 (1977) (remarks of Rep. Annunzio) (civil penalty provisions in House version of bill were "consistent with those in the [CCPA]"); Fair Debt Collection Practices Act: Hearings on S. 656 et al. before the Subcommittee on Consumer Affairs of the Senate Committee on Banking, Housing and Urban Affairs, 95th Cong., 1st Sess., 51, 707 (1977) (statement of Rep. Wylie) (describing "[c]ivil liability provisions" in the House bill as "the standard provisions that attach to all the titles of the [CCPA]").

[12] Although again not necessary to our conclusion, evidence from the legislative record suggests some Members of Congress understood the amendment to "clarif[y]" the meaning of TILA's bona fide error defense "to make clear that it applies to mechanical and computer errors, provided they are not the result of erroneous legal judgments as to the act's requirements." S.Rep. No. 96-73, pp. 7-8 (1979), U.S.Code Cong. & Admin.News 1980, pp. 280, 284-86; see also Lockhart, 153 A.L.R. Fed. 211-212, § 2[a] (1999) (amendment "was intended merely to clarify what was then the prevailing view, that the bona fide error defense applies to clerical errors, not including errors of legal judgment") (relying on S.Rep. No. 96-368, p. 32 (1979), U.S.Code Cong. & Admin.News 1980, pp. 236, 267).

The concurring and dissenting opinions perceive an inconsistency between these references to clerical errors, as well as similar references in the pre-FDCPA precedents interpreting TILA, n. 10, supra, and reading the FDCPA's bona fide error defense to include factual mistakes. Post, at 1626-1627, and n. 2 (opinion of SCALIA, J.); post, at 1638-1639 (KENNEDY, J., dissenting). The quoted legislative history sources, however, while stating expressly that the TILA defense excludes legal errors, do not discuss a distinction between clerical and factual errors. Similarly, the cited cases interpreting TILA do not address a distinction between factual and clerical errors; rather, the courts were presented with claims that the defense applied to mistakes of law or other nonfactual errors that the courts found not to be bona fide. See Ives, 522 F.2d, at 756-757; Haynes, 503 F.2d, at 1166-1167; Palmer, 502 F.2d, at 861. While factual mistakes might, in some circumstances, constitute bona fide errors and give rise to violations that are "not intentional" within the meaning of § 1692k(c), we need not and do not decide today the precise distinction between clerical and factual errors, or what kinds of factual mistakes qualify under the FDCPA's bona fide error defense. Cf. generally R. Hobbs, National Consumer Law Center, Fair Debt Collection § 7.2 (6th ed.2008 and Supp.2009) (surveying case law on scope of § 1692k(c)).

[13] The Government observes that several federal agencies have construed similar bona fide error defenses in statutes they administer to exclude errors of law. See Brief for United States as Amicus Curiae 28-30. The Secretary of Housing and Urban Development, for instance, has promulgated regulations specifying that the bona fide error defense in the Real Estate Settlement Procedures Act of 1974, 12 U.S.C. § 2607(d)(3), does not apply to "[a]n error of legal judgment," 24 CFR § 3500.15(b)(1)(ii) (2009). While administrative interpretations of other statutes do not control our reading of the FDCPA, we find it telling that no agency has adopted the view of the Court of Appeals. Of course, nothing in our opinion today addresses the validity of such regulations or the authority of agencies interpreting bona fide error provisions in other statutes to adopt a different reading. See National Cable & Telecommunications Assn. v. Brand X Internet Services, 545 U.S. 967, 982-983, 125 S.Ct. 2688, 162 L.Ed.2d 820 (2005).

[14] For instance, an amendment was proposed and rejected during the Senate Banking Committee's consideration of the FDCPA that would have required proof that a debt collector's violation was "knowin[g]." Senator Riegle, one of the Act's primary sponsors, opposed the change, explaining that the bill reflected the view that "certain things ought not to happen, period. . . . [W]hether somebody does it knowingly, willfully, you know, with a good heart, bad heart, is really quite incidental." See Senate Committee on Banking, Housing and Urban Affairs, Markup Session: S. 1130—Debt Collection Legislation 60 (July 26, 1977) (hereinafter Markup); see also ibid. ("We have left a way for these disputes to be adj[u]dicated if they are brought, where somebody can say, I didn't know that, or my computer malfunctioned, something happened, I didn't intend for the effect to be as it was"). To similar effect, a House Report on an earlier version of the bill explained the need for new legislation governing use of the mails for debt collection on grounds that existing statutes "frequently require[d]" a showing of "specific intent[,] which is difficult to prove." H.R.Rep. No. 95-131, p. 3 (1977). Elsewhere, to be sure, the legislative record contains statements more supportive of Carlisle's interpretation. In particular, a concern was raised in the July 26 markup session that the TILA bona fide error defense had been interpreted "as only protecting against a mathematical error," and that the FDCPA defense should "go beyond" TILA to "allow the courts discretion to dismiss a violation where it was a technical error." Markup 20. In response, a staffer explained that the FDCPA defense would "apply to any violation of the act which was unintentional," and answered affirmatively when the Chairman asked: "So it's not simply a mathematical error but any bona fide error without intent?" Id., at 21. Whatever the precise balance of these statements may be, we can conclude that this equivocal evidence from legislative history does not displace the clear textual and contextual authority discussed above.

[15] The dissent also cites several other consumer-protection statutes, such as TILA and the Fair Credit Reporting Act, 15 U.S.C. § 1681 et seq., which in its view create "incentives to file lawsuits even where no actual harm has occurred" and are illustrative of what the dissent perceives to be a "troubling dynamic of allowing certain actors in the system to spin even good-faith, technical violations of federal law into lucrative litigation." Post, at 1631. The dissent's concern is primarily with Congress' policy choice, embodied in statutory text, to authorize private rights of action and recovery of attorney's fees, costs, and in some cases, both actual and statutory damages. As noted, in one of the statutes the dissent cites, Congress explicitly barred reliance on a mistake-of-law defense notwithstanding the "highly technical" nature of the scheme. See 15 U.S.C. § 1640(c) (TILA); Ford Motor Credit Co. v. Milhollin, 444 U.S. 555, 566, 100 S.Ct. 790, 63 L.Ed.2d 22 (1980). Similarly, the plain text of the FDCPA authorizes a private plaintiff to recover not only "actual damage[s]" for harm suffered but also "such additional damages as the court may allow," § 1692k(a).

[16] The Courts of Appeals generally review a District Court's calculation of an attorney fee award under § 1692k for abuse of discretion. See, e.g., Carroll v. Wolpoff & Abramson, 53 F.3d 626, 628-629 (C.A.4 1995); Emanuel v. American Credit Exchange, 870 F.2d 805, 809 (C.A.2 1989). Many District Courts apply a lodestar method, permitting downward adjustments in appropriate circumstances. See, e.g., Schlacher v. Law Offices of Phillip J. Rotche & Assoc., P. C., 574 F.3d 852 (C.A.7 2009) (relying on Hensley v. Eckerhart, 461 U.S. 424, 103 S.Ct. 1933, 76 L.Ed.2d 40 (1983)); Ferland v. Conrad Credit Corp., 244 F.3d 1145, 1148-1151, and n. 4 (C.A.9 2001) (per curiam); see generally Hobbs, Fair Debt Collection § 6.8.6. In Schlacher, for instance, the court affirmed a downward adjustment for the "unnecessary use of multiple attorneys. . . in a straightforward, short-lived [FDCPA] case." 574 F.3d, at 854-855. In Carroll, the court found no abuse of discretion in a District Court's award of a $500 attorney's fee, rather than the lodestar amount, where the lawsuit had recovered only $50 in damages for "at most a technical violation" of the FDCPA. 53 F.3d, at 629-631.

Lower courts have taken different views about when, and whether, § 1692k requires an award of attorney's fees. Compare Tolentino v. Friedman, 46 F.3d 645 (C.A.7 1995) (award of fees to a successful plaintiff "mandatory"), and Emanuel, supra, at 808-809 (same, even where the plaintiff suffered no actual damages), with Graziano, 950 F.2d, at 114, and n. 13 (attorney's fees may be denied for plaintiff's "bad faith conduct"), and Johnson v. Eaton, 80 F.3d 148, 150-152 (C.A.5 1996) ("attorney's fees . . . are only available [under § 1692k] where the plaintiff has succeeded in establishing that the defendant is liable for actual and/or additional damages"; this reading "will deter suits brought only as a means of generating attorney's fees"). We need not resolve these issues today to express doubt that our reading of § 1692k(c) will impose unmanageable burdens on debt collecting lawyers.

[17] See Brief for Ohio Creditor's Attorneys Association et al. as Amici Curiae 4-6, and nn. 7-8 (identifying "134 state consumer protection and debt collection statutes," 42 of which expressly exclude legal errors from their defenses for bona fide errors).

[18] See, e.g., Kan. Stat. Ann. § 16a-5-201(7) (2007) (provision of Kansas Consumer Credit Code providing a defense for a "bona fide error of law or fact"); Ind. Code § 24-9-5-5 (West 2004) (defense for creditor's "bona fide error of law or fact" in Indiana Home Loan Practices Act).

[19] The dissent also downplays the predicate fact that respondents in this case brought a foreclosure lawsuit against Jerman for a debt she had already repaid. Neither the lower courts nor this Court have been asked to consider, and thus we express no view about, whether Carlisle could be subject to liability under the FDCPA for that uncontested error—regardless of how reasonably Carlisle may have acted after the mistake was pointed out by Jerman's (privately retained) lawyer.

[20] Compare Hartman v. Great Senaca Financial Corp., 569 F.3d 606, 614-615 (C.A.6 2009) (suggesting that reasonable procedures might include "perform[ing] ongoing FDCPA training, procur[ing] the most recent case law, or hav[ing] an individual responsible for continuing compliance with the FDCPA"), with Johnson v. Riddle, 443 F.3d 723, 730-731 (C.A.10 2006) (suggesting that researching case law and filing a test case might be sufficient, but remanding for a jury determination of whether the "limited [legal] analysis" undertaken was sufficient and whether the test case was in fact a "sham").

[21] The dissent adds in passing that today's decision "creates serious concerns . . . for First Amendment rights." Post, at 1635 (citing Legal Services Corporation v. Velazquez, 531 U.S. 533, 545, 121 S.Ct. 1043, 149 L.Ed.2d 63 (2001)). That claim was neither raised nor passed upon below, and was mentioned neither in the certiorari papers nor the parties' merits briefing to this Court. We decline to express any view on it. See Cutter v. Wilkinson, 544 U.S. 709, 718, n. 7, 125 S.Ct. 2113, 161 L.Ed.2d 1020 (2005).

[22] The FDCPA has been amended some eight times since its enactment in 1977; the most recent amendment addressed a concern not unrelated to the question we consider today, specifying that a pleading in a civil action is not an "initial communication" triggering obligations under § 1692g requiring a written notice to the consumer. Financial Services Regulatory Relief Act of 2006, § 802(a), 120 Stat. 2006 (codified at 15 U.S.C. § 1692g(d)).

[1] Of course where so many federal courts have read the language that way, the text was probably clear enough that resort to unexpressed congressional intent would be unnecessary. Or indeed it could be said that such uniform and longstanding judicial interpretation

had established the public meaning of the text, whether the Members of Congress were aware of the cases or not. That would be the understanding of the text by reasonable people familiar with its legal context.

[2] The page cited in the Senate Committee Report does not actually support the American Law Report's statement. It makes no mention of clarification or judicial interpretations; it merely states that the amendment is intended to "provide protection where errors are clerical or mechanical in nature," S.Rep. No. 96-368, p. 32 (1979), U.S.Code Cong. & Admin. News 1980, at p. 267.

CITATIONS

On a related note, this Court observes that the Supreme Court recently held that the "bona fide error" defense does not apply to "a violation resulting from a debt collector's mistaken interpretation of the legal requirements of the FDCPA." - in Bradshaw v. HILCO RECEIVABLES, LLC, 2010

If that were true, one could say that those decisions had established the public meaning of the term in this context-whether Congress knew of (or agreed with) that meaning or not. - in Merck & Co., Inc. v. Reynolds, 2010

In other words, a debt collector's conduct may be intentional even if he lacked the actual knowledge that his conduct violated the FDCPA. - in Bassett v. IC System, Inc., 2010

The sole basis for federal jurisdiction was the FDCPA, which was enacted "to eliminate abusive debt collection practices, to ensure that debt collectors who abstain from such practices are not competitively disadvantaged, and to promote consistent state action to protect consumers." - in Solomon v. HSBC MORTGAGE CORPORATION, 2010

This case does not involve statutory regulation of the activity of various market players, say, for example, of lawyers functioning as debt collectors. - in THE REAL ESTATE BAR v. NATIONAL REAL ESTATE INFO., 2010

"We have long recognized the 'common maxim, familiar to all minds, that ignorance of the law will not excuse any person, either civilly or criminally.' " - in UNITED STATES COURT OF APPEALS TENTH CIRCUIT

The FDCPA subjects debt collectors to civil liability for engaging in certain proscribed debt collection practices. - in AGUEROS v. HUDSON & KEYSE, LLC, 2010

"Among other things, the Act prohibits debt collectors from making false representations as to a debt's character, amount, or legal status, § 1692e (2)(A); communicating with consumers at an `unusual time or place' likely to be inconvenient to the consumer, § 1692c (a)(1); or using obscene or profane language or violence or the threat thereof, §§ 1692d (1),(2). " - in Bassett v. IC System, Inc., 2010

The bona fide defense may only be used in circumstances where a violation results from other causes, such as a clerical or factual mistake. - in Bradshaw v. HILCO RECEIVABLES, LLC, 2010

8

FDCPA AND FCRA OFFICIAL US CODE

Federal Trade Commission's Frequently Asked Questions (FAQ) Regarding Debt Collection

(Source: Federal Trade Commission Website www.ftc.gov)

What types of debts are covered?
The Act covers personal, family, and household debts, including money you owe on a personal credit card account, an auto loan, a medical bill, and your mortgage. The FDCPA doesn't cover debts you incurred to run a business.

Can a debt collector contact me any time or any place?
No. A debt collector may not contact you at inconvenient times or places, such as before 8 in the morning or after 9 at night, unless you agree to it. And collectors may not contact you at work if they're told (orally or in writing) that you're not allowed to get calls there.

How can I stop a debt collector from contacting me?
If a collector contacts you about a debt, you may want to talk to them at least once to see if you can resolve the matter – even if you don't think you owe the debt, can't repay it immediately, or think that the collector is contacting you by mistake. If you decide after contacting the debt collector that you don't want the collector to contact you again, tell the collector – in writing – to stop contacting you. Here's how to do that:

Make a copy of your letter. Send the original by certified mail, and pay for a "return receipt" so you'll be able to document what the collector received. Once the collector receives your letter, they may not contact you again, with two exceptions: a collector can contact you to tell you there will be no further contact or to let you know that they or the creditor intend to take a specific action, like filing a lawsuit. Sending such a letter to a debt collector you owe money to does not get rid of the debt, but it should stop the contact. The creditor or the debt collector still can sue you to collect the debt.

Can a debt collector contact anyone else about my debt?

If an attorney is representing you about the debt, the debt collector must contact the attorney, rather than you. If you don't have an attorney, a collector may contact other people – but only to find out your address, your home phone number, and where you work. Collectors usually are prohibited from contacting third parties more than once. Other than to obtain this location information about you, a debt collector generally is not permitted to discuss your debt with anyone other than you, your spouse, or your attorney.

What does the debt collector have to tell me about the debt?

Every collector must send you a written "validation notice" telling you how much money you owe within five days after they first contact you. This notice also must include the name of the creditor to whom you owe the money, and how to proceed if you don't think you owe the money.

Can a debt collector keep contacting me if I don't think I owe any money?

If you send the debt collector a letter stating that you don't owe any or all of the money, or asking for verification of the debt, that collector must stop contacting you. You have to send that letter within 30 days after you receive the validation notice. But a collector can begin contacting you again if they send you written verification of the debt, like a copy of a bill for the amount you owe.

What practices are off limits for debt collectors?

Harassment. Debt collectors may not harass, oppress, or abuse you or any third parties they contact. For example, they may not:

use threats of violence or harm;
publish a list of names of people who refuse to pay their debts (but they can give this information to the credit reporting companies);
use obscene or profane language; or
repeatedly use the phone to annoy someone.
False statements. Debt collectors may not lie when they are trying to collect a debt. For example, they may not:

falsely claim that they are attorneys or government representatives;
falsely claim that you have committed a crime;
falsely represent that they operate or work for a credit reporting company;
misrepresent the amount you owe;

indicate that papers they send you are legal forms if they aren't; or
indicate that papers they send to you aren't legal forms if they are.

Debt collectors also are prohibited from saying that:

you will be arrested if you don't pay your debt;
they'll seize, garnish, attach, or sell your property or wages unless they are permitted by law to take the action and intend to do so; or
legal action will be taken against you, if doing so would be illegal or if they don't intend to take the action.

Debt collectors may not:

give false credit information about you to anyone, including a credit reporting company;
send you anything that looks like an official document from a court or government agency if it isn't; or
use a false company name.

Unfair practices. Debt collectors may not engage in unfair practices when they try to collect a debt. For example, they may not:

try to collect any interest, fee, or other charge on top of the amount you owe unless the contract that created your debt – or your state law – allows the charge;
deposit a post-dated check early;
take or threaten to take your property unless it can be done legally; or
contact you by postcard.
Can I control which debts my payments apply to?
Yes. If a debt collector is trying to collect more than one debt from you, the collector must apply any payment you make to the debt you select. Equally important, a debt collector may not apply a payment to a debt you don't think you owe.

Can a debt collector garnish my bank account or my wages?
If you don't pay a debt, a creditor or its debt collector generally can sue you to collect. If they win, the court will enter a judgment against you. The judgment states the amount of money you owe, and allows the creditor or collector to get a garnishment order against you, directing a third party, like your bank, to turn over funds from your account to pay the debt.

Wage garnishment happens when your employer withholds part of your compensation to pay your debts. Your wages usually can be garnished only as the result of a court order. Don't ignore a lawsuit summons. If you do, you lose the opportunity to fight a wage garnishment.

Can federal benefits be garnished?
Many federal benefits are exempt from garnishment, including:

- Social Security Benefits
- Supplemental Security Income (SSI) Benefits
- Veterans' Benefits
- Civil Service and Federal Retirement and Disability Benefits
- Service Members' Pay
- Military Annuities and Survivors' Benefits
- Student Assistance
- Railroad Retirement Benefits
- Merchant Seamen Wages
- Longshoremen's and Harbor Workers' Death and Disability Benefits
- Foreign Service Retirement and Disability Benefits
- Compensation for Injury, Death, or Detention of Employees of U.S. Contractors Outside the U.S.
- Federal Emergency Management Agency Federal Disaster Assistance

But federal benefits may be garnished under certain circumstances, including to pay delinquent taxes, alimony, child support, or student loans.

Do I have any recourse if I think a debt collector has violated the law?
You have the right to sue a collector in a state or federal court within one year from the date the law was violated. If you win, the judge can require the collector to pay you for any damages you can prove you suffered because of the illegal collection practices, like lost wages and medical bills. The judge can require the debt collector to pay you up to $1,000, even if you can't prove that you suffered actual damages. You also can be reimbursed for your attorney's fees and court costs. A group of people also may sue a debt collector as part of a class action lawsuit and recover money for damages up to $500,000, or one percent of the collector's net worth, whichever amount is lower. Even if a debt collector violates the FDCPA in trying to collect a debt, the debt does not go away if you owe it.

What should I do if a debt collector sues me?
If a debt collector files a lawsuit against you to collect a debt, respond to the lawsuit, either personally or through your lawyer, by the date specified in the court papers to preserve your rights.

THE FAIR DEBT COLLECTION PRACTICES ACT TITLE 15, US CODE, SECTION §1692

As amended by Pub. L. 109-351, §§ 801-02, 120 Stat. 1966 (2006)

§ 801. Short Title

This title may be cited as the "Fair Debt Collection Practices Act."

§ 802. Congressional findings and declaration of purpose
(a) There is abundant evidence of the use of abusive, deceptive, and unfair debt collection practices by many debt collectors. Abusive debt collection practices contribute to the number of personal bankruptcies, to marital instability, to the loss of jobs, and to invasions of individual privacy.
(b) Existing laws and procedures for redressing these injuries are inadequate to protect consumers.
(c) Means other than misrepresentation or other abusive debt collection practices are

available for the effective collection of debts.

(d) Abusive debt collection practices are carried on to a substantial extent in interstate commerce and through means and instrumentalities of such commerce. Even where abusive debt collection practices are purely intrastate in character, they nevertheless directly affect interstate commerce.

(e) It is the purpose of this title to eliminate abusive debt collection practices by debt collectors, to insure that those debt collectors who refrain from using abusive debt collection practices are not competitively disadvantaged, and to promote consistent State action to protect consumers against debt collection abuses.

§ 803. Definitions

As used in this title—

(1) The term "Commission" means the Federal Trade Commission.

(2) The term "communication" means the conveying of information regarding a debt directly or indirectly to any person through any medium.

(3) The term "consumer" means any natural person obligated or allegedly obligated to pay any debt.

(4) The term "creditor" means any person who offers or extends credit creating a debt or to whom a debt is owed, but such term does not include any person to the extent that he receives an assignment or transfer of a debt in default solely for the purpose of facilitating col-lection of such debt for another.

(5) The term "debt" means any obligation or alleged obligation of a consumer to pay money arising out of a transaction in which the money, property, insurance or services which are the subject of the transaction are primarily for personal, family, or household purposes, whether or not such obligation has been reduced to judgment.

(6) The term "debt collector" means any person who uses any instrumentality of interstate commerce or the mails in any business the principal purpose of which is the collection of any debts, or who regularly collects or attempts to collect, directly or indirectly, debts owed or due or asserted to be owed or due another. Notwithstanding the exclusion provided by clause (F) of the last sentence of this paragraph, the term includes any creditor who, in the process of collecting his own debts, uses any name other than his own which would indicate that a third person is collecting or attempting to collect such debts. For the purpose of section 808(6), such term also includes any person who uses any instrumentality of interstate commerce or the mails in any business the principal purpose of which is the enforcement of security interests. The term does not include—

(A) any officer or employee of a creditor while, in the name of the creditor, collecting debts for such creditor;

(B) any person while acting as a debt collector for another person, both of whom are related by common ownership or affiliated by corporate control, if the person acting as a debt collector does so only for persons to whom it is so related or affiliated and if the

principal business of such person is not the collection of debts;
(C) any officer or employee of the United States or any State to the extent that collecting or attempting to collect any debt is in the performance of his official duties;
(D) any person while serving or attempting to serve legal process on any other person in connection with the judicial enforcement of any debt;
(E) any nonprofit organization which, at the request of consumers, performs bona fide consumer credit counseling and assists consumers in the liquidation of their debts by receiving payments from such consumers and distributing such amounts to creditors; and
(F) any person collecting or attempting to collect any debt owed or due or asserted to be owed or due another to the extent such activity
(i) is incidental to a bona fide fiduciary obligation or a bona fide escrow arrangement;
(ii) concerns a debt which was originated by such person;
(iii) concerns a debt which was not in default at the time it was obtained by such person;
or
(iv) concerns a debt obtained by such person as a secured party in a commercial credit transaction involving the creditor.
(7) The term "location information" means a consumer's place of abode and his telephone number at such place, or his place of employment.
(8) The term "State" means any State, territory, or possession of the United States, the District of Columbia, the Commonwealth of Puerto Rico, or any political subdivision of any of the foregoing.

§ 804. Acquisition of location information
Any debt collector communicating with any person other than the consumer for the purpose of acquiring location information about the consumer shall—
(1) identify himself, state that he is confirming or correcting location information concerning the consumer, and, only if expressly requested, identify his employer;
(2) not state that such consumer owes any debt;
(3) not communicate with any such person more than once unless requested to do so by such person or unless the debt collector reasonably believes that the earlier response of such person is erroneous or incomplete and that such person now has correct or complete location information;
(4) not communicate by post card;
(5) not use any language or symbol on any envelope or in the contents of any communication effected by the mails or telegram that indicates that the debt collector is in the debt collection business or that the communication relates to the collection of a debt; and
(6) after the debt collector knows the consumer is represented by an attorney with regard to the subject debt and has knowledge of, or can readily ascertain, such attorney's name and address, not communicate with any person other than that attorney, unless the attorney fails to respond within a reasonable period of time to the communication from the debt collector.

§ 805. Communication in connection with debt collection

(a) COMMUNICATION WITH THE CONSUMER GENER¬ALLY. Without the prior consent of the consumer given directly to the debt collector or the express permission of a court of competent jurisdiction, a debt collector may not communicate with a consumer in connection with the collection of any debt—

(1) at any unusual time or place or a time or place known or which should be known to be inconvenient to the consumer. In the absence of knowledge of circumstances to the contrary, a debt collector shall assume that the convenient time for communicating with a consumer is after 8 o'clock antimeridian and before 9 o'clock postmeridian, local time at the consumer's location;

(2) if the debt collector knows the consumer is represented by an attorney with respect to such debt and has knowledge of, or can readily ascertain, such attorney's name and address, unless the attorney fails to respond within a reasonable period of time to a communication from the debt collector or unless the attorney consents to direct communication with the consumer; or

(3) at the consumer's place of employment if the debt collector knows or has reason to know that the consumer's employer prohibits the consumer from receiving such communication.

(b) COMMUNICATION WITH THIRD PARTIES. Except as provided in section 804, without the prior consent of the consumer given directly to the debt collector, or the express permission of a court of competent jurisdiction, or as reasonably necessary to effectuate a postjudgment judicial remedy, a debt collector may not communicate, in connection with the collection of any debt, with any person other than a consumer, his attorney, a consumer reporting agency if otherwise permitted by law, the creditor, the attorney of the creditor, or the attorney of the debt collector.

(c) CEASING COMMUNICATION. If a consumer notifies a debt collector in writing that the consumer refuses to pay a debt or that the consumer wishes the debt collector to cease further communication with the consumer, the debt collector shall not communicate further with the consumer with respect to such debt, except—

(1) to advise the consumer that the debt collector's further efforts are being terminated;

(2) to notify the consumer that the debt collector or creditor may invoke specified remedies which are ordinarily invoked by such debt collector or creditor; or

(3) where applicable, to notify the consumer that the debt collector or creditor intends to invoke a specified remedy.

If such notice from the consumer is made by mail, notification shall be complete upon receipt.

(d) For the purpose of this section, the term "consumer" includes the consumer's spouse, parent (if the consumer is a minor), guardian, executor, or administrator.

§ 806. Harassment or abuse

A debt collector may not engage in any conduct the natural consequence of which is to harass, oppress, or abuse any person in connection with the collection of a debt. Without limiting the general application of the foregoing, the following conduct is a violation of this section:
(1) The use or threat of use of violence or other criminal means to harm the physical person, reputation, or property of any person.
(2) The use of obscene or profane language or language the natural consequence of which is to abuse the hearer or reader.
(3) The publication of a list of consumers who allegedly refuse to pay debts, except to a consumer reporting agency or to persons meeting the requirements of section 603(f) or 604(3)1 of this Act.
(4) The advertisement for sale of any debt to coerce payment of the debt.
(5) Causing a telephone to ring or engaging any person in telephone conversation repeatedly or continuously with intent to annoy, abuse, or harass any person at the called number.
(6) Except as provided in section 804, the placement of telephone calls without meaningful disclosure of the caller's identity.
1. Section 604(3) has been renumbered as Section 604(a)(3).
§ 807. False or misleading representations
A debt collector may not use any false, deceptive, or misleading representation or means in connection with the collection of any debt. Without limiting the general application of the foregoing, the following conduct is a violation of this section:
(1) The false representation or implication that the debt collector is vouched for, bonded by, or affiliated with the United States or any State, including the use of any badge, uniform, or facsimile thereof.
(2) The false representation of—
(A) the character, amount, or legal status of any debt; or
(B) any services rendered or compensation which may be lawfully received by any debt collector for the collection of a debt.
(3) The false representation or implication that any individual is an attorney or that any communication is from an attorney.
(4) The representation or implication that nonpayment of any debt will result in the arrest or imprisonment of any person or the seizure, garnishment, attachment, or sale of any property or wages of any person unless such action is lawful and the debt collector or creditor intends to take such action.
(5) The threat to take any action that cannot legally be taken or that is not intended to be taken.
(6) The false representation or implication that a sale, referral, or other transfer of any interest in a debt shall cause the consumer to—
(A) lose any claim or defense to payment of the debt; or
(B) become subject to any practice prohibited by this title.

(7) The false representation or implication that the consumer committed any crime or other conduct in order to disgrace the consumer.
(8) Communicating or threatening to communicate to any person credit information which is known or which should be known to be false, including the failure to communicate that a disputed debt is disputed.
(9) The use or distribution of any written communication which simulates or is falsely represented to be a document authorized, issued, or approved by any court, official, or agency of the United States or any State, or which creates a false impression as to its source, authorization, or approval.
(10) The use of any false representation or deceptive means to collect or attempt to collect any debt or to obtain information concerning a consumer.
(11) The failure to disclose in the initial written communication with the consumer and, in addition, if the initial communication with the consumer is oral, in that initial oral communication, that the debt collector is attempting to collect a debt and that any information obtained will be used for that purpose, and the failure to disclose in subsequent communications that the communication is from a debt collector, except that this paragraph shall not apply to a formal pleading made in connection with a legal action.
(12) The false representation or implication that accounts have been turned over to innocent purchasers for value.
(13) The false representation or implication that documents are legal process.
(14) The use of any business, company, or organization name other than the true name of the debt collector's business, company, or organization.
(15) The false representation or implication that documents are not legal process forms or do not require action by the consumer.
(16) The false representation or implication that a debt collector operates or is employed by a consumer reporting agency as defined by section 603(f) of this Act.
§ 808. Unfair practices
A debt collector may not use unfair or unconscionable means to collect or attempt to collect any debt. Without limiting the general application of the foregoing, the following conduct is a violation of this section:
(1) The collection of any amount (including any interest, fee, charge, or expense incidental to the principal obligation) unless such amount is expressly authorized by the agreement creating the debt or permitted by law.
(2) The acceptance by a debt collector from any person of a check or other payment instrument postdated by more than five days unless such person is notified in writing of the debt collector's intent to deposit such check or instrument not more than ten nor less than three business days prior to such deposit.
(3) The solicitation by a debt collector of any postdated check or other postdated payment instrument for the purpose of threatening or instituting criminal prosecution.
(4) Depositing or threatening to deposit any postdated check or other postdated payment instrument prior to the date on such check or instrument.

(5) Causing charges to be made to any person for communications by concealment of the true propose of the communication. Such charges include, but are not limited to, collect telephone calls and telegram fees.
(6) Taking or threatening to take any nonjudicial action to effect dispossession or disablement of property if—
(A) there is no present right to possession of the property claimed as collateral through an enforceable security interest;
(B) there is no present intention to take possession of the property; or
(C) the property is exempt by law from such dispossession or disablement.
(7) Communicating with a consumer regarding a debt by post card.
(8) Using any language or symbol, other than the debt collector's address, on any envelope when communicating with a consumer by use of the mails or by telegram, except that a debt collector may use his business name if such name does not indicate that he is in the debt collection business.
§ 809. Validation of debts
(a) Within five days after the initial communication with a consumer in connection with the collection of any debt, a debt collector shall, unless the following information is contained in the initial communication or the consumer has paid the debt, send the consumer a written notice containing—
(1) the amount of the debt;
(2) the name of the creditor to whom the debt is owed;
(3) a statement that unless the consumer, within thirty days after receipt of the notice, disputes the validity of the debt, or any portion thereof, the debt will be assumed to be valid by the debt collector;
(4) a statement that if the consumer notifies the debt collector in writing within the thirty-day period that the debt, or any portion thereof, is disputed, the debt collector will obtain verification of the debt or a copy of a judgment against the consumer and a copy of such verification or judgment will be mailed to the consumer by the debt collector; and
(5) a statement that, upon the consumer's written request within the thirty-day period, the debt collector will provide the consumer with the name and address of the original creditor, if different from the current creditor.
(b) If the consumer notifies the debt collector in writing within the thirty-day period described in subsection (a) that the debt, or any portion thereof, is disputed, or that the consumer requests the name and address of the original creditor, the debt collector shall cease collection of the debt, or any disputed portion thereof, until the debt collector obtains verification of the debt or any copy of a judgment, or the name and address of the original creditor, and a copy of such verification or judgment, or name and address of the original creditor, is mailed to the consumer by the debt collector. Collection activities and communications that do not otherwise violate this title may continue during the 30-day period referred to in subsection (a) unless the consumer has notified the debt collec-

tor in writing that the debt, or any portion of the debt, is disputed or that the consumer requests the name and address of the original creditor. Any collection activities and communication during the 30-day period may not overshadow or be inconsistent with the disclosure of the consumer's right to dispute the debt or request the name and address of the original creditor.

(c) The failure of a consumer to dispute the validity of a debt under this section may not be construed by any court as an admission of liability by the consumer.

(d) A communication in the form of a formal pleading in a civil action shall not be treated as an initial communication for purposes of subsection (a).

(e) The sending or delivery of any form or notice which does not relate to the collection of a debt and is expressly required by the Internal Revenue Code of 1986, title V of Gramm-Leach-Bliley Act, or any provision of Federal or State law relating to notice of data security breach or privacy, or any regulation prescribed under any such provision of law, shall not be treated as an initial communication in connection with debt collection for purposes of this section.

§ 810. Multiple debts

If any consumer owes multiple debts and makes any single payment to any debt collector with respect to such debts, such debt collector may not apply such payment to any debt which is disputed by the consumer and, where applicable, shall apply such payment in accordance with the consumer's directions.

§ 811. Legal actions by debt collectors

(a) Any debt collector who brings any legal action on a debt against any consumer shall—

(1) in the case of an action to enforce an interest in real property securing the consumer's obligation, bring such action only in a judicial district or similar legal entity in which such real property is located; or

(2) in the case of an action not described in paragraph (1), bring such action only in the judicial district or similar legal entity—

(A) in which such consumer signed the contract sued upon; or

(B) in which such consumer resides at the commencement of the action.

(b) Nothing in this title shall be construed to authorize the bringing of legal actions by debt collectors.

§ 812. Furnishing certain deceptive forms

(a) It is unlawful to design, compile, and furnish any form knowing that such form would be used to create the false belief in a consumer that a person other than the creditor of such consumer is participating in the collection of or in an attempt to collect a debt such consumer allegedly owes such creditor, when in fact such person is not so participating.

(b) Any person who violates this section shall be liable to the same extent and in the same manner as a debt collector is liable under section 813 for failure to comply with a provision of this title.

§ 813. Civil liability

(a) Except as otherwise provided by this section, any debt collector who fails to comply with any provision of this title with respect to any person is liable to such person in an amount equal to the sum of—

(1) any actual damage sustained by such person as a result of such failure;

(2) (A) in the case of any action by an individual, such additional damages as the court may allow, but not exceeding $1,000; or

(B) in the case of a class action,

(i) such amount for each named plaintiff as could be recovered under subparagraph (A), and

(ii) such amount as the court may allow for all other class members, without regard to a minimum individual recovery, not to exceed the lesser of $500,000 or 1 per centum of the net worth of the debt collector; and

(3) in the case of any successful action to enforce the foregoing liability, the costs of the action, together with a reasonable attorney's fee as determined by the court. On a finding by the court that an action under this section was brought in bad faith and for the purpose of harassment, the court may award to the defendant attorney's fees reasonable in relation to the work expended and costs.

(b) In determining the amount of liability in any action under subsection (a), the court shall consider, among other relevant factors—

(1) in any individual action under subsection (a)(2)(A), the frequency and persistence of noncompliance by the debt collector, the nature of such noncompliance, and the extent to which such noncompliance was intentional; or

(2) in any class action under subsection (a)(2)(B), the frequency and persistence of noncompliance by the debt collector, the nature of such noncompliance, the resources of the debt collector, the number of persons adversely affected, and the extent to which the debt collector's noncompliance was intentional.

(c) A debt collector may not be held liable in any action brought under this title if the debt collector shows by a preponderance of evidence that the violation was not intentional and resulted from a bona fide error notwithstanding the maintenance of procedures reasonably adapted to avoid any such error.

(d) An action to enforce any liability created by this title may be brought in any appropriate United States district court without regard to the amount in controversy, or in any other court of competent jurisdiction, within one year from the date on which the violation occurs.

(e) No provision of this section imposing any liability shall apply to any act done or omitted in good faith in conformity with any advisory opinion of the Commission, notwithstanding that after such act or omission has occurred, such opinion is amended, rescinded, or determined by judicial or other authority to be invalid for any reason.

§ 814. Administrative enforcement

(a) Compliance with this title shall be enforced by the Commission, except to the extent that enforcement of the requirements imposed under this title is specifically committed to another agency under subsection (b). For purpose of the exercise by the Commission of its functions and powers under the Federal Trade Commission Act, a violation of this title shall be deemed an unfair or deceptive act or practice in violation of that Act. All of the functions and powers of the Commission under the Federal Trade Commission Act are available to the Commission to enforce compliance by any person with this title, irrespective of whether that person is engaged in commerce or meets any other jurisdictional tests in the Federal Trade Commission Act, including the power to enforce the provisions of this title in the same manner as if the violation had been a violation of a Federal Trade Commission trade regulation rule.

(b) Compliance with any requirements imposed under this title shall be enforced under—

(1) section 8 of the Federal Deposit Insurance Act, in the case of—

(A) national banks, and Federal branches and Federal agencies of foreign banks, by the Office of the Comptroller of the Currency;

(B) member banks of the Federal Reserve System (other than national banks), branches and agencies of foreign banks (other than Federal branches, Federal agencies, and insured State branches of foreign banks), commercial lending companies owned or controlled by foreign banks, and organizations operating under section 25 or 25(a) of the Federal Reserve Act, by the Board of Governors of the Federal Reserve System; and

(C) banks insured by the Federal Deposit Insurance Corporation (other than members of the Federal Reserve System) and insured State branches of foreign banks, by the Board of Directors of the Federal Deposit Insurance Corporation;

(2) section 8 of the Federal Deposit Insurance Act, by the Director of the Office of Thrift Supervision, in the case of a savings association the deposits of which are insured by the Federal Deposit Insurance Corporation;

(3) the Federal Credit Union Act, by the Administrator of the National Credit Union Administration with respect to any Federal credit union;

(4) the Acts to regulate commerce, by the Secretary of Transportation, with respect to all carriers subject to the jurisdiction of the Surface Transportation Board;

(5) the Federal Aviation Act of 1958, by the Secretary of Transportation with respect to any air carrier or any foreign air carrier subject to that Act; and

(6) the Packers and Stockyards Act, 1921 (except as provided in section 406 of that Act), by the Secretary of Agriculture with respect to any activities subject to that Act.

The terms used in paragraph (1) that are not defined in this title or otherwise defined in section 3(s) of the Federal Deposit Insurance Act (12 U.S.C. 1813(s)) shall have the meaning given to them in section 1(b) of the International Banking Act of 1978 (12 U.S.C. 3101).

(c) For the purpose of the exercise by any agency referred to in subsection (b) of its powers under any Act referred to in that subsection, a violation of any requirement imposed under this title shall be deemed to be a violation of a requirement imposed under that Act. In addition to its powers under any provision of law specifically referred to in subsection (b), each of the agencies referred to in that subsection may exercise, for the purpose of enforcing compliance with any requirement imposed under this title any other authority conferred on it by law, except as provided in subsection (d).

(d) Neither the Commission nor any other agency referred to in subsection (b) may promulgate trade regulation rules or other regulations with respect to the collection of debts by debt collectors as defined in this title.

§ 815. Reports to Congress by the Commission

(a) Not later than one year after the effective date of this title and at one-year intervals thereafter, the Commission shall make reports to the Congress concerning the administration of its functions under this title, including such recommendations as the Commission deems necessary or appropriate. In addition, each report of the Commission shall include its assessment of the extent to which compliance with this title is being achieved and a summary of the enforcement actions taken by the Commission under section 814 of this title.

(b) In the exercise of its functions under this title, the Commission may obtain upon request the views of any other Federal agency which exercises enforcement functions under section 814 of this title.

§ 816. Relation to State laws

This title does not annul, alter, or affect, or exempt any person subject to the provisions of this title from complying with the laws of any State with respect to debt collection practices, except to the extent that those laws are inconsistent with any provision of this title, and then only to the extent of the inconsistency. For purposes of this section, a State law is not inconsistent with this title if the protection such law affords any consumer is greater than the protection provided by this title.

§ 817. Exemption for State regulation

The Commission shall by regulation exempt from the requirements of this title any class of debt collection practices within any State if the Commission determines that under the law of that State that class of debt collection practices is subject to requirements substantially similar to those imposed by this title, and that there is adequate provision for enforcement.

§ 818. Exception for certain bad check enforcement programs operated by private entities

(a) In General.—

(1) TREATMENT OF CERTAIN PRIVATE ENTITIES.—Subject to paragraph (2), a private entity shall be excluded from the definition of a debt collector, pursuant to the exception provided in section 803(6), with respect to the operation by the entity of a program described in paragraph (2)(A) under a contract described in paragraph (2)(B).

(2) CONDITIONS OF APPLICABILITY.—Paragraph (1) shall apply if—

(A) a State or district attorney establishes, within the jurisdiction of such State or district attorney and with respect to alleged bad check violations that do not involve a check described in subsection (b), a pretrial diversion program for alleged bad check offenders who agree to participate voluntarily in such program to avoid criminal prosecution;
(B) a private entity, that is subject to an administrative support services contract with a State or district attorney and operates under the direction, supervision, and control of such State or district attorney, operates the pretrial diversion program described in subparagraph (A); and
(C) in the course of performing duties delegated to it by a State or district attorney under the contract, the private entity referred to in subparagraph (B)—
(i) complies with the penal laws of the State;
(ii) conforms with the terms of the contract and directives of the State or district attorney;
(iii) does not exercise independent prosecutorial discretion;
(iv) contacts any alleged offender referred to in subparagraph (A) for purposes of participating in a program referred to in such paragraph—
(I) only as a result of any determination by the State or district attorney that probable cause of a bad check violation under State penal law exists, and that contact with the alleged offender for purposes of participation in the program is appropriate; and
(II) the alleged offender has failed to pay the bad check after demand for payment, pursuant to State law, is made for payment of the check amount;
(v) includes as part of an initial written communication with an alleged offender a clear and conspicuous statement that—
(I) the alleged offender may dispute the validity of any alleged bad check violation;
(II) where the alleged offender knows, or has reasonable cause to believe, that the alleged bad check violation is the result of theft or forgery of the check, identity theft, or other fraud that is not the result of the conduct of the alleged offender, the alleged offender may file a crime report with the appropriate law enforcement agency; and
(III) if the alleged offender notifies the private entity or the district attorney in writing, not later than 30 days after being contacted for the first time pursuant to clause (iv), that there is a dispute pursuant to this subsection, before further restitution efforts are pursued, the district attorney or an employee of the district attorney authorized to make such a determination makes a determination that there is probable cause to believe that a crime has been committed; and
(vi) charges only fees in connection with services under the contract that have been authorized by the contract with the State or district attorney.
(b) Certain Checks Excluded.—A check is described in this subsection if the check involves, or is subsequently found to involve—
(1) a postdated check presented in connection with a payday loan, or other similar transaction, where the payee of the check knew that the issuer had insufficient funds at the time the check was made, drawn, or delivered;

(2) a stop payment order where the issuer acted in good faith and with reasonable cause in stopping payment on the check;
(3) a check dishonored because of an adjustment to the issuer's account by the financial institution holding such account without providing notice to the person at the time the check was made, drawn, or delivered;
(4) a check for partial payment of a debt where the payee had previously accepted partial payment for such debt;
(5) a check issued by a person who was not competent, or was not of legal age, to enter into a legal contractual obligation at the time the check was made, drawn, or delivered; or
(6) a check issued to pay an obligation arising from a transaction that was illegal in the jurisdiction of the State or district attorney at the time the check was made, drawn, or delivered.
(c) Definitions.—For purposes of this section, the following definitions shall apply:
(1) STATE OR DISTRICT ATTORNEY.—The term "State or district attorney" means the chief elected or appointed prosecuting attorney in a district, county (as defined in section 2 of title 1, United States Code), municipality, or comparable jurisdiction, including State attorneys general who act as chief elected or appointed prosecuting attorneys in a district, county (as so defined), municipality or comparable jurisdiction, who may be referred to by a variety of titles such as district attorneys, prosecuting attorneys, commonwealth's attorneys, solicitors, county attorneys, and state's attorneys, and who are responsible for the prosecution of State crimes and violations of jurisdiction-specific local ordinances.
(2) CHECK.—The term "check" has the same meaning as in section 3(6) of the Check Clearing for the 21st Century Act.
(3) BAD CHECK VIOLATION.—The term "bad check violation" means a violation of the applicable State criminal law relating to the writing of dishonored checks.
§ 819. Effective date
This title takes effect upon the expiration of six months after the date of its enactment, but section 809 shall apply only with respect to debts for which the initial attempt to collect occurs after such effective date.

Legislative History

House Report: No. 95-131 (Comm. on Banking, Finance, and Urban Affairs)
Senate Report: No. 95-382 (Comm. on Banking, Housing and Urban Affairs)
Congressional Record, Vol. 123 (1977)
April 4, House considered and passed H.R. 5294.
Aug. 5, Senate considered and passed amended version of H.R. 5294.

Sept. 8, House considered and passed Senate version.
Enactment: Public Law 95-109 (Sept. 20, 1977)
Amendments: Public Law Nos.
99-361 (July 9, 1986)
101-73 (Aug. 9, 1989)
102-242 (Dec. 19, 1991)
102-550 (Oct. 28, 1992)
104-88 (Dec. 29, 1995)
104-208 (Sept. 30, 1996)
109-351 (Oct. 13, 2006)

FAIR CREDIT REPORTING ACT (FCRA) - TITLE 15, U.S. CODE, SECTION §1681

TABLE OF CONTENTS

§ 601. Short title
This title may be cited as the "Fair Credit Reporting Act".

§ 602. Congressional findings and statement of purpose [15 U.S.C. § 1681]
(a) Accuracy and fairness of credit reporting. The Congress makes the following findings:
(1) The banking system is dependent upon fair and accurate credit reporting. Inaccurate credit reports directly impair the efficiency of the banking system, and unfair credit reporting methods undermine the public confidence which is essential to the continued functioning of the banking system.
(2) An elaborate mechanism has been developed for investigating and evaluating the credit worthiness, credit standing, credit capacity, character, and general reputation of consumers.
(3) Consumer reporting agencies have assumed a vital role in assembling and evaluating consumer credit and other information on consumers.
(4) There is a need to insure that consumer reporting agencies exercise their grave responsibilities with fairness, impartiality, and a respect for the consumer's right to privacy.
(b) Reasonable procedures. It is the purpose of this title to require that consumer reporting agencies adopt reasonable procedures for meeting the needs of commerce for consumer credit, personnel, insurance, and other information in a manner which is fair and equitable to the consumer, with regard to the confidentiality, accuracy, relevancy, and proper utilization of such information in accordance with the requirements of this title.

§ 603. Definitions; rules of construction [15 U.S.C. § 1681a]
(a) Definitions and rules of construction set forth in this section are applicable for the purposes of this title.
(b) The term "person" means any individual, partnership, corporation, trust, estate, co-

operative, association, government or governmental subdivision or agency, or other entity.

(c) The term "consumer" means an individual.

(d) Consumer Report

(1) In general. The term "consumer report" means any written, oral, or other communication of any information by a consumer reporting agency bearing on a consumer's credit worthiness, credit standing, credit capacity, character, general reputation, personal characteristics, or mode of living which is used or expected to be used or collected in whole or in part for the purpose of serving as a factor in establishing the consumer's eligibility for

(A) credit or insurance to be used primarily for personal, family, or household purposes;

(B) employment purposes; or

(C) any other purpose authorized under section 604 [§ 1681b].

(2) Exclusions. Except as provided in paragraph (3), the term "consumer report" does not include

(A) subject to section 624, any

(i) report containing information solely as to transactions or experiences between the consumer and the person making the report;

(ii) communication of that information among persons related by common ownership or affiliated by corporate control; or

(iii) communication of other information among persons related by common ownership or affiliated by corporate control, if it is clearly and conspicuously disclosed to the consumer that the information may be communicated among such persons and the consumer is given the opportunity, before the time that the information is initially communicated, to direct that such information not be communicated among such persons;

(B) any authorization or approval of a specific extension of credit directly or indirectly by the issuer of a credit card or similar device;

(C) any report in which a person who has been requested by a third party to make a specific extension of credit directly or indirectly to a consumer conveys his or her decision with respect to such request, if the third party advises the consumer of the name and address of the person to whom the request was made, and such person makes the disclosures to the consumer required under section 615 [§ 1681m]; or

(D) a communication described in subsection (o) or (x).

(3) Restriction on sharing of medical information. Except for information or any communication of information disclosed as provided in section 604(g)(3), the exclusions in paragraph (2) shall not apply with respect to information disclosed

July 30, 2004 4

to any person related by common ownership or affiliated by corporate control, if the information is-¬

(A) medical information;

(B) an individualized list or description based on the payment transactions of the consumer for medical products or services; or

(C) an aggregate list of identified consumers based on payment transactions for medical products or services.

(e) The term "investigative consumer report" means a consumer report or portion thereof in which information on a consumer's character, general reputation, personal characteristics, or mode of living is obtained through personal interviews with neighbors, friends, or associates of the consumer reported on or with others with whom he is acquainted or who may have knowledge concerning any such items of information. However, such information shall not include specific factual information on a consumer's credit record obtained directly from a creditor of the consumer or from a consumer reporting agency when such information was obtained directly from a creditor of the consumer or from the consumer.

(f) The term "consumer reporting agency" means any person which, for monetary fees, dues, or on a cooperative nonprofit basis, regularly engages in whole or in part in the practice of assembling or evaluating consumer credit information or other information on consumers for the purpose of furnishing consumer reports to third parties, and which uses any means or facility of interstate commerce for the purpose of preparing or furnishing consumer reports.

(g) The term "file," when used in connection with information on any consumer, means all of the information on that consumer recorded and retained by a consumer reporting agency regardless of how the information is stored.

(h) The term "employment purposes" when used in connection with a consumer report means a report used for the purpose of evaluating a consumer for employment, promotion, reassignment or retention as an employee.

(i) The term "medical information" -¬

(1) means information or data, whether oral or recorded, in any form or medium, created by or derived from a health care provider or the consumer, that relates to-¬

(A) the past, present, or future physical, mental, or behavioral health or condition of an individual;

(B) the provision of health care to an individual; or

(C) the payment for the provision of health care to an individual.

(2) does not include the age or gender of a consumer, demographic information about the consumer, including a consumer's residence address or e-mail address, or any other information about a consumer that does not relate to the physical, mental, or behavioral health or condition of a consumer, including the existence or value of any insurance policy.

(j) Definitions Relating to Child Support Obligations

(1) The "overdue support" has the meaning given to such term in section 666(e) of title 42 [Social Security Act, 42 U.S.C. § 666(e)].

(2) The term "State or local child support enforcement agency" means a State or local

agency which administers a State or local program for establishing and enforcing child support obligations.

(k) Adverse Action

(1) Actions included. The term "adverse action"

(i) a denial or cancellation of, an increase in any charge for, or a reduction or other adverse or unfavorable change in the terms of coverage or amount of, any insurance, existing or applied for, in connection with the underwriting of insurance;

(ii) a denial of employment or any other decision for employment purposes that adversely affects any current or prospective employee;

(iii) a denial or cancellation of, an increase in any charge for, or any other adverse or unfavorable change in the terms of, any license or benefit described in section 604(a)(3)(D) [§ 1681b]; and

(iv) an action taken or determination that is

(I) made in connection with an application that was made by, or a transaction that was initiated by, any consumer, or in connection with a review of an account under section 604(a)(3)(F)(ii)[§ 1681b]; and

(II) adverse to the interests of the consumer.

(2) Applicable findings, decisions, commentary, and orders. For purposes of any determination of whether an action is an adverse action under paragraph (1)(A), all appropriate final findings, decisions, commentary, and orders issued under

section 701(d)(6) of the Equal Credit Opportunity Act by the Board of Governors of the Federal Reserve System or any court shall apply.

(l) The term "firm offer of credit or insurance" means any offer of credit or insurance to a consumer that will be honored if the consumer is determined, based on information in a consumer report on the consumer, to meet the specific criteria used to select the consumer for the offer, except that the offer may be further conditioned on one or more of the following:

(1) The consumer being determined, based on information in the consumer's application for the credit or insurance, to meet specific criteria bearing on credit worthiness or insurability, as applicable, that are established

(A) before selection of the consumer for the offer; and

(B) for the purpose of determining whether to extend credit or insurance pursuant to the offer.

(2) Verification

(A) that the consumer continues to meet the specific criteria used to select the consumer for the offer, by using information in a consumer report on the consumer, information in the consumer's application for the credit or insurance, or other information bearing on the credit worthiness or insurability of the consumer; or

(B) of the information in the consumer's application for the credit or insurance, to determine that the consumer meets the specific criteria bearing on credit worthiness or insurability.

(3) The consumer furnishing any collateral that is a requirement for the extension of the credit or insurance that was

(A) established before selection of the consumer for the offer of credit or insurance; and

(B) disclosed to the consumer in the offer of credit or insurance.

(m) The term "credit or insurance transaction that is not initiated by the consumer" does not include the use of a consumer report by a person with which the consumer has an account or insurance policy, for purposes of

(1) reviewing the account or insurance policy; or

(2) collecting the account.

(n) The term "State" means any State, the Commonwealth of Puerto Rico, the District of Columbia, and any territory or possession of the United States.

(o) Excluded communications. A communication is described in this subsection if it is a communication

(1) that, but for subsection (d)(2)(D), would be an investigative consumer report;

(2) that is made to a prospective employer for the purpose of

(A) procuring an employee for the employer; or

(B) procuring an opportunity for a natural person to work for the employer;

(3) that is made by a person who regularly performs such procurement;

(4) that is not used by any person for any purpose other than a purpose described in subparagraph (A) or (B) of paragraph (2); and

(5) with respect to which

(A) the consumer who is the subject of the communication

(i) consents orally or in writing to the nature and scope of the communication, before the collection of any information for the purpose of making the communication;

(ii) consents orally or in writing to the making of the communication to a prospective employer, before the making of the communication; and

(iii) in the case of consent under clause (i) or (ii) given orally, is provided written confirmation of that consent by the person making the communication, not later than 3 business days after the receipt of the consent by that person;

(B) the person who makes the communication does not, for the purpose of making the communication, make any inquiry that if made by a prospective employer of the consumer who is the subject of the communication would violate any applicable Federal or State equal employment opportunity law or regulation; and

(C) the person who makes the communication

(i) discloses in writing to the consumer who is the subject of the communication, not later than 5 business days after receiving any request from the consumer for such disclosure, the nature and substance of all information in the consumer's file at the time of the request, except that the sources of any information that is acquired solely for use in making the communication and is actually used for no other purpose, need not be disclosed other than under appropriate discovery procedures in any court of competent jurisdiction in which an action is brought; and

(ii) notifies the consumer who is the subject of the communication, in writing, of the consumer's right to request the information described in clause (i).

(p) The term "consumer reporting agency that compiles and maintains files on consumers on a nationwide basis" means a consumer reporting agency that regularly engages in the practice of assembling or evaluating, and maintaining, for the purpose of furnishing consumer reports to third parties bearing on a consumer's credit worthiness, credit standing, or credit capacity, each of the following regarding consumers residing nationwide:

(1) Public record information.

(2) Credit account information from persons who furnish that information regularly and in the ordinary course of business.

(q) Definitions relating to fraud alerts.

(1) The term "active duty military consumer" means a consumer in military service who -

(A) is on active duty (as defined in section 101(d)(1) of title 10, United States Code) or is a reservist performing duty under a call or order to active duty under a provision of law referred to in section 101(a)(13) of title 10, United States Code; and

(B) is assigned to service away from the usual duty station of the consumer.

(2) The terms "fraud alert" and "active duty alert" mean a statement in the file of a consumer that-¬

(A) notifies all prospective users of a consumer report relating to the consumer that the consumer may be a victim of fraud, including identity theft, or is an active duty military consumer, as applicable; and

(B) is presented in a manner that facilitates a clear and conspicuous view of the statement described in subparagraph (A) by any person requesting such consumer report.

(3) The term "identity theft" means a fraud committed using the identifying information of another person, subject to such further definition as the Commission may prescribe, by regulation.

(4) The term "identity theft report" has the meaning given that term by rule of the Commission, and means, at a minimum, a report-¬

(A) that alleges an identity theft;

(B) that is a copy of an official, valid report filed by a consumer with an appropriate Federal, State, or local law enforcement agency, including the United States Postal Inspection Service, or such other government agency deemed appropriate by the Commission; and

(C) the filing of which subjects the person filing the report to criminal penalties relating to the filing of false information if, in fact, the information in the report is false.

(5) The term "new credit plan" means a new account under an open end credit plan (as defined in section 103(i) of the Truth in Lending Act) or a new credit transaction not under

an open end credit plan.

(r) Credit and Debit Related Terms

(1) The term "card issuer" means-¬

(A) a credit card issuer, in the case of a credit card; and

(B) a debit card issuer, in the case of a debit card.

(2) The term "credit card" has the same meaning as in section 103 of the Truth in Lending Act.

(3) The term "debit card" means any card issued by a financial institution to a consumer for use in initiating an electronic fund transfer from the account of the consumer at such financial institution, for the purpose of transferring money between accounts or obtaining money, property, labor, or services.

(4) The terms "account" and "electronic fund transfer" have the same meanings as in section 903 of the Electronic Fund Transfer Act.

(5) The terms "credit" and "creditor" have the same meanings as in section 702 of the Equal Credit Opportunity Act.

(s) The term "Federal banking agency" has the same meaning as in section 3 of the Federal Deposit Insurance Act.

(t) The term "financial institution" means a State or National bank, a State or Federal savings and loan association, a mutual savings bank, a State or Federal credit union, or any other person that, directly or indirectly, holds a transaction account (as defined in section 19(b) of the Federal Reserve Act) belonging to a consumer.

(u) The term "reseller" means a consumer reporting agency that-¬

(1) assembles and merges information contained in the database of another consumer reporting agency or multiple consumer reporting agencies concerning any consumer for purposes of furnishing such information to any third party, to the extent of such activities; and

(2) does not maintain a database of the assembled or merged information from which new consumer reports are produced.

(v) The term "Commission" means the Federal Trade Commission.

(w) The term "nationwide specialty consumer reporting agency" means a consumer reporting agency that compiles and maintains files on consumers on a nationwide basis relating to-

(1) medical records or payments;

(2) residential or tenant history;

(3) check writing history;

(4) employment history; or

(5) insurance claims.

(x) Exclusion of Certain Communications for Employee Investigations

(1) A communication is described in this subsection if-¬

(A) but for subsection (d)(2)(D), the communication would be a consumer report;

(B) the communication is made to an employer in connection with an investigation of–

(i) suspected misconduct relating to employment; or

(ii) compliance with Federal, State, or local laws and regulations, the rules of a self-regulatory organization, or any preexisting written policies of the employer;

(C) the communication is not made for the purpose of investigating a consumer's credit worthiness, credit standing, or credit capacity; and

(D) the communication is not provided to any person except-

(i) to the employer or an agent of the employer;

(ii) to any Federal or State officer, agency, or department, or any officer, agency, or department of a unit of general local government;

(iii) to any self-regulatory organization with regulatory authority over the activities of the employer or employee;

(iv) as otherwise required by law; or

(v) pursuant to section 608.

(2) Subsequent disclosure. After taking any adverse action based in whole or in part on a communication described in paragraph (1), the employer shall disclose to the consumer a summary containing the nature and substance of the communication upon which the adverse action is based, except that the sources of information acquired solely for use in preparing what would be but for subsection (d)(2)(D) an investigative consumer report need not be disclosed.

(3) For purposes of this subsection, the term "self-regulatory organization" includes any self-regulatory organization (as defined in section 3(a)(26) of the Securities Exchange Act of 1934), any entity established under title I of the Sarbanes-Oxley Act of 2002, any board of trade designated by the Commodity Futures Trading Commission, and any futures association registered with such Commission.

§ 604. Permissible purposes of consumer reports [15 U.S.C. § 1681b]

(a) In general. Subject to subsection (c), any consumer reporting agency may furnish a consumer report under the following circumstances and no other:

(1) In response to the order of a court having jurisdiction to issue such an order, or a subpoena issued in connection with proceedings before a Federal grand jury.

(2) In accordance with the written instructions of the consumer to whom it relates.

(3) To a person which it has reason to believe

(A) intends to use the information in connection with a credit transaction involving the consumer on whom the information is to be furnished and involving the extension of credit to, or review or collection of an account of, the consumer; or

(B) intends to use the information for employment purposes; or

(C) intends to use the information in connection with the underwriting of insurance involving the consumer; or

(D) intends to use the information in connection with a determination of the consumer's eligibility for a license or other benefit granted by a governmental instrumentality required by law to consider an applicant's financial responsibility or status; or

(E) intends to use the information, as a potential investor or servicer, or current insurer, in connection with a valuation of, or an assessment of the credit or prepayment risks associated with, an existing credit obligation; or

(F) otherwise has a legitimate business need for the information

(i) in connection with a business transaction that is initiated by the consumer; or

(ii) to review an account to determine whether the consumer continues to meet the terms of the account.

(4) In response to a request by the head of a State or local child support enforcement agency (or a State or local government official authorized by the head of such an agency), if the person making the request certifies to the consumer reporting agency that

(A) the consumer report is needed for the purpose of establishing an individual's capacity to make child support payments or determining the appropriate level of such payments;

(B) the paternity of the consumer for the child to which the obligation relates has been established or acknowledged by the consumer in accordance with State laws under which the obligation arises (if required by those laws);

(C) the person has provided at least 10 days' prior notice to the consumer whose report is requested, by certified or registered mail to the last known address of the consumer, that the report will be requested; and

(D) the consumer report will be kept confidential, will be used solely for a purpose described in subparagraph (A), and will not be used in connection with any other civil, administrative, or criminal proceeding, or for any other purpose.

(5) To an agency administering a State plan under Section 454 of the Social Security Act (42 U.S.C. § 654) for use to set an initial or modified child support award.

(b) Conditions for Furnishing and Using Consumer Reports for Employment Purposes.

(1) Certification from user. A consumer reporting agency may furnish a consumer report for employment purposes only if

(A) the person who obtains such report from the agency certifies to the agency that

(i) the person has complied with paragraph (2) with respect to the consumer report, and the person will comply with paragraph (3) with respect to the consumer report if paragraph (3) becomes applicable; and

(ii) information from the consumer report will not be used in violation of any applicable Federal or State equal employment opportunity law or regulation; and

(B) the consumer reporting agency provides with the report, or has previously provided, a summary of the consumer's rights under this title, as prescribed by the Federal Trade Commission under section 609(c)(3) [§ 1681g].

(2) Disclosure to Consumer.

(A) In general. Except as provided in subparagraph (B), a person may not procure a consumer report, or cause a consumer report to be procured, for employment purposes with respect to any consumer, unless-¬

(i) a clear and conspicuous disclosure has been made in writing to the consumer at any time before the report is procured or caused to be procured, in a document that consists solely of the disclosure, that a consumer report may be obtained for employment purposes; and

(ii) the consumer has authorized in writing (which authorization may be made on the document referred to in clause (i)) the procurement of the report by that person.

(B) Application by mail, telephone, computer, or other similar means. If a consumer described in subparagraph (C) applies for employment by mail, telephone, computer, or other similar means, at any time before a consumer report is procured or caused to be procured in connection with that application-¬

(i) the person who procures the consumer report on the consumer for employment purposes shall provide to the consumer, by oral, written, or electronic means, notice that a consumer report may be obtained for employment purposes, and a summary of the consumer's rights under section 615(a)(3); and

(ii) the consumer shall have consented, orally, in writing, or electronically to the procurement of the report by that person.

(C) Scope. Subparagraph (B) shall apply to a person procuring a consumer report on a consumer in connection with the consumer's application for employment only if-¬

(i) the consumer is applying for a position over which the Secretary of Transportation has the power to establish qualifications and maximum hours of service pursuant to the provisions of section 31502 of title 49, or a position subject to safety regulation by a State transportation agency; and

(ii) as of the time at which the person procures the report or causes the report to be procured the only interaction between the consumer and the person in connection with that employment application has been by mail, telephone, computer, or other similar means.

(3) Conditions on use for adverse actions.

(A) In general. Except as provided in subparagraph (B), in using a consumer report for employment purposes, before taking any adverse action based in whole or in part on the report, the person intending to take such adverse action shall provide to the consumer to whom the report relates-¬

(i) a copy of the report; and

(ii) a description in writing of the rights of the consumer under this title, as prescribed by the Federal Trade Commission under section 609(c)(3).1

(B) Application by mail, telephone, computer, or other similar means.

(i) If a consumer described in subparagraph (C) applies for employment by mail, telephone, computer, or other similar means, and if a person who has procured a consumer report on the consumer for employment purposes takes adverse action on the employment application based in whole or in part on the report, then the person must provide to the consumer to whom the report relates, in lieu of the notices required under subparagraph (A) of this section and under section 615(a), within 3 business days of taking such action, an oral, written or electronic notification-¬

(I) that adverse action has been taken based in whole or in part on a consumer report received from a consumer reporting agency;

(II) of the name, address and telephone number of the consumer reporting agency that furnished the consumer report (including a toll-free telephone number established by the agency if the agency compiles and maintains files on consumers on a nationwide basis);

(III) that the consumer reporting agency did not make the decision to take the adverse action and is unable to provide to the consumer the specific reasons why the adverse action was taken; and

(IV) that the consumer may, upon providing proper identification, request a free copy of a report and may dispute with the consumer reporting agency the accuracy or completeness of any information in a report.

1The references in Sections 604(b)(3)(A) and 604(b)(3)(B) should be to Section 609(c)(1), not (c)(3) that no longer exists as the result of Congress' re-organization of Section 609(c) in 2003 (FACT Act).

(ii) If, under clause (B)(i)(IV), the consumer requests a copy of a consumer report from the person who procured the report, then, within 3 business days of receiving the consumer's request, together with proper identifi¬cation, the person must send or provide to the consumer a copy of a report and a copy of the consumer's rights as prescribed by the Federal Trade Commission under section 609(c)(3).

(C) Scope. Subparagraph (B) shall apply to a person procuring a consumer report on a consumer in connection with the consumer's application for employment only if-¬

(i) the consumer is applying for a position over which the Secretary of Trans¬portation has the power to establish qualifications and maximum hours of service pursuant to the provisions of section 31502 of title 49, or a position subject to safety regulation by a State transportation agency; and

(ii) as of the time at which the person procures the report or causes the report to be procured the only interaction between the consumer and the person in connection with that employment application has been by mail, telephone, computer, or other similar means.

(4) Exception for national security investigations.

(A) In general. In the case of an agency or department of the United States Government which seeks to obtain and use a consumer report for employ¬ment purposes, paragraph (3) shall not apply to any adverse action by such agency or department which is based in part on such consumer report, if the head of such agency or department makes a written finding that–

(i) the consumer report is relevant to a national security investigation of such agency or department;

(ii) the investigation is within the jurisdiction of such agency or department;

(iii) there is reason to believe that compliance with paragraph (3) will-¬

(I) endanger the life or physical safety of any person;

(II) result in flight from prosecution;

(III) result in the destruction of, or tampering with, evidence relevant to the investigation;

(IV) result in the intimidation of a potential witness relevant to the investigation;

(V) result in the compromise of classified information; or

(VI) otherwise seriously jeopardize or unduly delay the investigation or another official proceeding.

(B) Notification of consumer upon conclusion of investigation. Upon the conclusion of a national security investigation described in subparagraph (A), or upon the determination that the exception under subparagraph (A) is no longer required for the reasons set forth in such subparagraph, the official exercising the authority in such subparagraph shall provide to the consumer who is the subject of the consumer report with regard to which such finding was made-¬

(i) a copy of such consumer report with any classified information redacted as necessary;

(ii) notice of any adverse action which is based, in part, on the consumer report; and

(iii) the identification with reasonable specificity of the nature of the investigation for which the consumer report was sought.

(C) Delegation by head of agency or department. For purposes of subparagraphs (A) and (B), the head of any agency or department of the United States Government may delegate his or her authorities under this paragraph to an official of such agency or department who has personnel security responsibilities and is a member of the Senior Executive Service or equivalent civilian or military rank.

(D) Report to the Congress. Not later than January 31 of each year, the head of each agency and department of the United States Government that exercised authority under this paragraph during the preceding year shall submit a report to the Congress on the number of times the department or agency exercised such authority during the year.

(E) Definitions. For purposes of this paragraph, the following definitions shall apply:

(i) The term "classified information" means information that is protected from unauthorized disclosure under Executive Order No. 12958 or successor orders.

(ii) The term "national security investigation" means any official inquiry by an agency or department of the United States Government to determine the eligibility of a consumer to receive access or continued access to classified information or to determine whether classified information has been lost or compromised.

(c) Furnishing reports in connection with credit or insurance transactions that are not initiated by the consumer.

(1) In general. A consumer reporting agency may furnish a consumer report relating to any consumer pursuant to subparagraph (A) or (C) of subsection (a)(3) in connection with any credit or insurance transaction that is not initiated by the consumer only if

(A) the consumer authorizes the agency to provide such report to such person; or (B)(i) the transaction consists of a firm offer of credit or insurance;

(ii) the consumer reporting agency has complied with subsection (e); and

(iii) there is not in effect an election by the consumer, made in accordance with subsection (e), to have the consumer's name and address excluded from lists of names provided by the agency pursuant to this paragraph.

(2) Limits on information received under paragraph (1)(B). A person may receive pursuant to paragraph (1)(B) only

(A) the name and address of a consumer;

(B) an identifier that is not unique to the consumer and that is used by the person solely for the purpose of verifying the identity of the consumer; and

(C) other information pertaining to a consumer that does not identify the relationship or experience of the consumer with respect to a particular creditor or other entity.

(3) Information regarding inquiries. Except as provided in section 609(a)(5) [§1681g], a consumer reporting agency shall not furnish to any person a record of inquiries in connection with a credit or insurance transaction that is not initiated by a consumer.

(d) Reserved.

(e) Election of consumer to be excluded from lists.

(1) In general. A consumer may elect to have the consumer's name and address excluded from any list provided by a consumer reporting agency under subsection (c)(1)(B) in connection with a credit or insurance transaction that is not initiated by the consumer, by notifying the agency in accordance with paragraph (2) that the consumer does not consent to any use of a consumer report relating to the consumer in connection with any credit or insurance transaction that is not initiated by the consumer.

(2) Manner of notification. A consumer shall notify a consumer reporting agency under paragraph (1)

(A) through the notification system maintained by the agency under paragraph (5); or

(B) by submitting to the agency a signed notice of election form issued by the agency for purposes of this subparagraph.

(3) Response of agency after notification through system. Upon receipt of notification of the election of a consumer under paragraph (1) through the notification system maintained by the agency under paragraph (5), a consumer reporting agency shall

(A) inform the consumer that the election is effective only for the 5-year period following the election if the consumer does not submit to the agency a signed notice of election form issued by the agency for purposes of paragraph (2)(B); and

(B) provide to the consumer a notice of election form, if requested by the consumer, not later than 5 business days after receipt of the notification of the election through the system established under paragraph (5), in the case of a request made at the time the consumer provides notification through the system.

(4) Effectiveness of election. An election of a consumer under paragraph (1)

(A) shall be effective with respect to a consumer reporting agency beginning 5 business days after the date on which the consumer notifies the agency in accordance with paragraph (2);

(B) shall be effective with respect to a consumer reporting agency

(i) subject to subparagraph (C), during the 5-year period beginning 5 business days after the date on which the consumer notifies the agency of the election, in the case of an election for which a consumer notifies the agency only in accordance with paragraph (2)(A); or

(ii) until the consumer notifies the agency under subparagraph (C), in the case of an election for which a consumer notifies the agency in accordance with paragraph (2)(B);

(C) shall not be effective after the date on which the consumer notifies the agency, through the notification system established by the agency under paragraph (5), that the election is no longer effective; and

(D) shall be effective with respect to each affiliate of the agency.

(5) Notification System

(A) In general. Each consumer reporting agency that, under subsection (c)(1)(B), furnishes a consumer report in connection with a credit or insurance transaction that is not initiated by a consumer, shall

(i) establish and maintain a notification system, including a toll-free telephone number, which permits any consumer whose consumer report is maintained by the agency to notify the agency, with appropriate identification, of the consumer's election to have the consumer's name and address excluded from any such list of names and addresses provided by the agency for such a transaction; and

(ii) publish by not later than 365 days after the date of enactment of the Consumer Credit Reporting Reform Act of 1996, and not less than annually thereafter, in a publication of general circulation in the area served by the agency

(I) a notification that information in consumer files maintained by the agency may be used in connection with such transactions; and

(II) the address and toll-free telephone number for consumers to use to notify the agency of the consumer's election under clause (I).

(B) Establishment and maintenance as compliance. Establishment and maintenance of a notification system (including a toll-free telephone number) and publication by a consumer reporting agency on the agency's own behalf and on behalf of any of its affiliates in accordance with this paragraph is deemed to be compliance with this paragraph by each of those affiliates.

(6) Notification system by agencies that operate nationwide. Each consumer reporting agency that compiles and maintains files on consumers on a nationwide basis shall establish and maintain a notification system for purposes of paragraph (5) jointly with other such consumer reporting agencies.

(f) Certain use or obtaining of information prohibited. A person shall not use or obtain a consumer report for any purpose unless

(1) the consumer report is obtained for a purpose for which the consumer report is authorized to be furnished under this section; and

(2) the purpose is certified in accordance with section 607 [§ 1681e] by a prospective user of the report through a general or specific certification.

(g) Protection of Medical Information

(1) Limitation on consumer reporting agencies. A consumer reporting agency shall not furnish for employment purposes, or in connection with a credit or insurance transaction, a consumer report that contains medical information (other than medical contact information treated in the manner required under section 605(a)(6)) about a consumer, unless-¬

(A) if furnished in connection with an insurance transaction, the consumer affirmatively consents to the furnishing of the report;

(B) if furnished for employment purposes or in connection with a credit transaction-¬

(i) the information to be furnished is relevant to process or effect the employment or credit transaction; and

(ii) the consumer provides specific written consent for the furnishing of the report that describes in clear and conspicuous language the use for which the information will be furnished; or

(C) the information to be furnished pertains solely to transactions, accounts, or balances relating to debts arising from the receipt of medical services, products, or devises, where such information, other than account status or amounts, is restricted or reported using codes that do not identify, or do not provide information sufficient to infer, the specific provider or the nature of such services, products, or devices, as provided in section 605(a)(6).

(2) Limitation on creditors. Except as permitted pursuant to paragraph (3)(C) or regulations prescribed under paragraph (5)(A), a creditor shall not obtain or use medical information (other than medical contact information treated in the manner required under section 605(a)(6)) pertaining to a consumer in connection with any determination of the consumer's eligibility, or continued eligibility, for credit.

(3) Actions authorized by federal law, insurance activities and regulatory determinations. Section 603(d)(3) shall not be construed so as to treat information or any communication of information as a consumer report if the information or communication is disclosed-¬

(A) in connection with the business of insurance or annuities, including the activities described in section 18B of the model Privacy of Consumer Financial and Health Information Regulation issued by the National Association of Insurance Commissioners (as in effect on January 1, 2003);

(B) for any purpose permitted without authorization under the Standards for Individually Identifiable Health Information promulgated by the Department of Health and Human Services pursuant to the Health Insurance Portability and Accountability Act of 1996, or referred to under section 1179 of such Act, or described in section 502(e) of Public Law 106-102; or

(C) as otherwise determined to be necessary and appropriate, by regulation or order and subject to paragraph (6), by the Commission, any Federal banking agency or the National Credit Union Administration (with respect to any financial institution subject to the jurisdiction of such agency or Administration under paragraph (1), (2), or (3) of section 621(b), or the applicable State insurance authority (with respect to any person engaged in providing insurance or annuities).

(4) Limitation on redisclosure of medical information. Any person that receives medical information pursuant to paragraph (1) or (3) shall not disclose such information to any other person, except as necessary to carry out the purpose for which the information was initially disclosed, or as otherwise permitted by statute, regulation, or order.

(5) Regulations and Effective Date for Paragraph (2)

(A) Regulations required. Each Federal banking agency and the National Credit Union Administration shall, subject to paragraph (6) and after notice and opportunity for comment, prescribe regulations that permit transactions under paragraph (2) that are determined to be necessary and appropriate to protect legitimate operational, transactional, risk, consumer, and other needs (and which shall include permitting actions necessary for administrative verification purposes), consistent with the intent of paragraph (2) to restrict the use of medical information for inappropriate purposes.

(B) Final regulations required. The Federal banking agencies and the National Credit Union Administration shall issue the regulations required under subparagraph (A) in final form before the end of the 6-month period beginning on the date of enactment of the Fair and Accurate Credit Transactions Act of 2003.

(6) Coordination with other laws. No provision of this subsection shall be construed as altering, affecting, or superseding the applicability of any other provision of Federal law relating to medical confidentiality.

§ 605. Requirements relating to information contained in consumer reports [15 U.S.C. §1681c]

(a) Information excluded from consumer reports. Except as authorized under subsection

(b) of this section, no consumer reporting agency may make any consumer report containing any of the following items of information:

(1) Cases under title 11 [United States Code] or under the Bankruptcy Act that, from the date of entry of the order for relief or the date of adjudication, as the case may be, antedate the report by more than 10 years.

(2) Civil suits, civil judgments, and records of arrest that from date of entry, antedate the report by more than seven years or until the governing statute of limitations has expired, whichever is the longer period.

(3) Paid tax liens which, from date of payment, antedate the report by more than seven years.

(4) Accounts placed for collection or charged to profit and loss which antedate the report by more than seven years.2

2 The reporting periods have been lengthened for certain adverse information pertaining to U.S. Government insured or guaranteed student loans, or pertaining to national direct

student loans. See sections 430A(f) and 463(c)(3) of the Higher Education Act of 1965, 20 U.S.C. 1080a(f) and 20 U.S.C. 1087cc(c)(3), respectively.
July 30, 2004 22

(5) Any other adverse item of information, other than records of convictions of crimes which antedates the report by more than seven years.2
(6) The name, address, and telephone number of any medical information furnisher that has notified the agency of its status, unless-¬
(A) such name, address, and telephone number are restricted or reported using codes that do not identify, or provide information sufficient to infer, the specific provider or the nature of such services, products, or devices to a person other than the consumer; or
(B) the report is being provided to an insurance company for a purpose relating to engaging in the business of insurance other than property and casualty insurance.

(b) Exempted cases. The provisions of paragraphs (1) through (5) of subsection (a) of this section are not applicable in the case of any consumer credit report to be used in connection with
(1) a credit transaction involving, or which may reasonably be expected to involve, a principal amount of $150,000 or more;
(2) the underwriting of life insurance involving, or which may reasonably be expected to involve, a face amount of $150,000 or more; or
(3) the employment of any individual at an annual salary which equals, or which may reasonably be expected to equal $75,000, or more.
(c) Running of Reporting Period
(1) In general. The 7-year period referred to in paragraphs (4) and (6) 3 of subsection
(a) shall begin, with respect to any delinquent account that is placed for collection (internally or by referral to a third party, whichever is earlier), charged to profit and loss, or subjected to any similar action, upon the expiration of the 180-day period beginning on the date of the commencement of the delinquency which immediately preceded the collection activity, charge to profit and loss, or similar action.
(2) Effective date. Paragraph (1) shall apply only to items of information added to the file of a consumer on or after the date that is 455 days after the date of enactment of the Consumer Credit Reporting Reform Act of 1996.
(d) Information Required to be Disclosed

(1) Title 11 information. Any consumer reporting agency that furnishes a consumer report that contains information regarding any case involving the consumer that arises under title 11, United States Code, shall include in the report an
3This provision, added in September 1996, should read "paragraphs (4) and (5)...." Prior Section 605(a)(6) was amended and re-designated as Section 605(a)(5) in November 1998. The current Section 605(a)(6), added in December 2003 and now containing no reference to

any 7-year period, is obviously inapplicable.

July 30, 2004 23

identification of the chapter of such title 11 under which such case arises if provided by the source of the information. If any case arising or filed under title 11, United States Code, is withdrawn by the consumer before a final judgment, the consumer reporting agency shall include in the report that such case or filing was withdrawn upon receipt of documentation certifying such withdrawal.

(2) Key factor in credit score information. Any consumer reporting agency that fur¬nishes a consumer report that contains any credit score or any other risk score or predictor on any consumer shall include in the report a clear and conspicuous statement that a key factor (as defined in section 609(f)(2)(B)) that adversely affected such score or predictor was the number of enquiries, if such a predictor was in fact a key factor that adversely affected such score. This paragraph shall not apply to a check services company, acting as such, which issues authorizations for the purpose of approving or processing negotiable instruments, electronic fund transfers, or similar methods of payments, but only to the extent that such company is engaged in such activities.

(e) Indication of closure of account by consumer. If a consumer reporting agency is notified pursuant to section 623(a)(4) [§ 1681s-2] that a credit account of a consumer was voluntarily closed by the consumer, the agency shall indicate that fact in any consumer report that includes information related to the account.

(f) Indication of dispute by consumer. If a consumer reporting agency is notified pursuant to section 623(a)(3) [§ 1681s-2] that information regarding a consumer who was furnished to the agency is disputed by the consumer, the agency shall indicate that fact in each consumer report that includes the disputed information.

(g) Truncation of Credit Card and Debit Card Numbers

(1) In general. Except as otherwise provided in this subsection, no person that accepts credit cards or debit cards for the transaction of business shall print more than the last 5 digits of the card number or the expiration date upon any receipt provided to the cardholder at the point of the sale or transaction.

(2) Limitation. This subsection shall apply only to receipts that are electronically printed, and shall not apply to transactions in which the sole means of recording a credit card or debit card account number is by handwriting or by an imprint or copy of the card.

(3) Effective date. This subsection shall become effective-¬

(A) 3 years after the date of enactment of this subsection, with respect to any cash register or other machine or device that electronically prints receipts for cred¬it card or debit card transactions that is in use before January 1, 2005; and

(B) 1 year after the date of enactment of this subsection, with respect to any cash register or other machine or device that electronically prints receipts for credit card or debit card transactions that is first put into use on or after January 1, 2005.

(h) Notice of Discrepancy in Address

(1) In general. If a person has requested a consumer report relating to a consumer from a consumer reporting agency described in section 603(p), the request includes an address for the consumer that substantially differs from the addresses in the file of the consumer, and the agency provides a consumer report in response to the request, the consumer reporting agency shall notify the requester of the existence of the discrepancy.

(2) Regulations

(A) Regulations required. The Federal banking agencies, the National Credit Union Administration, and the Commission shall jointly, with respect to the entities that are subject to their respective enforcement authority under section 621, prescribe regulations providing guidance regarding reasonable policies and procedures that a user of a consumer report should employ when such user has received a notice of discrepancy under paragraph (1).

(B) Policies and procedures to be included. The regulations prescribed under subparagraph (A) shall describe reasonable policies and procedures for use by a user of a consumer report-¬

(i) to form a reasonable belief that the user knows the identity of the person to whom the consumer report pertains; and

(ii) if the user establishes a continuing relationship with the consumer, and the user regularly and in the ordinary course of business furnishes information to the consumer reporting agency from which the notice of discrepancy pertaining to the consumer was obtained, to reconcile the address of the consumer with the consumer reporting agency by furnishing such address to such consumer reporting agency as part of information regularly furnished by the user for the period in which the relationship is established.

§ 605A. Identity theft prevention; fraud alerts and active duty alerts [15 U.S.C. §1681c-1]

(a) One-call Fraud Alerts

(1) Initial alerts. Upon the direct request of a consumer, or an individual acting on behalf of or as a personal representative of a consumer, who asserts in good faith a suspicion that the consumer has been or is about to become a victim of fraud or related crime, including identity theft, a consumer reporting agency described in section 603(p) that maintains a file on the consumer and has received appropriate proof of the identity of the requester shall-¬

(A) include a fraud alert in the file of that consumer, and also provide that alert along with any credit score generated in using that file, for a period of not less than 90 days, beginning on the date of such request, unless the consumer or such representative requests that such fraud alert be removed before the end of such period, and the agency has received appropriate proof of the identity of the requester for such purpose; and

(B) refer the information regarding the fraud alert under this paragraph to each of the other consumer reporting agencies described in section 603(p), in accordance with procedures developed under section 621(f).

(2) Access to free reports. In any case in which a consumer reporting agency includes a fraud alert in the file of a consumer pursuant to this subsection, the consumer reporting agency shall-¬

(A) disclose to the consumer that the consumer may request a free copy of the file of the consumer pursuant to section 612(d); and

(B) provide to the consumer all disclosures required to be made under section 609, without charge to the consumer, not later than 3 business days after any request described in subparagraph (A).

(b) Extended Alerts

(1) In general. Upon the direct request of a consumer, or an individual acting on behalf of or as a personal representative of a consumer, who submits an identity theft report to a consumer reporting agency described in section 603(p) that maintains a file on the consumer, if the agency has received appropriate proof of the identity of the requester, the agency shall-¬

(A) include a fraud alert in the file of that consumer, and also provide that alert along with any credit score generated in using that file, during the 7-year period beginning on the date of such request, unless the consumer or such representative requests that such fraud alert be removed before the end of such period and the agency has received appropriate proof of the identity of the requester for such purpose;

(B) during the 5-year period beginning on the date of such request, exclude the consumer from any list of consumers prepared by the consumer reporting agency and provided to any third party to offer credit or insurance to the consumer as part of a transaction that was not initiated by the consumer, unless the consumer or such representative requests that such exclusion be rescinded before the end of such period; and

(C) refer the information regarding the extended fraud alert under this paragraph to each of the other consumer reporting agencies described in section 603(p), in accordance with procedures developed under section 621(f).

(2) Access to free reports. In any case in which a consumer reporting agency includes a fraud alert in the file of a consumer pursuant to this subsection, the consumer reporting agency shall-¬

(A) disclose to the consumer that the consumer may request 2 free copies of the file of the consumer pursuant to section 612(d) during the 12-month period beginning on the date on which the fraud alert was included in the file; and

(B) provide to the consumer all disclosures required to be made under section 609, without charge to the consumer, not later than 3 business days after any request described in subparagraph (A).

(c) Active duty alerts. Upon the direct request of an active duty military consumer, or an individual acting on behalf of or as a personal representative of an active duty military consumer, a consumer reporting agency described in section 603(p) that maintains a file on the active duty military consumer and has received appropriate proof of the identity of the requester shall-¬

(1) include an active duty alert in the file of that active duty military consumer, and also provide that alert along with any credit score generated in using that file, during a period of not less than 12 months, or such longer period as the Commission shall determine, by regulation, beginning on the date of the request, unless the active duty military consumer or such representative requests that such fraud alert be removed before the end of such period, and the agency has received appropriate proof of the identity of the requester for such purpose;

(2) during the 2-year period beginning on the date of such request, exclude the active duty military consumer from any list of consumers prepared by the consumer reporting agency and provided to any third party to offer credit or insurance to the consumer as part of a transaction that was not initiated by the consumer, unless the consumer requests that such exclusion be rescinded before the end of such period; and

(3) refer the information regarding the active duty alert to each of the other consumer reporting agencies described in section 603(p), in accordance with procedures developed under section 621(f).

(d) Procedures. Each consumer reporting agency described in section 603(p) shall establish policies and procedures to comply with this section, including procedures that inform consumers of the availability of initial, extended, and active duty alerts and procedures that allow consumers and active duty military consumers to request initial, extended, or active duty alerts (as applicable) in a simple and easy manner, including by telephone.

(e) Referrals of alerts. Each consumer reporting agency described in section 603(p) that receives a referral of a fraud alert or active duty alert from another consumer reporting agency pursuant to this section shall, as though the agency received the request from the consumer directly, follow the procedures required under-¬

(1) paragraphs (1)(A) and (2) of subsection (a), in the case of a referral under subsection (a)(1)(B);

(2) paragraphs (1)(A), (1)(B), and (2) of subsection (b), in the case of a referral under subsection (b)(1)(C); and

(3) paragraphs (1) and (2) of subsection (c), in the case of a referral under subsection (c)(3).

(f) Duty of reseller to reconvey alert. A reseller shall include in its report any fraud alert or active duty alert placed in the file of a consumer pursuant to this section by another consumer reporting agency.

(g) Duty of other consumer reporting agencies to provide contact information. If a consumer contacts any consumer reporting agency that is not described in section 603(p) to communicate a suspicion that the consumer has been or is about to become a victim of fraud or related crime, including identity theft, the agency shall provide information to the consumer on how to contact the Commission and the consumer reporting agencies described in section 603(p) to obtain more detailed information and request alerts under this section.

(h) Limitations on Use of Information for Credit Extensions

(1) Requirements for initial and active duty alerts-

(A) Notification. Each initial fraud alert and active duty alert under this section shall include information that notifies all prospective users of a consumer report on the consumer to which the alert relates that the consumer does not authorize the establishment of any new credit plan or extension of credit, other than under an open-end credit plan (as defined in section 103(i)), in the name of the consumer, or issuance of an additional card on an existing credit account requested by a consumer, or any increase in credit limit on an existing credit account requested by a consumer, except in accordance with subparagraph (B).

(B) Limitation on Users

(i) In general. No prospective user of a consumer report that includes an initial fraud alert or an active duty alert in accordance with this section may establish a new credit plan or extension of credit, other than under an open-end credit plan (as defined in section 103(i)), in the name of the consumer, or issue an additional card on an existing credit account requested by a consumer, or grant any increase in credit limit on an existing credit account requested by a consumer, unless the user utilizes reasonable policies and procedures to form a reasonable belief that the user knows the identity of the person making the request.

(ii) Verification. If a consumer requesting the alert has specified a telephone number to be used for identity verification purposes, before authorizing any new credit plan or extension described in clause (i) in the name of such consumer, a user of such consumer report shall contact the consumer using that telephone number or take reasonable steps to verify the consumer's identity and confirm that the application for a new credit plan is not the result of identity theft.

(2) Requirements for Extended Alerts

(A) Notification. Each extended alert under this section shall include information that provides all prospective users of a consumer report relating to a consumer with–

(i) notification that the consumer does not authorize the establishment of any new credit plan or extension of credit described in clause (i), other than under an open-end credit plan (as defined in section 103(i)), in the name of the consumer, or issuance of an additional card on an existing credit account requested by a consumer, or any increase in credit limit on an existing credit account requested by a consumer, except in accordance with subparagraph (B); and

(ii) a telephone number or other reasonable contact method designated by the consumer.

(B) Limitation on users. No prospective user of a consumer report or of a credit score generated using the information in the file of a consumer that includes an extended fraud alert in accordance with this section may establish a new credit plan or extension of credit, other than under an open-end credit plan (as defined in section 103(i)), in the name of the consumer, or issue an additional card on an existing credit account requested by a consumer, or any increase in credit limit on an existing credit account requested by a consumer, unless the user contacts the consumer in person or using the contact method described in subparagraph (A)(ii) to confirm that the application for a new credit plan or increase in credit limit, or request for an additional card is not the result of identity theft.

§ 605B. Block of information resulting from identity theft [15 U.S.C. §1681c-2]

(a) Block. Except as otherwise provided in this section, a consumer reporting agency shall block the reporting of any information in the file of a consumer that the consumer identifies as information that resulted from an alleged identity theft, not later than 4 business days after the date of receipt by such agency of-¬

(1) appropriate proof of the identity of the consumer;

(2) a copy of an identity theft report;

(3) the identification of such information by the consumer; and

(4) a statement by the consumer that the information is not information relating to any transaction by the consumer.

(b) Notification. A consumer reporting agency shall promptly notify the furnisher of information identified by the consumer under subsection (a)-¬

(1) that the information may be a result of identity theft;

(2) that an identity theft report has been filed;

(3) that a block has been requested under this section; and

(4) of the effective dates of the block.

(c) Authority to Decline or Rescind

(1) In general. A consumer reporting agency may decline to block, or may rescind any block, of information relating to a consumer under this section, if the consumer reporting agency reasonably determines that-¬

(A) the information was blocked in error or a block was requested by the consumer in error;

(B) the information was blocked, or a block was requested by the consumer, on the basis of a material misrepresentation of fact by the consumer relevant to the request to block; or

(C) the consumer obtained possession of goods, services, or money as a result of the blocked transaction or transactions.

(2) Notification to consumer. If a block of information is declined or rescinded under this subsection, the affected consumer shall be notified promptly, in the same manner as consumers are notified of the reinsertion of information under section 611(a)(5)(B).

(3) Significance of block. For purposes of this subsection, if a consumer reporting agency rescinds a block, the presence of information in the file of a consumer prior to the blocking of such information is not evidence of whether the consumer knew or should have known that the consumer obtained possession of any goods, services, or money as a result of the block.

(d) Exception for Resellers

(1) No reseller file. This section shall not apply to a consumer reporting agency, if the

consumer reporting agency-¬

(A) is a reseller;

(B) is not, at the time of the request of the consumer under subsection (a), otherwise furnishing or reselling a consumer report concerning the information identified by the consumer; and

(C) informs the consumer, by any means, that the consumer may report the identity theft to the Commission to obtain consumer information regarding identity theft.

(2) Reseller with file. The sole obligation of the consumer reporting agency under this section, with regard to any request of a consumer under this section, shall be to block the consumer report maintained by the consumer reporting agency from any subsequent use, if-

¬

(A) the consumer, in accordance with the provisions of subsection (a), identifies, to a consumer reporting agency, information in the file of the consumer that resulted from identity theft; and

(B) the consumer reporting agency is a reseller of the identified information.

(3) Notice. In carrying out its obligation under paragraph (2), the reseller shall promptly provide a notice to the consumer of the decision to block the file. Such notice shall contain the name, address, and telephone number of each consumer reporting agency from which the consumer information was obtained for resale.

(e) Exception for verification companies. The provisions of this section do not apply to a check services company, acting as such, which issues authorizations for the purpose of approving or processing negotiable instruments, electronic fund transfers, or similar methods of payments, except that, beginning 4 business days after receipt of information described in paragraphs (1) through (3) of subsection (a), a check services company shall not report to a national consumer reporting agency described in section 603(p), any information identified in the subject identity theft report as resulting from identity theft.

(f) Access to blocked information by law enforcement agencies. No provision of this sec¬tion shall be construed as requiring a consumer reporting agency to prevent a Federal, State, or local law enforcement agency from accessing blocked information in a consumer file to which the agency could otherwise obtain access under this title.

§ 606. Disclosure of investigative consumer reports [15 U.S.C. § 1681d]

(a) Disclosure of fact of preparation. A person may not procure or cause to be prepared an investigative consumer report on any consumer unless

(1) it is clearly and accurately disclosed to the consumer that an investigative consumer report including information as to his character, general reputation, personal characteristics and mode of living, whichever are applicable, may be made, and such disclosure

(A) is made in a writing mailed, or otherwise delivered, to the consumer, not later than three days after the date on which the report was first requested, and

(B) includes a statement informing the consumer of his right to request the additional disclosures provided for under subsection (b) of this section and the written summary of the rights of the consumer prepared pursuant to section 609(c) [§ 1681g]; and

(2) the person certifies or has certified to the consumer reporting agency that

(A) the person has made the disclosures to the consumer required by paragraph (1); and

(B) the person will comply with subsection (b).

(b) Disclosure on request of nature and scope of investigation. Any person who procures or causes to be prepared an investigative consumer report on any consumer shall, upon written request made by the consumer within a reasonable period of time after the receipt by him of the disclosure required by subsection (a)(1) of this section, make a complete and accurate disclosure of the nature and scope of the investigation requested. This disclosure shall be made in a writing mailed, or otherwise delivered, to the consumer not later than five days after the date on which the request for such disclosure was received from the consumer or such report was first requested, whichever is the later.

(c) Limitation on liability upon showing of reasonable procedures for compliance with provisions. No person may be held liable for any violation of subsection (a) or (b) of this section if he shows by a preponderance of the evidence that at the time of the violation he maintained reasonable procedures to assure compliance with subsection

(a) or (b) of this section.

(d) Prohibitions

(1) Certification. A consumer reporting agency shall not prepare or furnish investigative consumer report unless the agency has received a certification under subsection (a)(2) from the person who requested the report.

(2) Inquiries. A consumer reporting agency shall not make an inquiry for the purpose of preparing an investigative consumer report on a consumer for employment purposes if the making of the inquiry by an employer or prospective employer of the consumer would violate any applicable Federal or State equal employment opportunity law or regulation.

(3) Certain public record information. Except as otherwise provided in section 613 [§ 1681k], a consumer reporting agency shall not furnish an investigative con¬sumer report that includes information that is a matter of public record and that relates to an arrest, indictment, conviction, civil judicial action, tax lien, or out¬standing judgment, unless the agency has verified the accuracy of the information during the 30-day period ending on the date on which the report is furnished.

(4) Certain adverse information. A consumer reporting agency shall not prepare or furnish an investigative consumer report on a consumer that contains information that is adverse to the interest of the consumer and that is obtained through a personal interview with a neighbor, friend, or associate of the consumer or with another person with whom the consumer is acquainted or who has knowledge of such item of information, unless

(A) the agency has followed reasonable procedures to obtain confirmation of the information, from an additional source that has independent and direct knowledge of the information; or

(B) the person interviewed is the best possible source of the information. § 607. Compliance procedures [15 U.S.C. § 1681e]

(a) Identity and purposes of credit users. Every consumer reporting agency shall maintain reasonable procedures designed to avoid violations of section 605 [§ 1681c] and to limit the furnishing of consumer reports to the purposes listed under section 604 [§ 1681b] of this title. These procedures shall require that prospective users of the information iden¬tify themselves, certify the purposes for which the information is sought, and certify that the information will be used for no other purpose. Every consumer reporting agency shall make a reasonable effort to verify the identity of a new prospective user and the uses certified by such prospective user prior to furnishing such user a consumer report. No consumer reporting agency may furnish a consumer report to any person if it has reasonable grounds for believing that the consumer report will not be used for a purpose listed in section 604 [§ 1681b] of this title.

(b) Accuracy of report. Whenever a consumer reporting agency prepares a consumer report it shall follow reasonable procedures to assure maximum possible accuracy of the information concerning the individual about whom the report relates.

(c) Disclosure of consumer reports by users allowed. A consumer reporting agency may not prohibit a user of a consumer report furnished by the agency on a consumer from disclosing the contents of the report to the consumer, if adverse action against the consumer has been taken by the user based in whole or in part on the report.

(d) Notice to Users and Furnishers of Information

(1) Notice requirement. A consumer reporting agency shall provide to any person

(A) who regularly and in the ordinary course of business furnishes information to the agency with respect to any consumer; or

(B) to whom a consumer report is provided by the agency; a notice of such person's responsibilities under this title.

(2) Content of notice. The Federal Trade Commission shall prescribe the content of noti¬ces under paragraph (1), and a consumer reporting agency shall be in compliance with this subsection if it provides a notice under paragraph (1) that is substantially similar to the Federal Trade Commission prescription under this paragraph.

(e) Procurement of Consumer Report for Resale

(1) Disclosure. A person may not procure a consumer report for purposes of reselling the report (or any information in the report) unless the person discloses to the consumer reporting agency that originally furnishes the report

(A) the identity of the end-user of the report (or information); and

(B) each permissible purpose under section 604 [§ 1681b] for which the report is furnished to the end-user of the report (or information).

(2) Responsibilities of procurers for resale. A person who procures a consumer report

for purposes of reselling the report (or any information in the report) shall

(A) establish and comply with reasonable procedures designed to ensure that the report (or information) is resold by the person only for a purpose for which the report may be furnished under section 604 [§ 1681b], including by requiring that each person to which the report (or information) is resold and that resells or provides the report (or information) to any other person

(i) identifies each end user of the resold report (or information);

(ii) certifies each purpose for which the report (or information) will be used; and

(iii) certifies that the report (or information) will be used for no other purpose; and

(B) before reselling the report, make reasonable efforts to verify the identifications and certifications made under subparagraph (A).

(3) Resale of consumer report to a federal agency or department. Notwithstanding paragraph (1) or (2), a person who procures a consumer report for purposes of reselling the report (or any information in the report) shall not disclose the identity of the end-user of the report under paragraph (1) or (2) if-¬

(A) the end user is an agency or department of the United States Government which procures the report from the person for purposes of determining the eligibility of the consumer concerned to receive access or continued access to classified information (as defined in section 604(b)(4)(E)(i)); and

(B) the agency or department certifies in writing to the person reselling the report

that nondisclosure is necessary to protect classified information or the safety of persons employed by or contracting with, or undergoing investigation for work or contracting with the agency or department.

§ 608. Disclosures to governmental agencies [15 U.S.C. § 1681f]

Notwithstanding the provisions of section 604 [§ 1681b] of this title, a consumer reporting agency may furnish identifying information respecting any consumer, limited to his name, address, former addresses, places of employment, or former places of employment, to a governmental agency.

§ 609. Disclosures to consumers [15 U.S.C. § 1681g]

(a) Information on file; sources; report recipients. Every consumer reporting agency shall, upon request, and subject to 610(a)(1) [§ 1681h], clearly and accurately disclose to the consumer:

(1) All information in the consumer's file at the time of the request except that-¬

(2) The sources of the information; except that the sources of information acquired solely for use in preparing an investigative consumer report and actually use for no other purpose need not be disclosed: Provided, That in the event an action is brought under this title, such sources shall be available to the plaintiff under appropriate discovery procedures in the court in which the action is brought.

(3)(A) Identification of each person (including each end-user identified under section 607(e)(1) [§ 1681e]) that procured a consumer report

(i) for employment purposes, during the 2-year period preceding the date on which the request is made; or

(ii) for any other purpose, during the 1-year period preceding the date on which the request is made.

(B) An identification of a person under subparagraph (A) shall include

(i) the name of the person or, if applicable, the trade name (written in full) under which such person conducts business; and

(ii) upon request of the consumer, the address and telephone number of the person.

(C) Subparagraph (A) does not apply if-¬

(i) the end user is an agency or department of the United States Government that procures the report from the person for purposes of determining the eligibility of the consumer to whom the report relates to receive access or continued access to classified information (as defined in section 604(b)(4)(E)(i)); and

(ii) the head of the agency or department makes a written finding as prescribed under section 604(b)(4)(A).

(4) The dates, original payees, and amounts of any checks upon which is based any adverse characterization of the consumer, included in the file at the time of the disclosure.

(5) A record of all inquiries received by the agency during the 1-year period preceding the request that identified the consumer in connection with a credit or insurance transaction that was not initiated by the consumer.

(6) If the consumer requests the credit file and not the credit score, a statement that the consumer may request and obtain a credit score.

(b) Exempt information. The requirements of subsection (a) of this section respecting the disclosure of sources of information and the recipients of consumer reports do not apply to information received or consumer reports furnished prior to the effective date of this title except to the extent that the matter involved is contained in the files of the consumer reporting agency on that date.

(c) Summary of Rights to Obtain and Dispute Information in Consumer Reports and to Obtain Credit Scores

(1) Commission Summary of Rights Required

(A) In general. The Commission shall prepare a model summary of the rights of consumers under this title.

(B) Content of summary. The summary of rights prepared under subparagraph

(A) shall include a description of–

(i) the right of a consumer to obtain a copy of a consumer report under subsection (a) from each consumer reporting agency;

(ii) the frequency and circumstances under which a consumer is entitled to receive a consumer report without charge under section 612;

(iii) the right of a consumer to dispute information in the file of the consumer under section 611;

(iv) the right of a consumer to obtain a credit score from a consumer reporting agency, and a description of how to obtain a credit score;

(v) the method by which a consumer can contact, and obtain a consumer report from, a consumer reporting agency without charge, as provided in the regulations of the Commission prescribed under section 211(c) of the Fair and Accurate Credit Transactions Act of 2003; and

(vi) the method by which a consumer can contact, and obtain a consumer report from, a consumer reporting agency described in section 603(w), as provided in the regulations of the Commission prescribed under section 612(a)(1)(C).

(C) Availability of summary of rights. The Commission shall-¬

(i) actively publicize the availability of the summary of rights prepared under this paragraph;

(ii) conspicuously post on its Internet website the availability of such summary of rights; and

(iii) promptly make such summary of rights available to consumers, on request.

(2) Summary of rights required to be included with agency disclosures. A consumer reporting agency shall provide to a consumer, with each written disclosure by the agency to the consumer under this section-¬

(A) the summary of rights prepared by the Commission under paragraph (1);

(B) in the case of a consumer reporting agency described in section 603(p), a toll-free telephone number established by the agency, at which personnel are accessible to consumers during normal business hours;

(C) a list of all Federal agencies responsible for enforcing any provision of this title, and the address and any appropriate phone number of each such agency, in a form that will assist the consumer in selecting the appropriate agency;

(D) a statement that the consumer may have additional rights under State law, and that the consumer may wish to contact a State or local consumer protection agency or a State attorney general (or the equivalent thereof) to learn of those rights; and

(E) a statement that a consumer reporting agency is not required to remove accurate derogatory information from the file of a consumer, unless the information is outdated under section 605 or cannot be verified.

(d) Summary of Rights of Identity Theft Victims

(1) In general. The Commission, in consultation with the Federal banking agencies and the National Credit Union Administration, shall prepare a model summary of the rights of consumers under this title with respect to the procedures for remedying the effects of fraud or identity theft involving credit, an electronic fund transfer, or an account or transaction at

or with a financial institution or other creditor.

(2) Summary of rights and contact information. Beginning 60 days after the date on which the model summary of rights is prescribed in final form by the Commission pursuant to paragraph (1), if any consumer contacts a consumer reporting agency and expresses a belief that the consumer is a victim of fraud or identity theft

involving credit, an electronic fund transfer, or an account or transaction at or with a financial institution or other creditor, the consumer reporting agency shall, in addition to any other action that the agency may take, provide the consumer with a summary of rights that contains all of the information required by the Commission under paragraph (1), and information on how to contact the Commission to obtain more detailed information.

(e) Information Available to Victims

(1) In general. For the purpose of documenting fraudulent transactions resulting from identity theft, not later than 30 days after the date of receipt of a request from a victim in accordance with paragraph (3), and subject to verification of the identity of the victim and the claim of identity theft in accordance with paragraph (2), a business entity that has provided credit to, provided for consideration products, goods, or services to, accepted payment from, or otherwise entered into a commercial transaction for consideration with, a person who has allegedly made unauthorized use of the means of identification of the victim, shall provide a copy of application and business transaction records in the control of the business entity, whether maintained by the business entity or by another person on behalf of the business entity, evidencing any transaction alleged to be a result of identity theft to-¬

(A) the victim;

(B) any Federal, State, or local government law enforcement agency or officer specified by the victim in such a request; or

(C) any law enforcement agency investigating the identity theft and authorized by the victim to take receipt of records provided under this subsection.

(2) Verification of identity and claim. Before a business entity provides any informa¬tion under paragraph (1), unless the business entity, at its discretion, otherwise has a high degree of confidence that it knows the identity of the victim making a request under paragraph (1), the victim shall provide to the business entity-¬

(A) as proof of positive identification of the victim, at the election of the business entity–

(i) the presentation of a government-issued identification card;

(ii) personally identifying information of the same type as was provided to the business entity by the unauthorized person; or

(iii) personally identifying information that the business entity typically requests from new applicants or for new transactions, at the time of the victim's request for information, including any documentation described in clauses (i) and (ii); and

(B) as proof of a claim of identity theft, at the election of the business entity-¬

(i) a copy of a police report evidencing the claim of the victim of identity theft; and

(ii) a properly completed-¬

(I) copy of a standardized affidavit of identity theft developed and made available by the Commission; or

(II) an affidavit of fact that is acceptable to the business entity for that purpose.

(3) Procedures. The request of a victim under paragraph (1) shall-¬

(A) be in writing;

(B) be mailed to an address specified by the business entity, if any; and

(C) if asked by the business entity, include relevant information about any transaction alleged to be a result of identity theft to facilitate compliance with this section including–

(i) if known by the victim (or if readily obtainable by the victim), the date of the application or transaction; and

(ii) if known by the victim (or if readily obtainable by the victim), any other identifying information such as an account or transaction number.

(4) No charge to victim. Information required to be provided under paragraph (1) shall be so provided without charge.

(5) Authority to decline to provide information. A business entity may decline to provide information under paragraph (1) if, in the exercise of good faith, the business entity determines that-¬

(A) this subsection does not require disclosure of the information;

(B) after reviewing the information provided pursuant to paragraph (2), the business entity does not have a high degree of confidence in knowing the true identity of the individual requesting the information;

(C) the request for the information is based on a misrepresentation of fact by the individual requesting the information relevant to the request for information; or

(D) the information requested is Internet navigational data or similar information about a person's visit to a website or online service.

(6) Limitation on liability. Except as provided in section 621, sections 616 and 617 do not apply to any violation of this subsection.

(7) Limitation on civil liability. No business entity may be held civilly liable under any provision of Federal, State, or other law for disclosure, made in good faith pursuant to this subsection.

(8) No new recordkeeping obligation. Nothing in this subsection creates an obligation on the part of a business entity to obtain, retain, or maintain information or records that are not otherwise required to be obtained, retained, or maintained in the ordinary course of its business or under other applicable law.

(9) Rule of Construction

(A) In general. No provision of subtitle A of title V of Public Law 106-102, prohibiting the disclosure of financial information by a business entity to third parties shall be used to deny disclosure of information to the victim under this subsection.

(B) Limitation. Except as provided in subparagraph (A), nothing in this subsection permits a business entity to disclose information, including information to law enforcement under subparagraphs (B) and (C) of paragraph (1), that the business entity is otherwise prohibited from disclosing under any other applicable provision of Federal or State law.

(10) Affirmative defense. In any civil action brought to enforce this subsection, it is an affirmative defense (which the defendant must establish by a preponderance of the evidence) for a business entity to file an affidavit or answer stating that-¬

(A) the business entity has made a reasonably diligent search of its available business records; and

(B) the records requested under this subsection do not exist or are not reasonably available.

(11) Definition of victim. For purposes of this subsection, the term "victim" means a consumer whose means of identification or financial information has been used or transferred (or has been alleged to have been used or transferred) without the authority of that consumer, with the intent to commit, or to aid or abet, an identity theft or a similar crime.

(12) Effective date. This subsection shall become effective 180 days after the date of enactment of this subsection.

(13) Effectiveness study. Not later than 18 months after the date of enactment of this subsection, the Comptroller General of the United States shall submit a report to Congress assessing the effectiveness of this provision.

(f) Disclosure of Credit Scores

(1) In general. Upon the request of a consumer for a credit score, a consumer reporting agency shall supply to the consumer a statement indicating that the

information and credit scoring model may be different than the credit score that may be used by the lender, and a notice which shall include-¬

(A) the current credit score of the consumer or the most recent credit score of the consumer that was previously calculated by the credit reporting agency for a purpose related to the extension of credit;

(B) the range of possible credit scores under the model used;

(C) all of the key factors that adversely affected the credit score of the consumer in the model used, the total number of which shall not exceed 4, subject to paragraph (9);

(D) the date on which the credit score was created; and

(E) the name of the person or entity that provided the credit score or credit file upon which the credit score was created.

(2) Definitions. For purposes of this subsection, the following definitions shall apply:

(A) The term "credit score" -¬

(i) means a numerical value or a categorization derived from a statistical tool or modeling system used by a person who makes or arranges a loan to predict the likelihood of certain credit behaviors, including default (and the numerical value or the categorization derived from such analysis may also be referred to as a "risk predictor" or "risk score"); and

(ii) does not include-¬

(I) any mortgage score or rating of an automated underwriting system that considers one or more factors in addition to credit information, including the loan to value ratio, the amount of down payment, or the financial assets of a consumer; or

(II) any other elements of the underwriting process or underwriting decision.

(B) The term "key factors" means all relevant elements or reasons adversely affecting the credit score for the particular individual, listed in the order of their importance based on their effect on the credit score.

(3) Timeframe and manner of disclosure. The information required by this subsection shall be provided in the same timeframe and manner as the information described in subsection (a).

(4) Applicability to certain uses. This subsection shall not be construed so as to compel a consumer reporting agency to develop or disclose a score if the agency does not-¬

(A) distribute scores that are used in connection with residential real property loans; or

(B) develop scores that assist credit providers in understanding the general credit behavior of a consumer and predicting the future credit behavior of the consumer.

(5) Applicability to credit scores developed by another person.

(A) In general. This subsection shall not be construed to require a consumer reporting agency that distributes credit scores developed by another person or entity to provide a further explanation of them, or to process a dispute arising pursuant to section 611, except that the consumer reporting agency shall provide the consumer with the name and address and website for contacting the person or entity who developed the score or developed the methodology of the score.

(B) Exception. This paragraph shall not apply to a consumer reporting agency that develops or modifies scores that are developed by another person or entity.

(6) Maintenance of credit scores not required. This subsection shall not be construed to require a consumer reporting agency to maintain credit scores in its files.

(7) Compliance in certain cases. In complying with this subsection, a consumer reporting agency shall-¬

(A) supply the consumer with a credit score that is derived from a credit scoring model that is widely distributed to users by that consumer reporting agency in connection with residential real property loans or with a credit score that assists the consumer in understanding the credit scoring assessment of the credit behavior of the consumer and predictions about the future credit behavior of the consumer; and

(B) a statement indicating that the information and credit scoring model may be different than that used by the lender.

(8) Fair and reasonable fee. A consumer reporting agency may charge a fair and reasonable fee, as determined by the Commission, for providing the information required under this subsection.

(9) Use of enquiries as a key factor. If a key factor that adversely affects the credit score

of a consumer consists of the number of enquiries made with respect to a consumer report, that factor shall be included in the disclosure pursuant to paragraph (1)(C) without regard to the numerical limitation in such paragraph.

(g) Disclosure of Credit Scores by Certain Mortgage Lenders

(1) In general. Any person who makes or arranges loans and who uses a consumer credit score, as defined in subsection (f), in connection with an application initiated or sought by a consumer for a closed end loan or the establishment of an open end loan for a consumer purpose that is secured by 1 to 4 units of residential real property (hereafter in this subsection referred to as the "lender") shall provide the following to the consumer as soon as reasonably practicable:

(A) Information Required under Subsection (f)

(i) In general. A copy of the information identified in subsection (f) that was obtained from a consumer reporting agency or was developed and used by the user of the information.

(ii) Notice under subparagraph (D). In addition to the information provided to it by a third party that provided the credit score or scores, a lender is only required to provide the notice contained in subparagraph (D).

(B) Disclosures in Case of Automated Underwriting System

(i) In general. If a person that is subject to this subsection uses an auto¬mated underwriting system to underwrite a loan, that person may satisfy the obligation to provide a credit score by disclosing a credit score and associated key factors supplied by a consumer reporting agency.

(ii) Numerical credit score. However, if a numerical credit score is generated by an automated underwriting system used by an enterprise, and that score is disclosed to the person, the score shall be disclosed to the consumer consistent with subparagraph (C).

(iii) Enterprise defined. For purposes of this subparagraph, the term "enter¬prise" has the same meaning as in paragraph (6) of section 1303 of the Federal Housing Enterprises Financial Safety and Soundness Act of 1992.

(C) Disclosures of credit scores not obtained from a consumer reporting agency. A person that is subject to the provisions of this subsection and that uses a credit score, other than a credit score provided by a consumer reporting agency, may satisfy the obligation to provide a credit score by disclosing a credit score and associated key factors supplied by a consumer reporting agency.

(D) Notice to home loan applicants. A copy of the following notice, which shall include the name, address, and telephone number of each consumer reporting agency providing a credit score that was used:

"Notice To The Home Loan Applicant

"In connection with your application for a home loan, the lender must disclose to you the score that a consumer reporting agency distributed to users and the lender used in connection with your home loan, and the key factors affecting your credit scores.

"The credit score is a computer generated summary calculated at the time of the request and based on information that a consumer reporting agency or lender has on file. The scores are based on data about your credit history and payment patterns. Credit scores are important because they are used to assist the lender in determining whether you will obtain a loan. They may also be used to determine what interest rate you may be offered on the mortgage. Credit scores can change over time, depending on your conduct, how your credit history and payment patterns change, and how credit scoring technologies change.

"Because the score is based on information in your credit history, it is very important that you review the credit-related information that is being furnished to make sure it is accurate. Credit records may vary from one company to another.

"If you have questions about your credit score or the credit information that is furnished to you, contact the consumer reporting agency at the address and telephone number provided with this notice, or contact the lender, if the lender developed or generated the credit score. The consumer reporting agency plays no part in the decision to take any action on the loan application and is unable to provide you with specific reasons for the decision on a loan application.

"If you have questions concerning the terms of the loan, contact the lender."

(E) Actions not required under this subsection. This subsection shall not require any person to–

(i) explain the information provided pursuant to subsection (f);

(ii) disclose any information other than a credit score or key factors, as defined in subsection (f);

(iii) disclose any credit score or related information obtained by the user after a loan has closed;

(iv) provide more than 1 disclosure per loan transaction; or

(v) provide the disclosure required by this subsection when another person has made the disclosure to the consumer for that loan transaction.

(F) No Obligation for Content

(i) In general. The obligation of any person pursuant to this subsection shall be limited solely to providing a copy of the information that was received from the consumer reporting agency.

(ii) Limit on liability. No person has liability under this subsection for the content of that information or for the omission of any information within the report provided by the consumer reporting agency.

(G) Person defined as excluding enterprise. As used in this subsection, the term "person" does not include an enterprise (as defined in paragraph (6) of section 1303 of the

Federal Housing Enterprises Financial Safety and Soundness Act of 1992).

(2) Prohibition on Disclosure Clauses Null and Void

(A) In general. Any provision in a contract that prohibits the disclosure of a credit score by a person who makes or arranges loans or a consumer reporting agency is void.

(B) No liability for disclosure under this subsection- A lender shall not have liability under any contractual provision for disclosure of a credit score pursuant to this subsection.

§ 610. Conditions and form of disclosure to consumers [15 U.S.C. § 1681h]

(a) In General

(1) Proper identification. A consumer reporting agency shall require, as a condition of making the disclosures required under section 609 [§ 1681g], that the consumer furnish proper identification.

(2) Disclosure in writing. Except as provided in subsection (b), the disclosures required to be made under section 609 [§ 1681g] shall be provided under that section in writing.

(b) Other Forms of Disclosure

(1) In general. If authorized by a consumer, a consumer reporting agency may make the disclosures required under 609 [§ 1681g]

(A) other than in writing; and

(B) in such form as may be

(i) specified by the consumer in accordance with paragraph (2); and

(ii) available from the agency.

(2) Form. A consumer may specify pursuant to paragraph (1) that disclosures under section 609 [§ 1681g] shall be made

(A) in person, upon the appearance of the consumer at the place of business of the consumer reporting agency where disclosures are regularly provided, during normal business hours, and on reasonable notice;

(B) by telephone, if the consumer has made a written request for disclosure by telephone;

(C) by electronic means, if available from the agency; or

(D) by any other reasonable means that is available from the agency.

(c) Trained personnel. Any consumer reporting agency shall provide trained personnel to explain to the consumer any information furnished to him pursuant to section 609 [§ 1681g] of this title.

(d) Persons accompanying consumer. The consumer shall be permitted to be accompanied by one other person of his choosing, who shall furnish reasonable identification. A consumer reporting agency may require the consumer to furnish a written statement granting permission to the consumer reporting agency to discuss the consumer's file in such person's presence.

(e) Limitation of liability. Except as provided in sections 616 and 617 [§§ 1681n and 1681o] of this title, no consumer may bring any action or proceeding in the nature of defamation, invasion of privacy, or negligence with respect to the reporting of information against any consumer reporting agency, any user of information, or any person who furnishes information to a consumer reporting agency, based on information disclosed pursuant to section 609, 610, or 615 [§§ 1681g, 1681h, or 1681m] of this title or based on information disclosed by a user of a consumer report to or for a consumer against whom the user has taken adverse action, based in whole or in part on the report, except as to false information furnished with malice or willful intent to injure such consumer.

§ 611. Procedure in case of disputed accuracy [15 U.S.C. § 1681i]

(a) Reinvestigations of Disputed Information

(1) Reinvestigation Required

(A) In general. Subject to subsection (f), if the completeness or accuracy of any item of information contained in a consumer's file at a consumer reporting agency is disputed by the consumer and the consumer notifies the agency directly, or indirectly through a reseller, of such dispute, the agency shall, free of charge, conduct a reasonable reinvestigation to determine whether the disputed information is inaccurate and record the current status of the disputed information, or delete the item from the file in accordance with paragraph (5), before the end of the 30-day period beginning on the date on which the agency receives the notice of the dispute from the consumer or reseller.

(B) Extension of period to reinvestigate. Except as provided in subparagraph (C), the 30-day period described in subparagraph (A) may be extended for not more than 15 additional days if the consumer reporting agency receives information from the consumer during that 30-day period that is relevant to the reinvestigation.

(C) Limitations on extension of period to reinvestigate. Subparagraph (B) shall not apply to any reinvestigation in which, during the 30-day period

described in subparagraph (A), the information that is the subject of the reinvestigation is found to be inaccurate or incomplete or the consumer reporting agency determines that the information cannot be verified.

(2) Prompt Notice of Dispute to Furnisher of Information

(A) In general. Before the expiration of the 5-business-day period beginning on the date on which a consumer reporting agency receives notice of a dispute from any consumer or a reseller in accordance with paragraph (1), the agency shall provide notification of the dispute to any person who provided any item of information in dispute, at the address and in the manner established with the person. The notice shall include all relevant information regarding the dispute that the agency has received from the consumer or reseller.

(B) Provision of other information. The consumer reporting agency shall promptly provide to the person who provided the information in dispute all relevant information regarding the dispute that is received by the agency from the consumer or the reseller after the period referred to in subparagraph (A) and before the end of the period referred to in paragraph (1)(A).

(3) Determination That Dispute Is Frivolous or Irrelevant

(A) In general. Notwithstanding paragraph (1), a consumer reporting agency may terminate a reinvestigation of information disputed by a consumer under that paragraph if the agency reasonably determines that the dispute by the consumer is frivolous or irrelevant, including by reason of a failure by a consumer to provide sufficient information to investigate the disputed information.

(B) Notice of determination. Upon making any determination in accordance with subparagraph (A) that a dispute is frivolous or irrelevant, a consumer reporting agency shall notify the consumer of such determination not later than 5 business days after making such determination, by mail or, if authorized by the consumer for that purpose, by any other means available to the agency.

(C) Contents of notice. A notice under subparagraph (B) shall include

(i) the reasons for the determination under subparagraph (A); and

(ii) identification of any information required to investigate the disputed information, which may consist of a standardized form describing the general nature of such information.

(4) Consideration of consumer information. In conducting any reinvestigation under paragraph (1) with respect to disputed information in the file of any consumer, the consumer reporting agency shall review and consider all relevant information submitted by the consumer in the period described in paragraph (1)(A) with respect to such disputed information.

(5) Treatment of Inaccurate or Unverifiable Information

(A) In general. If, after any reinvestigation under paragraph (1) of any information disputed by a consumer, an item of the information is found to be inaccurate or incomplete or cannot be verified, the consumer reporting agency shall–

(i) promptly delete that item of information from the file of the consumer, or modify that item of information, as appropriate, based on the results of the reinvestigation; and

(ii) promptly notify the furnisher of that information that the information has been modified or deleted from the file of the consumer.

(B) Requirements Relating to Reinsertion of Previously Deleted Material

(i) Certification of accuracy of information. If any information is deleted from a consumer's file pursuant to subparagraph (A), the information may not be reinserted in the file by the consumer reporting agency unless the person who furnishes the information certifies that the information is complete and accurate.

(ii) Notice to consumer. If any information that has been deleted from a consumer's file pursuant to subparagraph (A) is reinserted in the file, the consumer reporting agency shall notify the consumer of the reinsertion in writing not later than 5 business days after the reinsertion or, if authorized by the consumer for that purpose, by any other means available to the agency.

(iii) Additional information. As part of, or in addition to, the notice under clause (ii), a consumer reporting agency shall provide to a consumer in writing not later than 5 business days after the date of the reinsertion

(I) a statement that the disputed information has been reinserted;

(II) the business name and address of any furnisher of information contacted and the telephone number of such furnisher, if reasonably available, or of any furnisher of information that contacted the consumer reporting agency, in connection with the reinsertion of such information; and

(III) a notice that the consumer has the right to add a statement to the consumer's file disputing the accuracy or completeness of the disputed information.

(C) Procedures to prevent reappearance. A consumer reporting agency shall maintain reasonable procedures designed to prevent the reappearance in a consumer's file, and in consumer reports on the consumer, of information that is deleted pursuant to this paragraph (other than information that is reinserted in accordance with subparagraph (B)(i)).

(D) Automated reinvestigation system. Any consumer reporting agency that compiles and maintains files on consumers on a nationwide basis shall implement an automated system through which furnishers of information to that consumer reporting agency may report the results of a reinvestigation that finds incomplete or inaccurate information in a consumer's file to other such consumer reporting agencies.

(6) Notice of Results of Reinvestigation

(A) In general. A consumer reporting agency shall provide written notice to a consumer of the results of a reinvestigation under this subsection not later than 5 business days after the completion of the reinvestigation, by mail or, if authorized by the consumer for that purpose, by other means available to the agency.

(B) Contents. As part of, or in addition to, the notice under subparagraph (A), a consumer reporting agency shall provide to a consumer in writing before the expiration of the 5-day period referred to in subparagraph (A)

(i) a statement that the reinvestigation is completed;

(ii) a consumer report that is based upon the consumer's file as that file is revised as a result of the reinvestigation;

(iii) a notice that, if requested by the consumer, a description of the procedure used to determine the accuracy and completeness of the information shall be provided to the consumer by the agency, including the business name and address of any furnisher of information contacted in connection with such information and the telephone number of such furnisher, if reasonably available;

(iv) a notice that the consumer has the right to add a statement to the consumer's file disputing the accuracy or completeness of the information; and

(v) a notice that the consumer has the right to request under subsection

(d) that the consumer reporting agency furnish notifications under that subsection.

(7) Description of reinvestigation procedure. A consumer reporting agency shall provide to a consumer a description referred to in paragraph (6)(B)(iii) by not later than 15 days after receiving a request from the consumer for that description.

(8) Expedited dispute resolution. If a dispute regarding an item of information in a con-

sumer's file at a consumer reporting agency is resolved in accordance with paragraph (5)(A) by the deletion of the disputed information by not later than 3 business days after the date on which the agency receives notice of the dispute from the consumer in accordance with paragraph (1)(A), then the agency shall not be required to comply with paragraphs (2), (6), and (7) with respect to that dispute if the agency

(A) provides prompt notice of the deletion to the consumer by telephone;

(B) includes in that notice, or in a written notice that accompanies a confirmation and consumer report provided in accordance with subparagraph (C), a statement of the consumer's right to request under subsection (d) that the agency furnish notifications under that subsection; and

(C) provides written confirmation of the deletion and a copy of a consumer report on the consumer that is based on the consumer's file after the deletion, not later than 5 business days after making the deletion.

(b) Statement of dispute. If the reinvestigation does not resolve the dispute, the consumer may file a brief statement setting forth the nature of the dispute. The consumer reporting agency may limit such statements to not more than one hundred words if it provides the consumer with assistance in writing a clear summary of the dispute.

(c) Notification of consumer dispute in subsequent consumer reports. Whenever a statement of a dispute is filed, unless there is reasonable grounds to believe that it is frivolous or irrelevant, the consumer reporting agency shall, in any subsequent report containing the information in question, clearly note that it is disputed by the consumer and provide either the consumer's statement or a clear and accurate codification or summary thereof.

(d) Notification of deletion of disputed information. Following any deletion of information which is found to be inaccurate or whose accuracy can no longer be verified or any notation as to disputed information, the consumer reporting agency shall, at the request of the consumer, furnish notification that the item has been deleted or the statement, codification or summary pursuant to subsection (b) or (c) of this section to any person specifically designated by the consumer who has within two years prior thereto received a consumer report for employment purposes, or within six months prior thereto received a consumer report for any other purpose, which contained the deleted or disputed information.

(e) Treatment of Complaints and Report to Congress

(1) In general. The Commission shall-¬

(A) compile all complaints that it receives that a file of a consumer that is maintained by a consumer reporting agency described in section 603(p) contains incomplete or inaccurate information, with respect to which, the consumer appears to have disputed the completeness or accuracy with the consumer reporting agency or otherwise utilized the procedures provided by subsection (a); and

(B) transmit each such complaint to each consumer reporting agency involved.

(2) Exclusion. Complaints received or obtained by the Commission pursuant to its investigative authority under the Federal Trade Commission Act shall not be subject to paragraph (1).

(3) Agency responsibilities. Each consumer reporting agency described in section 603(p) that receives a complaint transmitted by the Commission pursuant to paragraph (1) shall-¬

(A) review each such complaint to determine whether all legal obligations imposed on the consumer reporting agency under this title (including any obligation imposed by an applicable court or administrative order) have been met with respect to the subject matter of the complaint;

(B) provide reports on a regular basis to the Commission regarding the determinations of and actions taken by the consumer reporting agency, if any, in connection with its review of such complaints; and

(C) maintain, for a reasonable time period, records regarding the disposition of each such complaint that is sufficient to demonstrate compliance with this subsection.

(4) Rulemaking authority. The Commission may prescribe regulations, as appropriate to implement this subsection.

(5) Annual report. The Commission shall submit to the Committee on Banking, Housing, and Urban Affairs of the Senate and the Committee on Financial Services of the House of Representatives an annual report regarding information gathered by the Commission under this subsection.'.

(f) Reinvestigation Requirement Applicable to Resellers

(1) Exemption from general reinvestigation requirement. Except as provided in para¬graph (2), a reseller shall be exempt from the requirements of this section.

(2) Action required upon receiving notice of a dispute. If a reseller receives a notice from a consumer of a dispute concerning the completeness or accuracy of any item of information contained in a consumer report on such consumer produced by the reseller, the reseller shall, within 5 business days of receiving the notice, and free of charge–

(A) determine whether the item of information is incomplete or inaccurate as a result of an act or omission of the reseller; and

(B) if (i) the reseller determines that the item of information is incomplete or inaccurate as a result of an act or omission of the reseller, not later than 20 days after receiving the notice, correct the information in the consumer report or delete it; or

(ii) if the reseller determines that the item of information is not incomplete or inaccurate as a result of an act or omission of the reseller, convey the notice of the dispute, together with all relevant information provided by the consumer, to each consumer reporting agency that provided the reseller with the information that is the subject of the dispute, using an address or a notification mechanism specified by the consumer reporting agency for such notices.

(3) Responsibility of consumer reporting agency to notify consumer through reseller. Upon the completion of a reinvestigation under this section of a dispute concerning the

complete¬ness or accuracy of any information in the file of a consumer by a consumer reporting agency that received notice of the dispute from a reseller under paragraph (2)-¬

(A) the notice by the consumer reporting agency under paragraph (6), (7), or (8) of subsection (a) shall be provided to the reseller in lieu of the consumer; and

(B) the reseller shall immediately reconvey such notice to the consumer, including any notice of a deletion by telephone in the manner required under paragraph (8)(A).

(4) Reseller reinvestigations. No provision of this subsection shall be construed as prohibiting a reseller from conducting a reinvestigation of a consumer dispute directly.

§ 612. Charges for certain disclosures [15 U.S.C. § 1681j] See also 16 CFR Part 610 69 Fed. Reg. 35467 (06/24/04)

(a) Free Annual Disclosure

(1) Nationwide Consumer Reporting Agencies

(A) In general. All consumer reporting agencies described in subsections (p) and

(w) of section 603 shall make all disclosures pursuant to section 609 once during any 12-month period upon request of the consumer and without charge to the consumer.

(B) Centralized source. Subparagraph (A) shall apply with respect to a consumer reporting agency described in section 603(p) only if the request from the consumer is made using the centralized source established for such purpose in accordance with section 211(c) of the Fair and Accurate Credit Transactions Act of 2003.

(C) Nationwide Specialty Consumer Reporting Agency

(i) In general. The Commission shall prescribe regulations applicable to each consumer reporting agency described in section 603(w) to require the establishment of a streamlined process for consumers to request consumer reports under subparagraph (A), which shall include, at a minimum, the establishment by each such agency of a toll-free telephone number for such requests.

(ii) Considerations. In prescribing regulations under clause (i), the Commission shall consider–

(I) the significant demands that may be placed on consumer reporting agencies in providing such consumer reports;

(II) appropriate means to ensure that consumer reporting agencies can satisfactorily meet those demands, including the efficacy of a system of staggering the availability to consumers of such consumer reports; and

(III) the ease by which consumers should be able to contact consumer reporting agencies with respect to access to such consumer reports.

(iii) Date of issuance. The Commission shall issue the regulations required by this subparagraph in final form not later than 6 months after the date of enactment of the Fair and Accurate Credit Transactions Act of 2003.

(iv) Consideration of ability to comply. The regulations of the Commission under this subparagraph shall establish an effective date by which each nationwide specialty consumer reporting agency (as defined in section 603(w)) shall be required to comply with subsection (a), which effective date-¬

(I) shall be established after consideration of the ability of each nationwide specialty consumer reporting agency to comply with subsection (a); and

(II) shall be not later than 6 months after the date on which such regulations are issued in final form (or such additional period not to exceed 3 months, as the Commission determines appropriate).

(2) Timing. A consumer reporting agency shall provide a consumer report under paragraph (1) not later than 15 days after the date on which the request is received under paragraph (1).

(3) Reinvestigations. Notwithstanding the time periods specified in section 611(a)(1), a reinvestigation under that section by a consumer reporting agency upon a request of a consumer that is made after receiving a consumer report under this subsection shall be completed not later than 45 days after the date on which the request is received.

(4) Exception for first 12 months of operation. This subsection shall not apply to a consumer reporting agency that has not been furnishing consumer reports to third parties on a continuing basis during the 12-month period preceding a request under paragraph (1), with respect to consumers residing nationwide.

(b) Free disclosure after adverse notice to consumer. Each consumer reporting agency that maintains a file on a consumer shall make all disclosures pursuant to section 609 [§ 1681g] without charge to the consumer if, not later than 60 days after receipt by such consumer of a notification pursuant to section 615 [§ 1681m], or of a notification from a debt collection agency affiliated with that consumer reporting agency stating that the consumer's credit rating may be or has been adversely affected, the consumer makes a request under section 609 [§ 1681g].

(c) Free disclosure under certain other circumstances. Upon the request of the consumer, a consumer reporting agency shall make all disclosures pursuant to section 609 [§ 1681g] once during any 12-month period without charge to that consumer if the consumer certifies in writing that the consumer

(1) is unemployed and intends to apply for employment in the 60-day period beginning on the date on which the certification is made;

(2) is a recipient of public welfare assistance; or

(3) has reason to believe that the file on the consumer at the agency contains inaccurate information due to fraud.

(d) Free disclosures in connection with fraud alerts. Upon the request of a consumer, a consumer reporting agency described in section 603(p) shall make all disclosures pursuant to section 609 without charge to the consumer, as provided in subsections (a)(2) and (b)(2) of section 605A, as applicable.

(e) Other charges prohibited A consumer reporting agency shall not impose any charge on a consumer for providing any notification required by this title or making any disclosure required by this title, except as authorized by subsection (f).

(f) Reasonable Charges Allowed for Certain Disclosures

(1) In general. In the case of a request from a consumer other than a request that is covered by any of subsections (a) through (d), a consumer reporting agency may impose a reasonable charge on a consumer

(A) for making a disclosure to the consumer pursuant to section 609 [§ 1681g], which charge

(i) shall not exceed $8;4 and

(ii) shall be indicated to the consumer before making the disclosure; and

(B) for furnishing, pursuant to 611(d) [§ 1681i], following a reinvestigation under section 611(a) [§ 1681i], a statement, codification, or summary to a person designated by the consumer under that section after the 30-day period beginning on the date of notification of the consumer under paragraph (6) or (8) of section 611(a) [§ 1681i] with respect to the reinvestigation, which charge

(i) shall not exceed the charge that the agency would impose on each designated recipient for a consumer report; and

(ii) shall be indicated to the consumer before furnishing such information.

(2) Modification of amount. The Federal Trade Commission shall increase the amount referred to in paragraph (1)(A)(I) on January 1 of each year, based proportionally on changes in the Consumer Price Index, with fractional changes rounded to the nearest fifty cents.

4

The Federal Trade Commission increased the maximum allowable charge to $9.00, effective January 1, 2002. 66 Fed. Reg. 63545 (Dec. 7, 2001).

July 30, 2004 54

§ 613. Public record information for employment purposes [15 U.S.C. § 1681k]

(a) In general. A consumer reporting agency which furnishes a consumer report for employment purposes and which for that purpose compiles and reports items of information on consumers which are matters of public record and are likely to have an adverse effect upon a consumer's ability to obtain employment shall

(1) at the time such public record information is reported to the user of such consumer report, notify the consumer of the fact that public record information is being reported by the consumer reporting agency, together with the name and address of the person to whom such information is being reported; or

(2) maintain strict procedures designed to insure that whenever public record information which is likely to have an adverse effect on a consumer's ability to obtain employment is reported it is complete and up to date. For purposes of this paragraph, items of public record relating to arrests, indictments, convictions, suits, tax liens, and outstanding judgments shall be considered up to date if the current public record status of the item at the time of the report is reported.

(b) Exemption for national security investigations. Subsection (a) does not apply in the case of an agency or department of the United States Government that seeks to obtain and use a consumer report for employment purposes, if the head of the agency or department makes a written finding as prescribed under section 604(b)(4)(A).

§ 614. Restrictions on investigative consumer reports [15 U.S.C. § 1681l]

Whenever a consumer reporting agency prepares an investigative consumer report, no adverse information in the consumer report (other than information which is a matter of public record) may be included in a subsequent consumer report unless such adverse information has been verified in the process of making such subsequent consumer report, or the adverse information was received within the three-month period preceding the date the subsequent report is furnished.

§ 615. Requirements on users of consumer reports [15 U.S.C. § 1681m]

(a) Duties of users taking adverse actions on the basis of information contained in consumer reports. If any person takes any adverse action with respect to any consumer that is based in whole or in part on any information contained in a consumer report, the person shall

(1) provide oral, written, or electronic notice of the adverse action to the consumer;

(2) provide to the consumer orally, in writing, or electronically

(A) the name, address, and telephone number of the consumer reporting agency (including a toll-free telephone number established by the agency if the agency compiles and maintains files on consumers on a nationwide basis) that furnished the report to the person; and

(B) a statement that the consumer reporting agency did not make the decision to take the adverse action and is unable to provide the consumer the specific reasons why the adverse action was taken; and

(3) provide to the consumer an oral, written, or electronic notice of the consumer's right

(A) to obtain, under section 612 [§ 1681j], a free copy of a consumer report on the consumer from the consumer reporting agency referred to in paragraph (2), which notice shall include an indication of the 60-day period under that section for obtaining such a copy; and

(B) to dispute, under section 611 [§ 1681i], with a consumer reporting agency the accuracy or completeness of any information in a consumer report furnished by the agency.

(b) Adverse Action Based on Information Obtained from Third Parties Other than Consumer Reporting Agencies

(1) In general. Whenever credit for personal, family, or household purposes involving a consumer is denied or the charge for such credit is increased either wholly or partly because of information obtained from a person other than a consumer reporting agency bearing upon the consumer's credit worthiness, credit standing, credit capacity, character, general reputation, personal characteristics, or mode of living, the user of such information shall, within a reasonable period of time, upon the consumer's written request for the reasons for such adverse action received within sixty days after learning of such adverse action, disclose the nature of the information to the consumer. The user of such information shall

clearly and accurately disclose to the consumer his right to make such written request at the time such adverse action is communicated to the consumer.

(2) Duties of Person Taking Certain Actions Based on Information Provided by Affiliate

(A) Duties, generally. If a person takes an action described in subparagraph

(B) with respect to a consumer, based in whole or in part on information described in subparagraph (C), the person shall

(i) notify the consumer of the action, including a statement that the consumer may obtain the information in accordance with clause (ii); and

(ii) upon a written request from the consumer received within 60 days after transmittal of the notice required by clause (I), disclose to the consumer the nature of the information upon which the action is based by not later than 30 days after receipt of the request.

(B) Action described. An action referred to in subparagraph (A) is an adverse action described in section 603(k)(1)(A) [§ 1681a], taken in connection with a transaction initiated by the consumer, or any adverse action described in clause (i) or (ii) of section 603(k)(1)(B) [§ 1681a].

(C) Information described. Information referred to in subparagraph (A)

(i) except as provided in clause (ii), is information that

(I) is furnished to the person taking the action by a person related by common ownership or affiliated by common corporate control to the person taking the action; and

(II) bears on the credit worthiness, credit standing, credit capacity, character, general reputation, personal characteristics, or mode of living of the consumer; and

(ii) does not include

(I) information solely as to transactions or experiences between the consumer and the person furnishing the information; or

(II) information in a consumer report.

(c) Reasonable procedures to assure compliance. No person shall be held liable for any violation of this section if he shows by a preponderance of the evidence that at the time of the alleged violation he maintained reasonable procedures to assure compliance with the provisions of this section.

(d) Duties of Users Making Written Credit or Insurance Solicitations on the Basis of Information Contained in Consumer Files

(1) In general. Any person who uses a consumer report on any consumer in connection with any credit or insurance transaction that is not initiated by the consumer, that is provided to that person under section 604(c)(1)(B) [§ 1681b], shall provide with each written solicitation made to the consumer regarding the transaction a clear and conspicuous statement that

(A) information contained in the consumer's consumer report was used in connection with the transaction;

(B) the consumer received the offer of credit or insurance because the consumer satisfied the criteria for credit worthiness or insurability under which the consumer was selected for the offer;

(C) if applicable, the credit or insurance may not be extended if, after the consumer responds to the offer, the consumer does not meet the criteria used to select the consumer for the offer or any applicable criteria bearing on credit worthiness or insurability or does not furnish any required collateral;

(D) the consumer has a right to prohibit information contained in the consumer's file with any consumer reporting agency from being used in connection with any credit or insurance transaction that is not initiated by the consumer; and

(E) the consumer may exercise the right referred to in subparagraph (D) by notifying a notification system established under section 604(e) [§ 1681b].

(2) Disclosure of address and telephone number; format. A statement under paragraph

(1) shall-¬

(A) include the address and toll-free telephone number of the appropriate notification system established under section 604(e); and

(B) be presented in such format and in such type size and manner as to be simple and easy to understand, as established by the Commission, by rule, in consultation with the Federal banking agencies and the National Credit Union Administration.

(3) Maintaining criteria on file. A person who makes an offer of credit or insurance to a consumer under a credit or insurance transaction described in paragraph (1) shall maintain on file the criteria used to select the consumer to receive the offer, all criteria bearing on credit worthiness or insurability, as applicable, that are the basis for determining whether or not to extend credit or insurance pursuant to the offer, and any requirement for the furnishing of collateral as a condition of the extension of credit or insurance, until the expiration of the 3-year period beginning on the date on which the offer is made to the consumer.

(4) Authority of federal agencies regarding unfair or deceptive acts or practices not affected. This section is not intended to affect the authority of any Federal or State agency to enforce a prohibition against unfair or deceptive acts or practices, including the making of false or misleading statements in connection with a credit or insurance transaction that is not initiated by the consumer.

(e) Red Flag Guidelines and Regulations Required

(1) Guidelines. The Federal banking agencies, the National Credit Union Administration, and the Commission shall jointly, with respect to the entities that are subject to their respective enforcement authority under section 621–

(A) establish and maintain guidelines for use by each financial institution and each creditor regarding identity theft with respect to account holders at, or customers of, such entities, and update such guidelines as often as necessary;

(B) prescribe regulations requiring each financial institution and each creditor to establish reasonable policies and procedures for implementing the guidelines established pursuant to subparagraph (A), to identify possible risks to account holders or customers or to the safety and soundness of the institution or customers; and

(C) prescribe regulations applicable to card issuers to ensure that, if a card issuer receives notification of a change of address for an existing account, and within a short period of time (during at least the first 30 days after such notification is received) receives a request for an additional or replacement card for the same account, the card issuer may not issue the additional or replacement card, unless the card issuer, in accordance with reasonable policies and procedures-¬

(i) notifies the cardholder of the request at the former address of the cardholder and provides to the cardholder a means of promptly reporting incorrect address changes;

(ii) notifies the cardholder of the request by such other means of communication as the cardholder and the card issuer previously agreed to; or

(iii) uses other means of assessing the validity of the change of address, in accordance with reasonable policies and procedures established by the card issuer in accordance with the regulations prescribed under subparagraph (B).

(2) Criteria

(A) In general. In developing the guidelines required by paragraph (1)(A), the agencies described in paragraph (1) shall identify patterns, practices, and specific forms of activity that indicate the possible existence of identity theft.

(B) Inactive accounts. In developing the guidelines required by paragraph (1)(A), the agencies described in paragraph (1) shall consider including reasonable guidelines providing that when a transaction occurs with respect to a credit or deposit account that has been inactive for more than 2 years, the creditor or financial institution shall follow reasonable policies and procedures that provide for notice to be given to a consumer in a manner reasonably designed to reduce the likelihood of identity theft with respect to such account.

(3) Consistency with verification requirements. Guidelines established pursuant to paragraph (1) shall not be inconsistent with the policies and procedures required under section 5318(l) of title 31, United States Code.

(f) Prohibition on Sale or Transfer of Debt Caused by Identity Theft

(1) In general. No person shall sell, transfer for consideration, or place for collection a debt that such person has been notified under section 605B has resulted from identity theft.

(2) Applicability. The prohibitions of this subsection shall apply to all persons collecting a debt described in paragraph (1) after the date of a notification under paragraph (1).

(3) Rule of construction. Nothing in this subsection shall be construed to prohibit-¬

(A) the repurchase of a debt in any case in which the assignee of the debt requires such repurchase because the debt has resulted from identity theft;

(B) the securitization of a debt or the pledging of a portfolio of debt as collateral in connection with a borrowing; or

(C) the transfer of debt as a result of a merger, acquisition, purchase and assumption transaction, or transfer of substantially all of the assets of an entity.

(g) Debt collector communications concerning identity theft. If a person acting as a debt collector (as that term is defined in title VIII) on behalf of a third party that is a creditor or other user of a consumer report is notified that any information relating to a debt that the person is attempting to collect may be fraudulent or may be the result of identity theft, that person shall-¬

(1) notify the third party that the information may be fraudulent or may be the result of identity theft; and

(2) upon request of the consumer to whom the debt purportedly relates, provide to the consumer all information to which the consumer would otherwise be entitled if the consumer were not a victim of identity theft, but wished to dispute the debt under provisions of law applicable to that person.

(h) Duties of Users in Certain Credit Transactions

(1) In general. Subject to rules prescribed as provided in paragraph (6), if any person uses a consumer report in connection with an application for, or a grant, extension, or other provision of, credit on material terms that are materially less favorable than the most favorable terms available to a substantial proportion of consumers from or through that person, based in whole or in part on a consumer report, the person shall provide an oral, written, or electronic notice to the consumer in the form and manner required by regulations prescribed in accordance with this subsection.

(2) Timing. The notice required under paragraph (1) may be provided at the time of an application for, or a grant, extension, or other provision of, credit or the time of communication of an approval of an application for, or grant, extension, or other provision of, credit, except as provided in the regulations prescribed under paragraph (6).

(3) Exceptions. No notice shall be required from a person under this subsection if–

(A) the consumer applied for specific material terms and was granted those terms, unless those terms were initially specified by the person after the transaction was initiated by the consumer and after the person obtained a consumer report; or

(B) the person has provided or will provide a notice to the consumer under subsection (a) in connection with the transaction.

(4) Other notice not sufficient. A person that is required to provide a notice under subsection (a) cannot meet that requirement by providing a notice under this subsection.

(5) Content and delivery of notice. A notice under this subsection shall, at a minimum–

(A) include a statement informing the consumer that the terms offered to the consumer are set based on information from a consumer report;

(B) identify the consumer reporting agency furnishing the report;

(C) include a statement informing the consumer that the consumer may obtain a copy of a consumer report from that consumer reporting agency without charge; and

(D) include the contact information specified by that consumer reporting agency for obtaining such consumer reports (including a toll-free telephone number established by the agency in the case of a consumer reporting agency described in section 603(p)).

(6) Rulemaking

(A) Rules required. The Commission and the Board shall jointly prescribe rules.

(B) Content. Rules required by subparagraph (A) shall address, but are not limited to–

(i) the form, content, time, and manner of delivery of any notice under this subsection;

(ii) clarification of the meaning of terms used in this subsection, including what credit terms are material, and when credit terms are materially less favorable;

(iii) exceptions to the notice requirement under this subsection for classes of persons or transactions regarding which the agencies determine that notice would not significantly benefit consumers;

(iv) a model notice that may be used to comply with this subsection; and

(v) the timing of the notice required under paragraph (1), including the circumstances under which the notice must be provided after the terms offered to the consumer were set based on information from a consumer report.

(7) Compliance. A person shall not be liable for failure to perform the duties required by this section if, at the time of the failure, the person maintained reasonable policies and procedures to comply with this section.

(8) Enforcement

(A) No civil actions. Sections 616 and 617 shall not apply to any failure by any person to comply with this section.

(B) Administrative enforcement. This section shall be enforced exclusively under section 621 by the Federal agencies and officials identified in that section.

§ 616. Civil liability for willful noncompliance [15 U.S.C. § 1681n]

(a) In general. Any person who willfully fails to comply with any requirement imposed under this title with respect to any consumer is liable to that consumer in an amount equal to the sum of

(1) (A) any actual damages sustained by the consumer as a result of the failure or damages of not less than $100 and not more than $1,000; or

(B) in the case of liability of a natural person for obtaining a consumer report under false pretenses or knowingly without a permissible purpose, actual damages sustained by the consumer as a result of the failure or $1,000, whichever is greater;

(2) such amount of punitive damages as the court may allow; and

(3) in the case of any successful action to enforce any liability under this section, the costs of the action together with reasonable attorney's fees as determined by the court.

(b) Civil liability for knowing noncompliance. Any person who obtains a consumer report from a consumer reporting agency under false pretenses or knowingly without a permissible purpose shall be liable to the consumer reporting agency for actual damages sustained by the consumer reporting agency or $1,000, whichever is greater.

(c) Attorney's fees. Upon a finding by the court that an unsuccessful pleading, motion, or other paper filed in connection with an action under this section was filed in bad faith or for purposes of harassment, the court shall award to the prevailing party attorney's fees reasonable in relation to the work expended in responding to the pleading, motion, or other paper.

§ 617. Civil liability for negligent noncompliance [15 U.S.C. § 1681o]

(a) In general. Any person who is negligent in failing to comply with any requirement imposed under this title with respect to any consumer is liable to that consumer in an amount equal to the sum of

(1) any actual damages sustained by the consumer as a result of the failure; and

(2) in the case of any successful action to enforce any liability under this section, the costs of the action together with reasonable attorney's fees as determined by the court.

(b) Attorney's fees. On a finding by the court that an unsuccessful pleading, motion, or other paper filed in connection with an action under this section was filed in bad faith or for purposes of harassment, the court shall award to the prevailing party attorney's fees reasonable in relation to the work expended in responding to the pleading, motion, or other paper.

§ 618. Jurisdiction of courts; limitation of actions [15 U.S.C. § 1681p]

An action to enforce any liability created under this title may be brought in any appropriate United States district court, without regard to the amount in controversy, or in any other court of competent jurisdiction, not later than the earlier of (1) 2 years after the date of discovery by the plaintiff of the violation that is the basis for such liability; or (2) 5 years after the date on which the violation that is the basis for such liability occurs.

§ 619. Obtaining information under false pretenses [15 U.S.C. § 1681q]

Any person who knowingly and willfully obtains information on a consumer from a consumer reporting agency under false pretenses shall be fined under title 18, United States Code, imprisoned for not more than 2 years, or both.

§ 620. Unauthorized disclosures by officers or employees [15 U.S.C. § 1681r]

Any officer or employee of a consumer reporting agency who knowingly and willfully provides information concerning an individual from the agency's files to a person not authorized to receive that information shall be fined under title 18, United States Code, imprisoned for not more than 2 years, or both.

§ 621. Administrative enforcement [15 U.S.C. § 1681s]

(a) (1) Enforcement by Federal Trade Commission. Compliance with the requirements imposed under this title shall be enforced under the Federal Trade Commission Act [15 U.S.C. §§ 41 et seq.] by the Federal Trade Commission with respect to consumer reporting agencies and all other persons subject thereto, except to the extent that enforcement of the requirements imposed under this title is specifically committed to some other government agency under subsection (b) hereof. For the purpose of the exercise by the Federal Trade Commission of its functions and powers under the Federal Trade Commission Act, a violation of any requirement or prohibition imposed under this title shall constitute an unfair or deceptive act or practice in commerce in violation of section 5(a) of the Federal Trade Commission Act [15 U.S.C. § 45(a)] and shall be subject to enforcement by the Federal Trade Commission under section 5(b) thereof [15 U.S.C. § 45(b)] with respect to any consumer reporting agency or person subject to enforcement by the Federal Trade Commission pursuant to this subsection, irrespective of whether that person is engaged in commerce or meets any other jurisdictional tests in the Federal Trade Commission Act. The Federal Trade Commission shall have such procedural, investigative, and enforcement powers, including the power to issue procedural rules in enforcing compliance with the requirements imposed under this title and to require the filing of reports, the production of documents, and the appearance of witnesses as though the applicable terms and conditions of the Federal Trade Commission Act were part of this title. Any person violating any of the provisions of this title shall be subject to the penalties and entitled to the privileges and immunities provided in the Federal Trade Commission Act as though the applicable terms and provisions thereof were part of this title.

(2) (A) In the event of a knowing violation, which constitutes a pattern or practice of violations of this title, the Commission may commence a civil action to recover a civil penalty in a district court of the United States against any person that violates this title. In such action, such person shall be liable for a civil penalty of not more than $2,500 per violation.

(B) In determining the amount of a civil penalty under subparagraph (A), the court shall take into account the degree of culpability, any history of prior such conduct, ability to pay, effect on ability to continue to do business, and such other matters as justice may require.

(3) Notwithstanding paragraph (2), a court may not impose any civil penalty on a person for a violation of section 623(a)(1) [§ 1681s-2] unless the person has been enjoined from committing the violation, or ordered not to commit the violation, in an action or proceeding brought by or on behalf of the Federal Trade Commission, and has violated the injunction or order, and the court may not impose any civil penalty for any violation occurring before the date of the violation of the injunction or order.

(b) Enforcement by other agencies. Compliance with the requirements imposed under this title with respect to consumer reporting agencies, persons who use consumer reports from such agencies, persons who furnish information to such agencies, and users of information that are subject to subsection (d) of section 615 [§ 1681m] shall be enforced under

(1) section 8 of the Federal Deposit Insurance Act [12 U.S.C. § 1818], in the case of

(A) national banks, and Federal branches and Federal agencies of foreign banks, by the Office of the Comptroller of the Currency;

(B) member banks of the Federal Reserve System (other than national banks), branches and agencies of foreign banks (other than Federal branches, Federal agencies, and insured State branches of foreign banks), commercial lending companies owned or controlled by foreign banks, and organizations operating under section 25 or 25A of the Federal Reserve Act [12 U.S.C. §§ 601 et seq., §§ 611 et seq], by the Board of Governors of the Federal Reserve System; and

(C) banks insured by the Federal Deposit Insurance Corporation (other than members of the Federal Reserve System) and insured State branches of foreign banks, by the Board of Directors of the Federal Deposit Insurance Corporation;

(2) section 8 of the Federal Deposit Insurance Act [12 U.S.C. § 1818], by the Director of the Office of Thrift Supervision, in the case of a savings association the deposits of which are insured by the Federal Deposit Insurance Corporation;

(3) the Federal Credit Union Act [12 U.S.C. §§ 1751 et seq.], by the Administrator of the National Credit Union Administration [National Credit Union Administration Board] with respect to any Federal credit union;

(4) subtitle IV of title 49 [49 U.S.C. §§ 10101 et seq.], by the Secretary of Transportation, with respect to all carriers subject to the jurisdiction of the Surface Transportation Board;

(5) the Federal Aviation Act of 1958 [49 U.S.C. Appx §§ 1301 et seq.], by the Secretary of Transportation with respect to any air carrier or foreign air carrier subject to that Act [49 U.S.C. Appx §§ 1301 et seq.]; and

(6) the Packers and Stockyards Act, 1921 [7 U.S.C. §§ 181 et seq.] (except as provided in section 406 of that Act [7 U.S.C. §§ 226 and 227]), by the Secretary of Agriculture with respect to any activities subject to that Act.

The terms used in paragraph (1) that are not defined in this title or otherwise defined in sec¬tion 3(s) of the Federal Deposit Insurance Act (12 U.S.C. §1813(s)) shall have the meaning given to them in section 1(b) of the International Banking Act of 1978 (12 U.S.C. § 3101).

(c) State Action for Violations

(1) Authority of states. In addition to such other remedies as are provided under State law, if the chief law enforcement officer of a State, or an official or agency designated by a State, has reason to believe that any person has violated or is violating this title, the State

(A) may bring an action to enjoin such violation in any appropriate United States district court or in any other court of competent jurisdiction;

(B) subject to paragraph (5), may bring an action on behalf of the residents of the State to recover

(i) damages for which the person is liable to such residents under sections 616 and 617 [§§ 1681n and 1681o] as a result of the violation;

(ii) in the case of a violation described in any of paragraphs (1) through (3) of section 623(c), damages for which the person would, but for section 623(c) [§ 1681s-2], be liable to such residents as a result of the violation; or

(iii) damages of not more than $1,000 for each willful or negligent violation; and

(C) in the case of any successful action under subparagraph (A) or (B), shall be awarded the costs of the action and reasonable attorney fees as determined by the court.

(2) Rights of federal regulators. The State shall serve prior written notice of any action under paragraph (1) upon the Federal Trade Commission or the appropriate Federal regulator determined under subsection (b) and provide the Commission or appropriate Federal regulator with a copy of its complaint, except in any case in which such prior notice is not feasible, in which case the State shall serve such notice immediately upon instituting such action. The Federal Trade Commission or appropriate Federal regulator shall have the right

(A) to intervene in the action;

(B) upon so intervening, to be heard on all matters arising therein;

(C) to remove the action to the appropriate United States district court; and

(D) to file petitions for appeal.

(3) Investigatory powers. For purposes of bringing any action under this subsection, nothing in this subsection shall prevent the chief law enforcement officer, or an official or agency designated by a State, from exercising the powers conferred on the chief law enforcement officer or such official by the laws of such State to conduct investigations or to administer oaths or affirmations or to compel the attendance of witnesses or the production of documentary and other evidence.

(4) Limitation on state action while federal action pending. If the Federal Trade Commission or the appropriate Federal regulator has instituted a civil action or an administrative action under section 8 of the Federal Deposit Insurance Act for a violation of this title, no State may, during the pendency of such action, bring an action under this section against any defendant named in the complaint of the Commission or the appropriate Federal regulator for any violation of this title that is alleged in that complaint.

(5) Limitations on State Actions for Certain Violations

(A) Violation of injunction required. A State may not bring an action against a person under paragraph (1)(B) for a violation described in any of paragraphs (1) through (3) of section 623(c), unless

(i) the person has been enjoined from committing the violation, in an action brought by the State under paragraph (1)(A); and

(ii) the person has violated the injunction.

(B) Limitation on damages recoverable. In an action against a person under paragraph (1)(B) for a violation described in any of paragraphs (1) through

(3) of section 623(c), a State may not recover any damages incurred before the date of the violation of an injunction on which the action is based.

(d) Enforcement under other authority. For the purpose of the exercise by any agency referred to in subsection (b) of this section of its powers under any Act referred to in that subsection, a violation of any requirement imposed under this title shall be deemed to be a violation of a requirement imposed under that Act. In addition to its powers under any provision of law specifically referred to in subsection (b) of this section, each of the agencies referred to in that subsection may exercise, for the purpose of enforcing compliance with any requirement imposed under this title any other authority conferred on it by law.

(e) Regulatory authority

(1) The Federal banking agencies referred to in paragraphs (1) and (2) of subsection

(b) shall jointly prescribe such regulations as necessary to carry out the purposes of this Act with respect to any persons identified under paragraphs (1) and (2) of subsection (b), and the Board of Governors of the Federal Reserve System shall have authority to prescribe regulations consistent with such joint regulations with respect to bank holding companies and affiliates (other than depository institutions and consumer reporting agencies) of such holding companies.

(2) The Board of the National Credit Union Administration shall prescribe such regula-

tions as necessary to carry out the purposes of this Act with respect to any persons identified under paragraph (3) of subsection (b).

(f) Coordination of Consumer Complaint Investigations

(1) In general. Each consumer reporting agency described in section 603(p) shall develop and maintain procedures for the referral to each other such agency of any consumer complaint received by the agency alleging identity theft, or requesting a fraud alert under section 605A or a block under section 605B.

(2) Model form and procedure for reporting identity theft. The Commission, in consultation with the Federal banking agencies and the National Credit Union Administration, shall develop a model form and model procedures to be used by consumers who are victims of identity theft for contacting and informing creditors and consumer reporting agencies of the fraud.

(3) Annual summary reports. Each consumer reporting agency described in section 603(p) shall submit an annual summary report to the Commission on consumer complaints received by the agency on identity theft or fraud alerts.

(g) FTC regulation of coding of trade names. If the Commission determines that a person described in paragraph (9) of section 623(a) has not met the requirements of such paragraph, the Commission shall take action to ensure the person's compliance with such paragraph, which may include issuing model guidance or prescribing reasonable policies and procedures, as necessary to ensure that such person complies with such paragraph.

§ 622. Information on overdue child support obligations [15 U.S.C. § 1681s-1]

Notwithstanding any other provision of this title, a consumer reporting agency shall include in any consumer report furnished by the agency in accordance with section 604 [§ 1681b] of this title, any information on the failure of the consumer to pay overdue support which

(1) is provided

(A) to the consumer reporting agency by a State or local child support enforcement agency; or

(B) to the consumer reporting agency and verified by any local, State, or Federal government agency; and

(2) antedates the report by 7 years or less.

§ 623. Responsibilities of furnishers of information to consumer reporting agencies [15 U.S.C. § 1681s-2]

(a) Duty of Furnishers of Information to Provide Accurate Information

(1) Prohibition

(A) Reporting information with actual knowledge of errors. A person shall not furnish any information relating to a consumer to any consumer reporting agency if the person knows or has reasonable cause to believe that the information is inaccurate.

(B) Reporting information after notice and confirmation of errors. A person shall not furnish information relating to a consumer to any consumer reporting agency if

(i) the person has been notified by the consumer, at the address specified by the person for such notices, that specific information is inaccurate; and

(ii) the information is, in fact, inaccurate.

(C) No address requirement. A person who clearly and conspicuously specifies to the consumer an address for notices referred to in subparagraph (B) shall not be subject to subparagraph (A); however, nothing in subparagraph (B) shall require a person to specify such an address.

(D) Definition. For purposes of subparagraph (A), the term "reasonable cause to believe that the information is inaccurate" means having specific knowledge, other than solely allegations by the consumer, that would cause a reasonable person to have substantial doubts about the accuracy of the information.

(2) Duty to correct and update information. A person who

(A) regularly and in the ordinary course of business furnishes information to one or more consumer reporting agencies about the person's transactions or experiences with any consumer; and

(B) has furnished to a consumer reporting agency information that the person determines is not complete or accurate, shall promptly notify the consumer reporting agency of that determination and provide to the agency any corrections to that information, or any additional information, that is necessary to make the information provided by the person to the agency complete and accurate, and shall not thereafter furnish to the agency any of the information that remains not complete or accurate.

(3) Duty to provide notice of dispute. If the completeness or accuracy of any informa¬tion furnished by any person to any consumer reporting agency is disputed to such person by a consumer, the person may not furnish the information to any consumer reporting agency without notice that such information is disputed by the consumer.

(4) Duty to provide notice of closed accounts. A person who regularly and in the ordinary course of business furnishes information to a consumer reporting agency regarding a consumer who has a credit account with that person shall notify the agency of the voluntary closure of the account by the consumer, in information regularly furnished for the period in which the account is closed.

(5) Duty to Provide Notice of Delinquency of Accounts

(A) In general. A person who furnishes information to a consumer reporting agency regarding a delinquent account being placed for collection, charged to profit or loss, or subjected to any similar action shall, not later than 90 days after furnishing the information, notify the agency of the date of delinquency on the account, which shall be the month and year of the commencement of the delinquency on the account that immediately preceded the action.

(B) Rule of construction. For purposes of this paragraph only, and provided that the consumer does not dispute the information, a person that furnishes information on a delinquent account that is placed for collection, charged for profit or loss, or subjected to any similar action, complies with this paragraph, if-¬

(i) the person reports the same date of delinquency as that provided by the creditor to which the account was owed at the time at which the commencement of the delinquency occurred, if the creditor previously reported that date of delinquency to a consumer reporting agency;

(ii) the creditor did not previously report the date of delinquency to a consumer reporting agency, and the person establishes and follows reasonable procedures to obtain the date of delinquency from the creditor or another reliable source and reports that date to a consumer reporting agency as the date of delinquency; or

(iii) the creditor did not previously report the date of delinquency to a consumer reporting agency and the date of delinquency cannot be reasonably obtained as provided in clause (ii), the person establishes and follows reasonable procedures to ensure the date reported as the date of delinquency precedes the date on which the account is placed for collection, charged to profit or loss, or subjected to any similar action, and reports such date to the credit reporting agency.

(6) Duties of Furnishers Upon Notice of Identity Theft-Related Information

(A) Reasonable procedures. A person that furnishes information to any consumer reporting agency shall have in place reasonable procedures to respond to any notification that it receives from a consumer reporting agency under section 605B relating to information resulting from identity theft, to prevent that person from refurnishing such blocked information.

(B) Information alleged to result from identity theft. If a consumer submits an identity theft report to a person who furnishes information to a consumer reporting agency at the address specified by that person for receiving such reports stating that information maintained by such person that purports to relate to the consumer resulted from identity theft, the person may not furnish such information that purports to relate to the consumer to any consumer reporting agency, unless the person subsequently knows or is informed by the consumer that the information is correct.

(7) Negative Information

(A) Notice to Consumer Required

(i) In general. If any financial institution that extends credit and regularly and in the ordinary course of business furnishes information to a con¬sumer reporting agency described in section 603(p) furnishes negative information to such an agency regarding credit extended to a customer, the financial institution shall provide a notice of such furnishing of negative information, in writing, to the customer.

(ii) Notice effective for subsequent submissions. After providing such notice, the financial institution may submit additional negative information to a consumer reporting agency described in section 603(p) with respect to the same transaction, extension of credit, account, or customer without providing additional notice to the customer.

(B) Time of Notice

(i) In general. The notice required under subparagraph (A) shall be provided to the customer prior to, or no later than 30 days after, furnishing the negative information to a consumer reporting agency described in section 603(p).

(ii) Coordination with new account disclosures. If the notice is provided to the customer prior to furnishing the negative information to a consumer reporting agency, the notice may not be included in the initial disclosures provided under section 127(a) of the Truth in Lending Act.

(C) Coordination with other disclosures-The notice required under subparagraph (A)-¬

(i) may be included on or with any notice of default, any billing statement, or any other materials provided to the customer; and

(ii) must be clear and conspicuous.

(D) Model Disclosure

(i) Duty of board to prepare. The Board shall prescribe a brief model disclosure a financial institution may use to comply with subparagraph (A), which shall not exceed 30 words.

(ii) Use of model not required. No provision of this paragraph shall be construed as requiring a financial institution to use any such model form prescribed by the Board.

(iii) Compliance using model. A financial institution shall be deemed to be in compliance with subparagraph (A) if the financial institution uses any such model form prescribed by the Board, or the financial institution uses any such model form and rearranges its format.

(E) Use of notice without submitting negative information. No provision of this paragraph shall be construed as requiring a financial institution that has provided a customer with a notice described in subparagraph (A) to furnish negative information about the customer to a consumer reporting agency.

(F) Safe harbor. A financial institution shall not be liable for failure to perform the duties required by this paragraph if, at the time of the failure, the financial institution maintained reasonable policies and procedures to comply with this paragraph or the financial institution reasonably believed that the institution is prohibited, by law, from contacting the consumer.

(G) Definitions. For purposes of this paragraph, the following definitions shall apply:

(i) The term "negative information" means information concerning a customer's delinquencies, late payments, insolvency, or any form of default.

(ii) The terms "customer" and "financial institution" have the same meanings as in section 509 Public Law 106-102.

(8) Ability of Consumer to Dispute Information Directly with Furnisher

(A) In general. The Federal banking agencies, the National Credit Union Administration, and the Commission shall jointly prescribe regulations that shall identify the circumstances under which a furnisher shall be required to reinvestigate a dispute concerning the accuracy of information contained in a consumer report on the consumer, based on a direct request of a consumer.

(B) Considerations. In prescribing regulations under subparagraph (A), the agencies shall weigh-¬

(i) the benefits to consumers with the costs on furnishers and the credit reporting system;

(ii) the impact on the overall accuracy and integrity of consumer reports of any such requirements;

(iii) whether direct contact by the consumer with the furnisher would likely result in the most expeditious resolution of any such dispute; and

(iv) the potential impact on the credit reporting process if credit repair organizations, as defined in section 403(3) [15 U.S.C. §1679a(3)], including entities that would be a credit repair organization, but for section 403(3)(B)(i), are able to circumvent the prohibition in subparagraph (G).

(C) Applicability. Subparagraphs (D) through (G) shall apply in any circumstance identified under the regulations promulgated under subparagraph (A).

(D) Submitting a notice of dispute-A consumer who seeks to dispute the accuracy of information shall provide a dispute notice directly to such person at the address specified by the person for such notices that-¬

(i) identifies the specific information that is being disputed;

(ii) explains the basis for the dispute; and

(iii) includes all supporting documentation required by the furnisher to substantiate the basis of the dispute.

(E) Duty of person after receiving notice of dispute. After receiving a notice of dispute from a consumer pursuant to subparagraph (D), the person that provided the information in dispute to a consumer reporting agency shall-¬

(i) conduct an investigation with respect to the disputed information;

(ii) review all relevant information provided by the consumer with the notice;

(iii) complete such person's investigation of the dispute and report the results of the investigation to the consumer before the expiration of the period under section 611(a)(1) within which a consumer reporting agency would be required to complete its action if the consumer had elected to dispute the information under that section; and

(iv) if the investigation finds that the information reported was inaccurate, promptly notify each consumer reporting agency to which the person furnished the inaccurate information of that determination and provide to the agency any correction to that information that is necessary to make the information provided by the person accurate.

(F) Frivolous or Irrelevant Dispute

(i) In general. This paragraph shall not apply if the person receiving a notice of a dispute from a consumer reasonably determines that the dispute is frivolous or irrelevant, including-¬

(I) by reason of the failure of a consumer to provide sufficient information to investigate the disputed information; or

(II) the submission by a consumer of a dispute that is substantially the same as a dispute previously submitted by or for the consumer, either directly to the person or through a consumer reporting agency under subsection (b), with respect to which the person has already performed the person's duties under this paragraph or subsection (b), as applicable.

(ii) Notice of determination. Upon making any determination under clause

(i) that a dispute is frivolous or irrelevant, the person shall notify the consumer of such determination not later than 5 business days after making such determination, by mail or, if authorized by the consumer for that purpose, by any other means available to the person.

(iii) Contents of notice. A notice under clause (ii) shall include-¬

(I) the reasons for the determination under clause (i); and

(II) identification of any information required to investigate the disputed information, which may consist of a standardized form describing the general nature of such information.

(G) Exclusion of credit repair organizations. This paragraph shall not apply if the notice of the dispute is submitted by, is prepared on behalf of the consumer by, or is submitted on a form supplied to the consumer by, a credit repair organization, as defined in section 403(3), or an entity that would be a credit repair organization, but for section 403(3)(B)(i).

(9) Duty to provide notice of status as medical information furnisher. A person whose primary business is providing medical services, products, or devices, or the person's agent or assignee, who furnishes information to a consumer reporting agency on a consumer shall be considered a medical information furnisher for purposes of this title, and shall notify the agency of such status.

(b) Duties of Furnishers of Information upon Notice of Dispute

(1) In general. After receiving notice pursuant to section 611(a)(2) [§ 1681i] of a dispute with regard to the completeness or accuracy of any information provided by a person to a consumer reporting agency, the person shall

(A) conduct an investigation with respect to the disputed information;

(B) review all relevant information provided by the consumer reporting agency pursuant to section 611(a)(2) [§ 1681i];

(C) report the results of the investigation to the consumer reporting agency;

(D) if the investigation finds that the information is incomplete or inaccurate, report those results to all other consumer reporting agencies to which the person furnished the information and that compile and maintain files on consumers on a nationwide basis; and

(E) if an item of information disputed by a consumer is found to be inaccurate or incomplete or cannot be verified after any reinvestigation under paragraph (1), for purposes of reporting to a consumer reporting agency only, as appropriate, based on the results of the reinvestigation promptly–

(i) modify that item of information;

(ii) delete that item of information; or

(iii) permanently block the reporting of that item of information.

(2) Deadline. A person shall complete all investigations, reviews, and reports required under paragraph (1) regarding information provided by the person to a consumer reporting agency, before the expiration of the period under section 611(a)(1) [§ 1681i] within which the consumer reporting agency is required to complete actions required by that section re-

garding that information.

(c) Limitation on liability. Except as provided in section 621(c)(1)(B), sections 616 and 617 do not apply to any violation of-¬

(1) subsection (a) of this section, including any regulations issued thereunder;

(2) subsection (e) of this section, except that nothing in this paragraph shall limit, expand, or otherwise affect liability under section 616 or 617, as applicable, for violations of subsection (b) of this section; or

(3) subsection (e) of section 615.

(d) Limitation on enforcement. The provisions of law described in paragraphs (1) through

(3) of subsection (c) (other than with respect to the exception described in paragraph

(2) of subsection (c)) shall be enforced exclusively as provided under section 621 by the Federal agencies and officials and the State officials identified in section 621.

(e) Accuracy Guidelines and Regulations Required

(1) Guidelines. The Federal banking agencies, the National Credit Union Administration, and the Commission shall, with respect to the entities that are subject to their respective enforcement authority under section 621, and in coordination as described in paragraph (2)-¬

(A) establish and maintain guidelines for use by each person that furnishes information to a consumer reporting agency regarding the accuracy and integrity of the information relating to consumers that such entities furnish to consumer reporting agencies, and update such guidelines as often as necessary; and

(B) prescribe regulations requiring each person that furnishes information to a consumer reporting agency to establish reasonable policies and procedures for implementing the guidelines established pursuant to subparagraph (A).

(2) Coordination. Each agency required to prescribe regulations under paragraph (1) shall consult and coordinate with each other such agency so that, to the extent possible, the regulations prescribed by each such entity are consistent and comparable with the regulations prescribed by each other such agency.

(3) Criteria. In developing the guidelines required by paragraph (1)(A), the agencies described in paragraph (1) shall-¬

(A) identify patterns, practices, and specific forms of activity that can compromise the accuracy and integrity of information furnished to consumer reporting agencies;

(B) review the methods (including technological means) used to furnish information relating to consumers to consumer reporting agencies;

(C) determine whether persons that furnish information to consumer reporting agencies maintain and enforce policies to assure the accuracy and integrity of information furnished to consumer reporting agencies; and

(D) examine the policies and processes that persons that furnish information to consumer reporting agencies employ to conduct reinvestigations and correct inaccurate information relating to consumers that has been furnished to consumer reporting agencies.

July 30, 2004 68
§ 624. Affiliate sharing [15 U.S.C. § 1681s-3]

(a) Special Rule for Solicitation for Purposes of Marketing

(1) Notice. Any person that receives from another person related to it by common ownership or affiliated by corporate control a communication of information that would be a consumer report, but for clauses (i), (ii), and (iii) of section 603(d)(2)(A), may not use the information to make a solicitation for marketing purposes to a consumer about its products or services, unless-¬

(A) it is clearly and conspicuously disclosed to the consumer that the information may be communicated among such persons for purposes of making such solicitations to the consumer; and

(B) the consumer is provided an opportunity and a simple method to prohibit the making of such solicitations to the consumer by such person.

(2) Consumer Choice

(A) In general. The notice required under paragraph (1) shall allow the consumer the opportunity to prohibit all solicitations referred to in such paragraph, and may allow the consumer to choose from different options when electing to prohibit the sending of such solicitations, including options regarding the types of entities and information covered, and which methods of delivering solicitations the consumer elects to prohibit.

(B) Format. Notwithstanding subparagraph (A), the notice required under paragraph (1) shall be clear, conspicuous, and concise, and any method provided under paragraph (1)(B) shall be simple. The regulations prescribed to implement this section shall provide specific guidance regarding how to comply with such standards.

(3) Duration

(A) In general. The election of a consumer pursuant to paragraph (1)(B) to prohibit the making of solicitations shall be effective for at least 5 years, beginning on the date on which the person receives the election of the consumer, unless the consumer requests that such election be revoked.

(B) Notice upon expiration of effective period. At such time as the election of a consumer pursuant to paragraph (1)(B) is no longer effective, a person may not use information that the person receives in the manner described in paragraph (1) to make any solicitation for marketing purposes to the consumer, unless the consumer receives a notice and an opportunity, using a simple method, to extend the opt-out for another period of at least 5 years, pursuant to the procedures described in paragraph (1).

(4) Scope. This section shall not apply to a person–

(A) using information to make a solicitation for marketing purposes to a consumer with whom the person has a pre-existing business relationship;

(B) using information to facilitate communications to an individual for whose benefit the person provides employee benefit or other services pursuant to a contract with an employer related to and arising out of the current employment relationship or status of the individual as a participant or beneficiary of an employee benefit plan;

(C) using information to perform services on behalf of another person related by common ownership or affiliated by corporate control, except that this subparagraph shall not be construed as permitting a person to send solicitations on behalf of another person, if such other person would not be permitted to send the solicitation on its own behalf as a result of the election of the consumer to prohibit solicitations under paragraph (1)(B);

(D) using information in response to a communication initiated by the consumer;

(E) using information in response to solicitations authorized or requested by the consumer; or

(F) if compliance with this section by that person would prevent compliance by that person with any provision of State insurance laws pertaining to unfair discrimination in any State in which the person is lawfully doing business.

(5) No retroactivity. This subsection shall not prohibit the use of information to send a solicitation to a consumer if such information was received prior to the date on which persons are required to comply with regulations implementing this subsection.

(b) Notice for other purposes permissible. A notice or other disclosure under this section may be coordinated and consolidated with any other notice required to be issued under any other provision of law by a person that is subject to this section, and a notice or other disclosure that is equivalent to the notice required by subsection (a), and that is provided by a person described in subsection (a) to a consumer together with disclosures required by any other provision of law, shall satisfy the requirements of subsection (a).

(c) User requirements. Requirements with respect to the use by a person of information received from another person related to it by common ownership or affiliated by corporate control, such as the requirements of this section, constitute requirements with respect to the exchange of information among persons affiliated by common ownership or common corporate control, within the meaning of section 625(b)(2).

(d) Definitions. For purposes of this section, the following definitions shall apply:

(1) The term "pre-existing business relationship" means a relationship between a person, or a person's licensed agent, and a consumer, based on-¬

(A) a financial contract between a person and a consumer which is in force;

(B) the purchase, rental, or lease by the consumer of that person's goods or services, or a financial transaction (including holding an active account or a policy in force or having another continuing relationship) between the consumer and that person during the 18-month period immediately preceding the date on which the consumer is sent a solicitation covered by this section;

(C) an inquiry or application by the consumer regarding a product or service offered by that person, during the 3-month period immediately preceding the date on which the consumer is sent a solicitation covered by this section; or

(D) any other pre-existing customer relationship defined in the regulations implementing this section.

(2) The term "solicitation" means the marketing of a product or service initiated by a person to a particular consumer that is based on an exchange of information described in subsection (a), and is intended to encourage the consumer to purchase such product or service, but does not include communications that are directed at the general public or determined not to be a solicitation by the regulations prescribed under this section.

July 30, 2004 76
§ 625. Relation to State laws [15 U.S.C. § 1681t]

(a) In general. Except as provided in subsections (b) and (c), this title does not annul, alter, affect, or exempt any person subject to the provisions of this title from complying with the laws of any State with respect to the collection, distribution, or use of any information on consumers, or for the prevention or mitigation of identity theft, except to the extent that those laws are inconsistent with any provision of this title, and then only to the extent of the inconsistency.

(b) General exceptions. No requirement or prohibition may be imposed under the laws of any State

(1) with respect to any subject matter regulated under

(A) subsection (c) or (e) of section 604 [§ 1681b], relating to the prescreening of consumer reports;

(B) section 611 [§ 1681i], relating to the time by which a consumer reporting agency must take any action, including the provision of notification to a consumer or other person, in any procedure related to the disputed accuracy of information in a consumer's file, except that this subparagraph shall not apply to any State law in effect on the date of enactment of the Consumer Credit Reporting Reform Act of 1996;

(C) subsections (a) and (b) of section 615 [§ 1681m], relating to the duties of a person who takes any adverse action with respect to a consumer;

(D) section 615(d) [§ 1681m], relating to the duties of persons who use a consumer report of a consumer in connection with any credit or insurance transaction that is not initiated by the consumer and that consists of a firm offer of credit or insurance;

(E) section 605 [§ 1681c], relating to information contained in consumer reports, except that this subparagraph shall not apply to any State law in effect on the date of enactment of the Consumer Credit Reporting Reform Act of 1996;

(F) section 623 [§ 1681s-2], relating to the responsibilities of persons who furnish information to consumer reporting agencies, except that this paragraph shall not apply

(i) with respect to section 54A(a) of chapter 93 of the Massachusetts Annotated Laws (as in effect on the date of enactment of the Consumer Credit Reporting Reform Act of 1996); or

(ii) with respect to section 1785.25(a) of the California Civil Code (as in effect on the date of enactment of the Consumer Credit Reporting Reform Act of 1996);

(G) section 609(e), relating to information available to victims under section 609(e);

(H) section 624, relating to the exchange and use of information to make a solicitation for marketing purposes; or

(I) section 615(h), relating to the duties of users of consumer reports to provide notice with respect to terms in certain credit transactions;

(2) with respect to the exchange of information among persons affiliated by common ownership or common corporate control, except that this paragraph shall not apply with respect to subsection (a) or (c)(1) of section 2480e of title 9, Vermont Statutes Annotated (as in effect on the date of enactment of the Consumer Credit Reporting Reform Act of 1996);

(3) with respect to the disclosures required to be made under subsection (c), (d), (e), or (g) of section 609, or subsection (f) of section 609 relating to the disclosure of credit scores for credit granting purposes, except that this paragraph-¬

(A) shall not apply with respect to sections 1785.10, 1785.16, and 1785.20.2 of the California Civil Code (as in effect on the date of enactment of the Fair and Accurate Credit Transactions Act of 2003) and section 1785.15 through section 1785.15.2 of such Code (as in effect on such date);

(B) shall not apply with respect to sections 5-3-106(2) and 212-14.3-104.3 of the Colorado Revised Statutes (as in effect on the date of enactment of the Fair and Accurate Credit Transactions Act of 2003); and

(C) shall not be construed as limiting, annulling, affecting, or superseding any provision of the laws of any State regulating the use in an insurance activity, or regulating disclosures concerning such use, of a credit-based insurance score of a consumer by any person engaged in the business of insurance;

(4) with respect to the frequency of any disclosure under section 612(a), except that this paragraph shall not apply–

(A) with respect to section 12-14.3-105(1)(d) of the Colorado Revised Statutes (as in effect on the date of enactment of the Fair and Accurate Credit Transactions Act of 2003);

(B) with respect to section 10-1-393(29)(C) of the Georgia Code (as in effect on the date of enactment of the Fair and Accurate Credit Transactions Act of 2003);

(C) with respect to section 1316.2 of title 10 of the Maine Revised Statutes (as in effect on the date of enactment of the Fair and Accurate Credit Transactions Act of 2003);

(D) with respect to sections 14-1209(a)(1) and 14-1209(b)(1)(i) of the Commercial Law Article of the Code of Maryland (as in effect on the date of enactment of the Fair and Accurate Credit Transactions Act of 2003);

(E) with respect to section 59(d) and section 59(e) of chapter 93 of the General Laws of Massachusetts (as in effect on the date of enactment of the Fair and Accurate Credit Transactions Act of 2003);

(F) with respect to section 56:11-37.10(a)(1) of the New Jersey Revised Statutes (as in effect on the date of enactment of the Fair and Accurate Credit Transactions Act of 2003); or

(G) with respect to section 2480c(a)(1) of title 9 of the Vermont Statutes Annotated (as in effect on the date of enactment of the Fair and Accurate Credit Transactions Act of 2003); or

(5) with respect to the conduct required by the specific provisions of-¬

(A) section 605(g);

(B) section 605A;

(C) section 605B;

(D) section 609(a)(1)(A);

(E) section 612(a);

(F) subsections (e), (f), and (g) of section 615;

(G) section 621(f);

(H) section 623(a)(6); or

(I) section 628.

(c) Definition of firm offer of credit or insurance. Notwithstanding any definition of the term "firm offer of credit or insurance" (or any equivalent term) under the laws of any State, the definition of that term contained in section 603(l) [§ 1681a] shall be construed to apply in the enforcement and interpretation of the laws of any State governing consumer reports.

(d) Limitations. Subsections (b) and (c) do not affect any settlement, agreement, or consent judgment between any State Attorney General and any consumer reporting agency in effect on the date of enactment of the Consumer Credit Reporting Reform Act of 1996.

§ 626. Disclosures to FBI for counterintelligence purposes [15 U.S.C. § 1681u]

(a) Identity of financial institutions. Notwithstanding section 604 [§ 1681b] or any other provision of this title, a consumer reporting agency shall furnish to the Federal Bureau of Investigation the names and addresses of all financial institutions (as that term is defined in section 1101 of the Right to Financial Privacy Act of 1978 [12

U.S.C. § 3401]) at which a consumer maintains or has maintained an account, to the extent that information is in the files of the agency, when presented with a written request for that information, signed by the Director of the Federal Bureau of Investigation, or the Director's designee in a position not lower than Deputy Assistant Director at Bureau headquarters or a Special Agent in Charge of a Bureau field office designated by the Director, which certifies compliance with this section. The Director or the Director's designee may make such a certification only if the Director or the Director's designee has determined in writing, that such information is sought for the conduct of an authorized investigation to protect against international terrorism or clandestine intelligence activities, provided that such an investigation of a United States person is not conducted solely upon the basis of activities protected by the first amendment to the Constitution of the United States.

(b) Identifying information. Notwithstanding the provisions of section 604 [§ 1681b] or any other provision of this title, a consumer reporting agency shall furnish identifying information respecting a consumer, limited to name, address, former addresses, places of employment, or former places of employment, to the Federal Bureau of Investigation when presented with a written request, signed by the Director or the Director's designee, which certifies compliance with this subsection. The Director or the Director's designee in a position not lower than Deputy Assistant Director at Bureau headquarters or a Special Agent in Charge of a Bureau field office designated by the Director may make such a certification only if the Director or the Director's designee has determined in writing that such information is sought for the conduct of an authorized investigation to protect against international terrorism or clandestine intelligence activities, provided that such an investigation of a United States person is not conducted solely upon the basis of activities protected by the first amendment to the Constitution of the United States.

(c) Court order for disclosure of consumer reports. Notwithstanding section 604 [§ 1681b] or any other provision of this title, if requested in writing by the Director of the Federal Bureau of Investigation, or a designee of the Director in a position not lower than Deputy Assistant Director at Bureau headquarters or a Special Agent in Charge of a Bureau field office designated by the Director, a court may issue an order ex parte directing a consumer reporting agency to furnish a consumer report to the Federal Bureau of Investigation, upon a showing in camera that the consumer report is sought for the conduct of an authorized investigation to protect against international terrorism or clandestine intelligence activities, provided that such an investigation of a United States person is not conducted solely upon the basis of activities protected by the first amendment to the Constitution of the United States. The terms of an order issued under this subsection shall not disclose that the order is issued for purposes of a counterintelligence investigation.

(d) Confidentiality. No consumer reporting agency or officer, employee, or agent of a consumer reporting agency shall disclose to any person, other than those officers, employees, or agents of a consumer reporting agency necessary to fulfill the requirement to disclose information to the Federal Bureau of Investigation under this section, that the Federal Bureau of Investigation has sought or obtained the identity of financial institutions or a consumer report respecting any consumer under subsection (a), (b), or (c), and no consumer reporting agency or officer, employee, or agent of a consumer reporting agency shall include in any consumer report any information that would indicate that the Federal Bureau of Investigation has sought or obtained such information or a consumer report.

(e) Payment of fees. The Federal Bureau of Investigation shall, subject to the availability of appropriations, pay to the consumer reporting agency assembling or providing report or information in accordance with procedures established under this section a fee for reimbursement for such costs as are reasonably necessary and which have been directly incurred in searching, reproducing, or transporting books, papers, records, or other data required or requested to be produced under this section.

(f) Limit on dissemination. The Federal Bureau of Investigation may not disseminate information obtained pursuant to this section outside of the Federal Bureau of Investigation, except to other Federal agencies as may be necessary for the approval or conduct of a foreign counterintelligence investigation, or, where the information concerns a person subject to the Uniform Code of Military Justice, to appropriate investigative authorities within the military department concerned as may be necessary for the conduct of a joint foreign counterintelligence investigation.

(g) Rules of construction. Nothing in this section shall be construed to prohibit information from being furnished by the Federal Bureau of Investigation pursuant to a subpoena or court order, in connection with a judicial or administrative proceeding to enforce the provisions of this Act. Nothing in this section shall be construed to authorize or permit the withholding of information from the Congress.

(h) Reports to Congress. On a semiannual basis, the Attorney General shall fully inform the Permanent Select Committee on Intelligence and the Committee on Banking, Finance and Urban Affairs of the House of Representatives, and the Select Committee on Intelligence and the Committee on Banking, Housing, and Urban Affairs of the Senate concerning all requests made pursuant to subsections (a), (b), and (c).

(i) Damages. Any agency or department of the United States obtaining or disclosing any consumer reports, records, or information contained therein in violation of this section is liable to the consumer to whom such consumer reports, records, or information relate in an amount equal to the sum of

(1) $100, without regard to the volume of consumer reports, records, or information involved;

(2) any actual damages sustained by the consumer as a result of the disclosure;

(3) if the violation is found to have been willful or intentional, such punitive damages as a court may allow; and

(4) in the case of any successful action to enforce liability under this subsection, the costs of the action, together with reasonable attorney fees, as determined by the court.

(j) Disciplinary actions for violations. If a court determines that any agency or department of the United States has violated any provision of this section and the court finds that the circumstances surrounding the violation raise questions of whether or not an officer or employee of the agency or department acted willfully or intentionally with respect to the violation, the agency or department shall promptly initiate a proceeding to determine whether or not disciplinary action is warranted against the officer or employee who was responsible for the violation.

(k) Good-faith exception. Notwithstanding any other provision of this title, any consumer reporting agency or agent or employee thereof making disclosure of consumer reports or identifying information pursuant to this subsection in good-faith reliance upon a certification of the Federal Bureau of Investigation pursuant to provisions of this section shall not be liable to any person for such disclosure under this title, the constitution of any State, or any law or regulation of any State or any political subdivision of any State.

(l) Limitation of remedies. Notwithstanding any other provision of this title, the remedies and sanctions set forth in this section shall be the only judicial remedies and sanctions for violation of this section.

(m) Injunctive relief. In addition to any other remedy contained in this section, injunctive relief shall be available to require compliance with the procedures of this section. In the event of any successful action under this subsection, costs together with reasonable attorney fees, as determined by the court, may be recovered.

§ 627. Disclosures to governmental agencies for counterterrorism purposes [15 U.S.C. §1681v]

(a) Disclosure. Notwithstanding section 604 or any other provision of this title, a consumer reporting agency shall furnish a consumer report of a consumer and all other information in a consumer's file to a government agency authorized to conduct investigations of, or intelligence or counterintelligence activities or analysis related to, international terrorism when presented with a written certification by such government agency that such information is necessary for the agency's conduct or such investigation, activity or analysis.

(b) Form of certification. The certification described in subsection (a) shall be signed by a supervisory official designated by the head of a Federal agency or an officer of a Federal agency whose appointment to office is required to be made by the President, by and with the advice and consent of the Senate.

(c) Confidentiality. No consumer reporting agency, or officer, employee, or agent of such consumer reporting agency, shall disclose to any person, or specify in any consumer report, that a government agency has sought or obtained access to information under subsection (a).

(d) Rule of construction. Nothing in section 626 shall be construed to limit the authority of the Director of the Federal Bureau of Investigation under this section.

(e) Safe harbor. Notwithstanding any other provision of this title, any consumer report¬ing agency or agent or employee thereof making disclosure of consumer reports or other information pursuant to this section in good-faith reliance upon a certification

of a governmental agency pursuant to the provisions of this section shall not be liable to any person for such disclosure under this subchapter, the constitution of any State, or any law or regulation of any State or any political subdivision of any State.

§ 628. Disposal of records [15 U.S.C. §1681w]

(a) Regulations

(1) In general. Not later than 1 year after the date of enactment of this section, the Federal banking agencies, the National Credit Union Administration, and the Commission with respect to the entities that are subject to their respective enforcement authority under section 621, and the Securities and Exchange Commission, and in coordination as described in paragraph (2), shall issue final regulations requiring any person that maintains or otherwise possesses consumer information, or any compilation of consumer information, derived from consumer reports for a business purpose to properly dispose of any such information or compilation.

(2) Coordination. Each agency required to prescribe regulations under paragraph (1)

shall–

(A) consult and coordinate with each other such agency so that, to the extent possible, the regulations prescribed by each such agency are consistent and comparable with the regulations by each such other agency; and

(B) ensure that such regulations are consistent with the requirements and regulations issued pursuant to Public Law 106-102 and other provisions of Federal law.

(3) Exemption authority. In issuing regulations under this section, the Federal banking agencies, the National Credit Union Administration, the Commission, and the Securities and Exchange Commission may exempt any person or class of persons from application of those regulations, as such agency deems appropriate to carry out the purpose of this section.

(b) Rule of construction. Nothing in this section shall be construed-¬

(1) to require a person to maintain or destroy any record pertaining to a consumer that is not imposed under other law; or

(2) to alter or affect any requirement imposed under any other provision of law to maintain or destroy such a record.

§ 629. Corporate and technological circumvention prohibited [15 U.S.C. §1681x]

The Commission shall prescribe regulations, to become effective not later than 90 days after the date of enactment of this section, to prevent a consumer reporting agency from circumventing or evading treatment as a consumer reporting agency described in section 603(p) for purposes of this title, including-¬

(1) by means of a corporate reorganization or restructuring, including a merger, ac¬quisition, dissolution, divestiture, or asset sale of a consumer reporting agency; or

(2) by maintaining or merging public record and credit account information in a manner that is substantially equivalent to that described in paragraphs (1) and (2) of section 603(p), in the manner described in section 603(p).

See also 16 CFR Part 611 69 Fed. Reg. 8531 (02/24/04) 69 Fed. Reg. 29061 (05/20/04)

Legislative History

House Reports: No. 91-975 (Comm. on Banking and Currency) and No. 91-1587 (Comm. of Conference)

Senate Reports: No. 91-1139 accompanying S. 3678 (Comm. on Banking and Currency)

Congressional Record, Vol. 116 (1970)

May 25, considered and passed House. Sept. 18, considered and passed Senate, amended. Oct. 9, Senate agreed to conference report. Oct. 13, House agreed to conference report.

Enactment: Public Law No. 91-508 (October 26, 1970):

Amendments: Public Law Nos. 95-473 (October 17, 1978) 95-598 (November 6, 1978) 98-443 (October 4, 1984) 101-73 (August 9, 1989) 102-242 (December 19, 1991) 102-537 (October 27, 1992) 102-550 (October 28, 1992) 103-325 (September 23, 1994) 104-88 (December 29, 1995) 104-93 (January 6, 1996) 104-193 (August 22, 1996) 104-208 (September 30, 1996) 105-107 (November 20, 1997) 105-347 (November 2, 1998) 106-102 (November 12, 1999) 107-56 (October 26, 2001) 108-159 (December 4, 2003)

9

CONCLUSION

All consumers have a right not to be abused by anyone. This book should help you exact justice (and money) from abusive companies. I sincerely hope that you put my knowledge to use and show collection companies that you refuse to accept any abuse on their part.

Consumers have the power to force change on the collection industry, until such time that a majority of consumers do fight back, we must take our issues to the courtroom and force accountability on companies that refuse to comply with the law.

I would love to hear your own personal stories of victory over abusive collection agencies. You may contact me through the contact form at http://smarterotti.com.

With that, I wish you the best of luck in pursuing bad collection companies that have harassed or abused you. You now have the knowledge on how to fight back. Use it to your benefit.

CONCLUSION

DISCLAIMER

This book is offered to the User conditionally on acceptance by the user without modification of the terms, conditions, and notices contained herein. Use of the content presented in book constitutes the User's agreement to abide by the following terms and conditions. This book is for informational purposes only and may not in any way, shape, or form be construed as legal advice.

Copyright Notices

Disclaimer

ALL MATERIALS INCLUDED IN THIS BOOK ARE PROVIDED "AS IS" WITHOUT WARRANTY OF ANY KIND. THE CONTENT PUBLISHED MAY INCLUDE INACCURACIES OR TYPOGRAPHICAL ERRORS. CHANGES ARE PERIODICALLY MADE TO THE INFORMATION HEREIN. ALLEN HARKLEROAD MAY MAKE IMPROVEMENTS AND/OR CHANGES TO THE BOOK AT ANY TIME. ALLEN HARKLEROAD MAKE NO REPRESENTATIONS AND, TO THE FULLEST EXTENT ALLOWED BY LAW DISCLAIM ALL WARRANTIES, EXPRESS OR IMPLIED, INCLUDING, BUT NOT LIMITED TO WARRANTIES OF MERCHANTABILITY AND FITNESS FOR A PARTICULAR PURPOSE REGARDING THE SUITABILITY OF THE INFORMATION; THE ACCURACY, RELIABILITY, COMPLETENESS OR TIMELINESS OF THE CONTENT, SERVICES, PRODUCTS, TEXT, GRAPHICS, LINKS, OR OTHER ITEMS CONTAINED WITHIN THE BOOK, OR THE RESULTS OBTAINED FROM ACCESSING AND USING THIS BOOK AND/OR THE CONTENT CONTAINED HEREIN. ALLEN HARKLEROAD DOES

NOT WARRANT THAT THE FUNCTIONS CONTAINED IN THE MATERIALS WILL BE UNINTERRUPTED OR ERROR-FREE, THAT DEFECTS WILL BE CORRECTED. Use of this book is at your own risk.

This book may contain advice, opinions, and statements of various information providers and content providers. Allen Harkleroad does not represent or endorse the accuracy or reliability of any advice, opinion, statement or other information provided by any information provider or content provider, or any user of this book or other person or entity. Reliance upon any such opinion, advice, statement, or other information shall also be at your own risk. Neither Allen Harkleroad or his affiliates, nor any of their respective agents, employees, information providers or content providers shall be liable to any user or anyone else for any inaccuracy, error, omission, interruption, timeliness, completeness, deletion, defect, failure of performance, alteration of, or use of any content herein, regardless of cause, for any damages resulting therefrom. Allen Harkleroad, his affiliates, information providers and his content providers shall not have any liability for investment or legal decisions based upon, or the results obtained from, the information provided. Allen Harkleroad, his affiliates, information providers and content providers do not guarantee or warrant the timeliness, sequence, accuracy, or completeness of any such information. Nothing contained in this book is intended to be, nor shall it be construed as investment or legal advice.

User agrees to indemnify and hold harmless Allen Harkleroad and all officers, directors, shareholders, employees, authorized representatives and agents form and against all claims and expenses, including attorneys' fees, arising out of any use or misuse of information contained in this book .

Modification

Allen Harkleroad shall have the right, at its discretion, to change, modify, add, or remove terms of this agreement at any time. Notification of any such changes shall be made herein. Changes shall be effective immediately, and subsequent use by you of this site shall constitute your acceptance of them.

Termination

This agreement is effective until terminated by Allen Harkleroad, at any time without notice.

Indemnity/Limitation of Liability

Under no circumstances, including, but not limited to, negligence, shall Allen Harkleroad, or his affiliates be liable for any direct, indirect, incidental, special or consequential damages that result from the use of, or the inability to use the information contained in this book. As a condition of use of this book, the user agrees to indemnify Allen Harkleroad and his suppliers from and against any and all liabilities, expenses and damages arising out of claims resulting from user's use of this book, including without limitation any claims alleging facts that if true would constitute a breach by user of these terms and conditions. If you are dissatisfied with any the books material, or with any of books terms and conditions, your sole and exclusive remedy is to discontinue using the book.

General

Allen Harkleroad reserves the right to make any and all changes to this book at his sole discretion without notice to the User. This Agreement shall be deemed to include all other notices, policies, disclaimers, and other terms contained in this book; provided, however, that in the event of a conflict between such other terms and the terms of this Agreement, the terms of this Agreement shall control. This Agreement has been made in and shall be construed and enforced in accordance with Georgia law. Any action to enforce this agreement shall be brought in the federal or state courts located in Bulloch County Georgia. If any provision is deemed unlawful or unenforceable, that shall not affect the validity and enforceability of the remaining provisions.

Made in the USA
Monee, IL
21 March 2025

14380478R00155